The Citizens' Guide to Geologic Hazards

A guide to understanding geologic hazards — including asbestos, radon, swelling soils, earthquakes, volcanoes, landslides, subsidence, floods and coastal hazards

Prepared by

The American Institute of Professi

Authors

Edward B. Nuhfer, University of Colorado at Denver; **Richard J. Proctor**, Independent Consultant, Arcadia, California; and **Paul H. Moser**, Geological Survey of Alabama

with

John E. Allen, James T. Bales, Jr., Janet M. Blabaum, Richard C. Benson, Jerome DeGraff, Jeffrey L. Hynes, William V. Knight, John Mayberry, Edith McKee, John Montagne, Douglas A. Sprinkel and **Jerry D. Vineyard**

aided by the comments and contributions of
Technical Reviewers
Bernard Amadei, Dwight Crandell, Phillip Gerla, Linda Gundersen, Philip LaMoreaux, Eugene L. Lecomte, Francis V. Reilly, Malcolm Ross and **Richard Waugh**

and the editorship of
Mary P. Dalles, Thomas Z. Jones, Charles Wm. Dimmick and **Wendy J. Davidson**

Order from A.I.P.G. 7828 Vance Drive, Suite 103, Arvada, CO 80003. Phone (303) 431-0831. Sets of 35 mm slides of photos and line drawings of hazards depicted in this book are available.

NOTICE to READER

Publication of this book was aided by the generous financial support of

Russell G. Slayback, CPG
James A. Gibbs, CPG
William V. Knight, CPG

who made designated contributions through the
AIPG Foundation, Inc.

The Citizens' Guide to Geologic Hazards - 134 pages, illustrated, annotated bibliographies, index

Key word list for indexing: *acid drainage, asbestos, avalanches, coastal hazards, disasters, earthquakes, engineering geology, environmental geology, floods, gas hazards, geologic hazards, geologists, geology, landslides, property insurance, radon, reactive aggregates, shoreline erosion, slope stability, storm surge, subsidence, swelling soils, tsunamis, videotapes, volcanoes*

The American Institute of Professional Geologists, 7828 Vance Drive, Arvada, CO 80003, Phone (303) 431-0831
© 1993 by the American Institute of Professional Geologists.
All rights reserved.
Printed in the United States of America
96 95 94 93   5 4 3 2 1
Library of Congress Catalog Card Number 92-073848

ISBN 0-933637-10-1

The **American Institute of Professional Geologists**
dedicates this book to the memory of

Maurice and Katia Krafft

who through their books and films conveyed their love of geology, and brought awareness of the beauty and hazards of volcanoes to the public of many nations.

Katia and Maurice Krafft, the French geologists who devoted their lives to documenting the major volcanic eruptions through movies, photographs and books for the public. The husband and wife team perished in June, 1991, at the eruption of Mount Unzen, Japan. (This photo was taken August, 1983, in Jakarta, Indonesia, at the symposium on the occasion of the 100th anniversary of the 1883 eruption of Krakatau Volcano, courtesy of Dr. Richard S. Fiske, Smithsonian Institution.)

Table of Contents

PREFACE

If you have wondered about the actual dangers of asbestos, radon, earthquakes, etc., that are mentioned but not explained very well in the news, then this book is certainly for you. The book was commissioned by The American Institute of Professional Geologists to give readers knowledge that will save lives and dollars. It explains geologic hazards, the risks these hazards pose, and how professional geologists help to mitigate these risks. We wrote this book for non-scientists, especially planners, contractors, homeowners, elected officials, insurance underwriters, lenders and financiers, realtors, science teachers, and students. Although geologists have the knowledge that can help reduce the risks, the value of this knowledge will increase greatly when the majority of citizens also understand the hazards and can upgrade public policies that will guarantee that available knowledge is used. Many of the losses that you will read about in this book are preventable if present-day knowledge is applied by the public. Knowledge and the will to act on the knowledge can prevent scenarios like he following:

A young couple in Pennsylvania use their entire savings to make a down-payment on their first house. Two months later the ground settles beneath the northeast corner of their brick home. The foundation disintegrates, doors shift out of line, windows break, walls crack and the house is finally condemned. The couple find that their homeowners' insurance does not cover the subsidence damage. Insurance that would have covered losses due to subsidence into an abandoned mine was available in Pennsylvania; the young homeowners simply never realized why they might need it. Mine subsidence was not a topic discussed in any class they had taken in school.

In a new neighborhood in Colorado, sidewalks and driveways start to heave and buckle. Two years later several houses on the block begin to experience cracked foundations as a result of the same swelling soils on which the development has been built. Property values in the area plummet. Maps showing the locations of the swelling soils had been available for years, but they were never consulted by a single home buyer.

A retainer wall is built of limestone blocks at the base of fill in western Illinois. Pressure builds against the wall. One evening, the material slumps and limestone blocks are hurled onto parked cars below the wall. Two young occupants in one vehicle are killed.

Homes and public buildings in northwestern Armenia are constructed of stone masonry and composite concrete frame. In the dead of winter, an earthquake destroys these structures. At a time when 25,000 people are killed in collapsing buildings and another 15,000 are injured, only 20% of the medical personnel in this area are left alive to deal with the casualties. The other 80% lie crushed beneath the collapsed concrete panels of their hospitals. Utilities are destroyed and a half million people are left homeless, without heat or water, in sub-freezing temperatures. The homes and hospitals were inadequately designed to resist tremors despite a well-documented history of severe quakes in the region.

The causes of these misfortunes, all based on actual cases, are **geologic hazards**—geologic phenomena that present common risks to life or property. They resulted when individuals or whole communities made plans based on insufficient consideration of the geological characteristics of the area. Ignorance is the primary catalyst that gives geologic hazards special power to injure. Citizens who acquire an education in geology are not as prone to experience loss of life and property from geologic hazards, nor are they as likely to purchase land that is actually unsuited for the uses for which it is intended.

Too often, available geological expertise and knowledge are not considered in policy decisions that affect water quality, land use, waste disposal, and domestic and industrial hygiene standards. This may be the result of too few Americans obtaining enough education in geology to enable them to appreciate the importance of that science in environmental applications.

An example of the benefits that arise from an educated public can be found in the field of health. Longevity and well-being have not resulted simply from medical breakthroughs and knowledge held by a few experts. Widespread benefits became possible only after an educated populace understood the causes of disease and took action themselves by practicing hygiene, mandating vaccination, and consulting experts directly regarding medication. Education fails most severely when knowledge pertinent to public welfare is not effectively delivered from experts to the public at large. The years 1990 - 2000 have been designated as the **International Decade of Hazards Reductions**. As we approach the 21st Century, we find that education in the earth sciences has not reached the American public to any degree comparable with that of life or health sciences. Geological illiteracy is compounded wherever earth science courses that are available are poorly taught. Some schools, even colleges, have presumed that "Anyone can teach earth science." W. Phillips (*Geotimes*, v. 36 n. 2, February 1991, pp. 56 - 57) noted that 50% of teachers now providing "earth science" courses have themselves taken only two courses or less in earth science. This leads to standards not tolerated in the science disciplines of mathematics, biology, chemistry and physics—namely teachers without degrees or significant training in a specific science assuming the responsibility for teaching it.

One reason that many geological processes pose as hazards is that the understanding and ordering of events in terms of geologic time or **deep time** (immense spans of time that encompass natural events that are seen to recur every few centuries, every few thousand years or even through tens of millions of years) is not taught to many citizens. When one understands the way these processes act through time, then one really understands the degree of risk, without being drawn into either the complacency produced by ignorance or the worry produced by wild speculation and exaggeration.

This book is a very practical kind of science book because it is designed to allow the reader to use the interesting information, evaluate whether the hazards threaten one's own property and then obtain help in making detailed assessment, planning remediation and even in obtaining insurance protection. Sources of help are primarily in Appendices A and B. Preliminary drafts of this book have been used in college courses for civil engineering students as their first introduction to the science of geology in its applied aspects.

The text is augmented by many color illustrations, and a person without geological training can quickly comprehend the content. Because geologic hazards are not covered in many introductory earth science or geology courses, this book is a useful supplement in these courses. Lists of additional references follow the discussions, and these should satisfy the extended curiosity of even the college professor of geology. In accord with the common availability of video-cassette players in homes and schools, we have also compiled lists of videotapes available on the topics of geologic hazards. Educators will find the listing of videotapes particularly useful.

Water pollution, waste disposal, and probably global warming and ozone depletion are technological hazards that require thorough knowledge of geology in order to understand and deal with them. These broad areas are also interdisciplinary with biology, engineering, chemistry and environmental science. Here, we focus primarily on those natural hazards that lie well within the area of geology.

Each chapter in this book was reviewed by a specialist, and the statements given in these chapters are based on the best resources that were available at the time of writing. Some topics such as asbestos and radon are controversial, and we have attempted to present the conflicting arguments in the most balanced manner possible. The statements made herein reflect the authors' best representation of current knowledge, but do not represent any official policy or endorsement of the American Institute of Professional Geologists.

Geological phenomena are fascinating, and the attraction to learn more about them sends geologists into the field, sometimes scurrying up active volcanoes, or into the laboratories where even late at night it becomes difficult to tear one's attention away from the thrill of discovery and learning. Geologic hazards make fascinating science, as you, the reader, will soon discover. You will enter the subsequent pages for a guided tour of a dynamic planet as it affects the sites where we live and work, and you'll emerge from these pages seeing local homes, hill slopes, highways, dams, rivers and seashores in ways that you never saw them before. Welcome to a wonderful and useful learning adventure!

Acknowledgments

Publication of a full color book of this magnitude is a serious financial undertaking for an organization the size of the American Institute of Professional Geologists (AIPG). The courage and commitment of the Executive Director and the Executive Committees of AIPG from 1990 through 1993 insured that this book became an actual product for the general public, rather than a mere aspiration. Funding to produce and publish this book was provided primarily by AIPG. Funding paid my living expenses to work at AIPG headquarters during the summer of 1991 to prepare the manuscript from my materials and from files furnished by co-authors listed on the title page. I thank the staff of AIPG Headquarters for their kindness and helpful discussions. Time was also provided for me to plan a format and produce an earlier draft by a sabbatical leave granted during 1988 and 1989 by my former employer, the University of Wisconsin at Platteville. I should also like to thank my employer, The University of Colorado at Denver, for their support for completing this project.

The employees of the United States Geological Survey (USGS) deserve special recognition for maintaining an excellent photographic collection at the Denver Federal Center. This provided us with a rich source of illustrations. Joe McGregor, Chloe MacDonald, and Carol Edwards of the USGS Special Collections library were especially helpful to the senior author. Michael Moore of the USGS Special Collections library in Menlo Park, CA, is commended for his initiating a collection of video tapes on geology; this is a tremendous service to the public and to educators. His help in sharing lists of video titles added much to my own compilations and is truly appreciated. David Wieprecht of the USGS Cascades Volcano Observatory also provided hard-to-obtain photographs in 1991 of Mount Pinatubo. The special expertise of USGS technical reviewers Dwight Crandell (volcanoes), Linda Gundersen (radon), and Malcolm Ross (asbestos) was greatly appreciated.

Lindsay McCleeland and Lee Siebert (Smithsonian Institution), John Lundberg, Roger Free and Donald Collins (Federal Emergency Management Administration—FEMA), David Wingerd (U.S. Army Corps of Engineers), and Linda Kremkau (Office of Meteorology) and Scott Kroczynski (Office of Hydrology), both with the National Weather Service, contributed or edited data that appears in parts of text, tables and appendices. Francis V. Reilly of the National Flood Insurance Program of FEMA provided many helpful editorial suggestions on the topics of floods and insurance.

Professors Bernard Amadei (University of Colorado at Boulder), Phillip Gerla (University of North Dakota) and David M. Bush (Duke University) provided review expertise and/or illustrations in the respective chapters on landslides, reactive minerals and coastal hazards. Richard Waugh of University of Wisconsin at Platteville was generous in providing photographs of hazards and in reviewing the chapter on coastal hazards. Earl McCullough and Richard Wetzel of the University of Wisconsin at Platteville's Department of Civil Engineering helped with illustrations for the landslide and flood chapters. Dave Morton, librarian at University of Colorado at Boulder's Natural Hazards Research and Applications Information Center, helped us acquire information and contacts for more information. Professionals from private industry who provided further review expertise and further contacts with experts include Philip LaMoreaux (LaMoreaux Associates—floods), Peter van Aartrijk, Jr. (Insurance Information Institute) and E. L. Lecomte (National Committee on Property Insurance).

Readability of this book was greatly aided by William Jackson and Abigail Jackson, two secondary school students who marked passages that were difficult, boring or simply needed rewriting. Editing and proofreading for grammar and style were done primarily by Mary Dalles, English Department of University Of Wisconsin at Platteville. Charles Dimmick, Central Connecticut State University; and Thomas Z. Jones, Columbus College, Columbus, Georgia, followed up with additional suggestions and recommendations for changes. Thomas Jones was AIPG National Editor during 1991 and 1992 when most of the review work was done, and I am very grateful for his encouragement and support. Good final polish in editing was provided by Carolyn Cott Stollman, Ruth Anna and Curtis Hart.

The manuscript was laid out in typeset form by me, but its final form also owes much to Wendy Davidson of AIPG Headquarters who served as my colleague and mentor of layout. The cover design was done primarily by Wendy Davidson. Masters for printing were output from files created on a Macintosh computer. All printing was done in the U.S.A. at Dubuque, Iowa.

It has been my greatest pleasure to have learned from each of these people and from my co-authors.

Edward B. Nuhfer, 1993

Everyone is affected by geologic hazards in some way. This "tropical snowfall," which is actually volcanic ash from Mount Pinatubo in the Philippines, forced the closing of nearby Clark Air Base in summer of 1991. Those viewing red sunsets through the latter part of 1991 and early 1992 saw Mount Pinatubo's ash still drifting in the upper atmosphere. Volcanic ash in the upper atmosphere reflects sunlight that would otherwise be absorbed and converted to heat on planet Earth. The Pinatubo eruption was also high in its sulfur content, which scientists deduced in 1992 as being at least as important to climate modification as ash content. Scientists in summer of 1991 anticipated a world-wide cooler summer for 1992 as a result of Pinatubo's erupted ash, and the results in 1992 validated that anticipation. Pinatubo affected global climate in that year more than any eruption since the 1883 eruption of Krakatau in Indonesia. (Photo courtesy of USGS Cascade Volcano Observatory, Vancouver, Washington.)

Part I - Geology, Geologists and Geologic Hazards

Geologic hazards annually take more than 100,000 lives and wrench billions of dollars from the world's economy. It has been demonstrated repeatedly that involvement of professional geologists can minimize hazards and reduce losses.

Geology is a science of *materials, processes, and change through immense expanses of time* (**deep time**). Materials include the solids, liquids and gases of the planet, and the processes include the physical and chemical transformations that occur on and within the planet. Geology includes the history of life and the interaction between living organisms, including humans, and the planet on which they live. In particular, geology considers the rates of change, the nature of change, and the ordering of events of change through the planet's history.

Geologists are those who are trained in and work in any branch of the geological sciences. The American Institute of Professional Geologists considers acquisition of a baccalaureate degree with 36 semester credits of courses in geology as the minimum educational qualifications needed to be a professional geologist. Many states now require licensing, certification or registration of geologists who practice as professionals in areas of geology that relate to public safety and welfare. Geologists who work with groundwater, waste disposal sites, engineering foundation assessments and assessment of geologic hazards are practicing in specialty areas related to public welfare.

Here a geologist records data from an outcropping of rock that will lead to production of a geologic map. Such maps are indispensable for general land use planning and also for dealing with geologic hazards. Dealing with geologic hazards usually begins with field studies of geology. Such studies may be the beginning of gathering general data to produce regional maps or to gather samples and data that pertain to a specific site. (photo by Paul Moser)

University geologists engaged in the study of effects of airborne volcanic ash from Mount Saint Helens on nearby lakes recover a year's sample accumulation from a time-marking collection device that was placed in Merrill Lake, Washington, USA. (photo by Walter E. Dean)

CASUALTIES FROM SPECIFIC GEOLOGIC HAZARDS COMPARED WITH FAMILIAR SOCIETAL CATASTROPHES

SOURCES of CASUALTIES	NUMBERS of CASUALTIES
Wars versus Earthquakes	
U.S. Battle Deaths in World War II	292,131
Atomic Bomb, Hiroshima, Japan 1945	80,000 to 200,000
EARTHQUAKE, Tangshan, China, 1976	242,000
U.S. Murders versus Single Volcanic Eruption	
Total murders U. S. , 1990	20,045
VOLCANIC ERUPTION, Colombia, 1985	22,000
AIDS Deaths in United States versus Single Landslide Event	
Total AIDS deaths U. S., through April, 1992	141,200
LANDSLIDES, Kansu, China, 1920	200,000
Greatest Atrocity versus Greatest Flood Events	
The Holocaust, Europe, 1939-1945	6,000,000
FLOOD Yellow River, China, 1887	900,000 to 6,000,000
FLOOD Yangtze River, China, 1931	3,700,000

(data on familiar societal catastrophes from *The World Almanac*, 1993, New York, Pharos Books; and *The Universal Almanac,* 1993, Kansas City, Andrews and McMeel; geological catastrophes compiled from Tufty, 1969, and Office of Foreign Disaster Assistance, 1992, *Disaster History*.)

The costs of geological ignorance are staggering. These losses are mostly preventable but will occur whenever necessary geological evaluation is omitted or performed poorly by someone without suitable training. Citizens who associate geology with only the study of dinosaurs, the production of oil and gas, or prospecting for precious metals are not likely to think of consulting a geologist when property is purchased, land use zoning decisions are made, environmental legislation is passed, or building codes are drafted. Yet these are everyday areas of life in which expertise of geologists can prevent severe losses.

Geologists are essential for making regional plans to deal with major geologic hazards. The data that geologists provide about the history and immediate nature of any major geologic hazard establish the basis for risk assessment, emergency preparedness, land-use planning and public awareness programs. The principal tasks of professional geologists in regional projects are (1) to determine what hazards are likely to exist in the area under study; (2) to investigate them thoroughly enough to provide all the necessary data required to characterize the hazard and its anticipated impacts; (3) to compile and communicate the pertinent information in a concise and comprehensive manner to other team members (such as engineers, planners, government representatives, and land owners); and (4) to ensure that the hazards are addressed in any final project plan.

Geologists are also indispensable investigators in local site evaluations. Site evaluations precede many projects which may range in magnitude from a single-family home to a nuclear power plant. Geologists work productively with site landowners, civil engineers, architects, contractors and regulatory personnel. The geologist will answer at least two important questions: *"How will the geologic conditions affect the success of the proposed use of the site?"* (Example— Will a home built here likely complete its expected useful life?) and *"How might the developed site eventually cause adverse impact through its geologic setting?"* (Example— If the storage tank sited here eventually leaks, is it likely to contaminate groundwater supplies over a wide area?)

Hazardous geological materials include **swelling soils**, which expand in the presence of water and can exert pressures sufficient to shatter pavements and building foundations; **toxic minerals,** such as certain types of asbestos, that can cause health hazards; and **toxic gases**, which may include radon gas.

Hazardous geological processes most familiar to the public are those that occur as rapid events. **Earthquakes** produced by the process of rapid snapping movements along faults, **volcanoes** produced by upward-migrating magma, **landslides** produced by instantaneous failure of rock masses under the stress of gravity, and **floods** produced by a combination of weather events and land use – all produce massive fatalities and make overnight headlines. Other geologic processes, such as **soil creep** (slow downslope movement of soils that often produces disalignment of fence posts or cracked foundations of older buildings), **frost heave** (upheaval of ground due to seasonal freezing of the upper few feet) and land subsidence act more slowly and over wider regions. These slower processes take a toll on the economy. Human interaction can be an important factor in triggering or hastening the natural processes.

Lack of awareness of events through deep time induces human complacency which sometimes proves fatal. It is difficult to perceive of natural dangers in any area where we and preceding generations have spent our lives in security and comforting familiarity. This is because most catastrophic geologic hazards do not occur on a timetable that makes them easily perceived by direct experience in a single lifetime. Yet development within a hazardous area inevitably produces consequences for some inhabitants. Hundreds of thousands of unfortunate people who perished in geological catastrophes such as landslides, floods or volcanic eruptions undoubtedly felt safe up until their final moments. In June, 1991, Clark Air Base in the Philippines was evacuated when Mount Pinatubo, a volcano dormant for over 600 years, began to erupt and put property and lives at risk.

Geologic hazards are not trivial or forgiving; in terms of loss of life, geologic hazards can compare with the most severe catastrophes of contemporary society. Single geological events have, in minutes, killed more people than now live in Madison, the capital of Wisconsin, (pop. 176,000). Where urban density increases and land is extensively developed, the potential severity of loss of life and property from geologic hazards increases.

Some geologic hazards, such as radon gas and asbestos, have only recently been recognized as hazards. Their eventual costs to our society and the degree of danger these actually pose remain, at present, questions

ECONOMIC COSTS of GEOLOGIC HAZARDS in the U.S.

GEOLOGIC HAZARD	COST in 1990 Dollars*	SOURCE(S)
HAZARDS from MATERIALS		
Swelling Soils	$6 to 11 billion annually	Jones and Holtz, 1973, Civil Engrg. v. 43, n. 8, pp. 49-51; Krohn and Slosson, 1980, ASCE Proc. 4th Intnl. Conf. Swelling Soils pp. 596-608.
Reactive Aggregates 1	No estimate	———
Acid Drainage	$365 million annually to control; $13 to 54 billion cumulative to repair	USBM, 1985, IC 9027; Senate Report, 1977, 95-128
Asbestos	$12 to 75 billion cumulative for remediation of rental & commercial buildings; total well above $100 billion including litigation and enforcement	Croke and others, 1989, The Environmental Professional, v. 11, pp. 256-263. Malcolm Ross, USGS, 1993, personal communication. Costs depend on extent and kind of remediation done; removal is most expensive option.
Radon	$100 billion ultimately to bring levels to EPA recommended levels of 4 PCi/L	Estimate based on remediating about 1/3 of American homes at $2500 each plus costs for energy and public buildings.
HAZARDS from PROCESSES		
Earthquakes	$230 million annually decade prior to 1989; over $6 billion in 1989	USGS, 1978, Prof. Paper 950; Ward and Page, 1990, USGS Pamphlet, "The Loma Prieta Earthquake of October 17, 1989"
Volcanoes	$4 billion in 1980; Several million annually in aircraft damage	USGS Circular 1065, 1991, and Circular 1073, 1992
Landslides/Avalanches	$2 billion /$0.5 million annually	Schuster & Fleming, 1986, Bull. Assoc. Engrg. Geols., v. 23, pp. 11-28/ Armstrong & Williams, 1986, *The Avalanche Book*
Subsidence 2 and Permafrost 3	At least $125 million annually for human-caused subsidence; $5 million annually from natural karst subsidence	Holzer, 1984, GSA Reviews in Engrg. Geology VI; FEMA, 1980, Subsidence Task Force Report
Floods	$ 3 to 4 billion annually	USGS Prof. Paper 950
Storm Surge 4 and Coastal Hazards	$700 million annually in coastal erosion; over $40 billion in hurricanes & storm surge 1989 - early 1993	Sorensen and Mitchell, 1975 Univ. CO Institute of Behavioral Sci., NSF-RA-E-75-014; Inst. of Behavioral Sci., personal comm.

*Costs from dates reported in "SOURCE(S)" column have been reported in terms of 1990 dollars. This neglects changes in population and land use practice since the original study was done but gives a reasonable comparative approximation between hazards. [1]**Aggregates** are substances such as sand, gravel or crushed stone that are commonly mixed with cement to make concrete. [2]**Subsidence** is local downward settling of land due to insufficient support in the subsurface. [3]**Permafrost** consists of normally frozen ground in polar or alpine regions that may thaw briefly due to warm seasons or human activities and flow . [4]**Storm surge** occurs when meteorological conditions cause a sudden local rise in sea level that results in water piling up along a coast, particularly when strong shoreward winds coincide with periods of high tide. Extensive flooding then occurs over low-lying riverine flood plains and coastal plains.

without clear answers. Yet substantial sums of money are already being spent to remedy perceived hazards. Some of this expenditure may prove needless. The magnitude of risk must be accurately known in order to tell if costs to remedy a hazard are worth the expenditures.

We are often faced with the decision about whether we can wisely live in areas where geologic forces may actively oppose otherwise pleasant living conditions. An informed decision can be based on several choices.

(1) *Avoid an area where known hazards exist.* Avoidance or abandonment of a large area is usually neither practical nor necessary. The accurate mapping of geologic hazards delineates those very specific areas which should be avoided for particular kinds of development. Otherwise hazardous sites may make excellent green belt space or parks. Towns such as Janesville, Wisconsin, have created beautiful parks in areas zoned as floodplains, thus avoiding placing expensive structures where flooding will cause damage.

(2) *Evaluate the potential risk of a hazard, if activated.* Risks can never be entirely eliminated, and the process of reducing risk requires expenditures of effort and money. Assuming, without study, that a hazard will not be serious is insufficient. Life then proceeds as though the hazard were not present at all. "It can't happen here" expresses the view that is responsible for some of the greatest losses. Yet it is equally important not to expend major amounts of society's resources to remedy a hazard for which the risk is actually trivial.

(3) *Minimize the effect of the hazards by engineering design and appropriate zoning.* Civil engineers who have learned to work with geologists as team members can be solid and effective contributors to minimizing effects of geologic hazards. More structures today fail as a result of incorrectly assessing (or ignoring) the geological conditions at the site than fail due to errors in engineering design. This fact has led many jurisdictions to mandate that geological site assessments be performed by a qualified geologist. Taking geological conditions into account when writing building codes can have a profound benefit. The December, 1988, earthquake in northwestern Armenia that killed 25,000 people was smaller in magnitude (about 40% smaller) than the October, 1989, Loma Prieta earthquake in California. The latter actually occurred in an area of higher population density but produced just 67 fatalities. Good construction and design practice in California was rewarded by preservation of lives and property.

In some colleges, civil engineers are not required to take any courses in geology, and there is a need to make geology, taught by qualified geologists, a part of the education of far more civil and environmental engineers. Engineers should be cognizant of the benefits of geological assessment and be able to communicate well with professional geologists. It is no more practical for an engineer without considerable formal training and experience in geology to perform geological site investigations than it is for someone without considerable formal training in engineering to practice engineering.

Sign marks allocation of flood plain as part of the Green Belt of Janesville, Wisconsin, now known as "the city of parks." Many of the parks lie in flood plain that might otherwise have been developed with peril to future owners and liability to the public. Zoning of land prone to flooding or other geologic hazards into low-development use is one effective action that local governments can take to prevent future disaster. (photo from City of Janesville Leisure Services Division)

California, in 1968, became the first American state to require professional geological investigations of construction sites and has reaped proven benefits for that decision. Since then many states have enacted legislation to insure that qualified geologists perform critical site evaluations of the geology beneath prospective structures such as housing developments and landfills. Most of these laws were enacted after 1980.

Zoning ordinances and building codes that are based on sound information and that are conscientiously enforced are the most effective legal documents for minimizing destruction from geologic hazards. After a severe flood, citizens have often been relocated back to the same site with funding by a sympathetic government. This is an example of "living with a geologic hazard" in the illogical sense. A less costly alternative might be to zone most floodplains out of residential use and to financially encourage communities or neighborhoods that suffer repeated damage to relocate to more suitable ground. When damage or injuries occur from a geologic hazard in a residential area, the "solution" is often a lawsuit brought against a developer. The problem has not truly been remedied; the costs of the mistake have simply been transferred to a more luckless party—the future purchasers of liability and homeowners' insurance at higher premiums. A solution would be a map that clearly delineates those hazardous areas where residential development is forbidden. A suitable alternative would be a statute requiring site assessment by a qualified geologist before an area can be developed. Sound land use that takes geology into account can prevent unreasonable insurance premiums, litigation, and repeated government disaster assistance payments for the same mistakes.

An example of tragedy from design, the upper deck of the Nimitz Freeway Interstate 880 overpass in Oakland, California, collapsed during the 1989 Loma Prieta earthquake. Column supports failed during shaking, and reinforcing bars popped from the concrete posts and peeled away like spaghetti. Elsewhere, support columns wrapped in iron withstood the vibration. These columns were due to be wrapped, but over 40 lives were lost in this collapse before action could be taken. The affected area fared well for a quake of this size, primarily due to good earthquake design practice. (photo by H. G. Wilshire, USGS)

(4) Develop a network of insurance and contingency plans to cover potential loss or damage from hazards. Planners and homeowners need not be geologists, but it is useful to them to be able to recognize the geological conditions of the area in which they live, and to realize when they need the services of a geologist. A major proportion of earthquake damage is not covered by insurance. Despite public awareness about earthquakes in California, the 1987 Whittier quake produced 358 million dollars worth of damage of which only 30 million dollars of this covered by insurance. Many property owners really do not realize that they may be uninsured against pertinent geological hazards.

For the property owner, especially the prospective homeowner, a geological site assessment may answer the following:

Is the site in an area where landslides, earthquakes, volcanoes or floods have occurred during historic time? Has the area had past underground mining or a history of production from wells? Did the land ever have a previous use that might have utilized underground workings or storage tanks that might now be buried? Does the site rest on fill, and is the quality of the fill and the ground beneath it known? Are there swelling soils in the area? Have geologic hazards damaged structures elsewhere in the same rock and soil formations which underlie the site in question? Has the home ever been checked for radon? If the home is on a domestic well, has the water quality been recently checked? Is the property on the flood plain of a stream? Is the property adjoining a body of water such as a lake or ocean where there have been severe shoreline erosion problems after infrequent (such as 20-year or 50-year) storms?

The answers to these questions are not always obvious. Individuals who assumed that they lived in areas that never flooded have often been surprised with great uninsured losses. A start in the home owner's assessment may be contact with the state geological survey or a local consulting geologist (Appendix A).

Insurance agents are not always familiar with local geological hazards. After risks have been assessed, the individual can then consult with insurance professionals (agents, brokers, salespersons) to learn which firms offer coverage that would include pertinent risks. *(Note: homeowners policies do not routinely cover geologic hazards such as subsidence or earthquake damage.)* Consulting with the state insurance boards and commissioners (Appendix B) can assist one in finding insurers who provide pertinent coverage.

Compaction and settling of soft sediment formations beneath Anchorage, Alaska, led to destruction of the central part of town in the earthquake of 1964. Note the elevation difference between two sides of the street. (photo from USGS Photo Library, Denver, CO)

Living with a geologic hazard can be done well or poorly. Relocation of unmodified structures back to sites that flood repeatedly is living with the hazard in the illogical sense. This invites a future drain on the economy through disaster relief or insurance payouts. Relocation or elevation of structures may be a wiser long-term economic choice. (photo from Alabama Geological Survey)

Local governments should make plans for zoning and for contingency measures such as evacuations with involvement from a professional geologist. The first line of help for local governments lies in their own state geological surveys. (See Appendix A.) Geologists there are employed for service to the public. While they cannot, by law, normally serve as consultants, they can provide much of the available information that is known about the site or region in question and can direct the inquirer to other additional resources. In many cases, the information which the state geological survey can supply will be sufficient. Geologic maps and reports from public and private agencies are most useful in the hands of those trained to interpret them. Significant evidence that reveals a potential geologic hazard may be present in the reports and maps, but it may not be evident to the user with only an introductory background in geology. If significant risks of hazards are thought to exist, then consultation with a professional geologist may be warranted.

Applied Ignorance *versus* Applied Science

"Planning" sometimes includes ignoring or missing the available geological reports. An example is the Turnagain Heights residential area in Anchorage, Alaska. Two geologists had made available a preliminary map and report in 1950 on the quick clays (fine-grained sediments that can be solid one moment but flow like a liquid after disturbance or shaking) that underlay Anchorage. The U.S. Geological Survey (USGS) published a further report on this hazard in 1959. The report mentioned the presence of quick clays below the city, and southern Alaska was well known as an area of frequent quakes. Planners and developers were unaware of, or ignored, this information. Therefore "planning" did not provide an awareness of what would likely occur to structures built above the clay when it settled and shifted during an earthquake. Contractors and developers proceeded to build in the hazardous area and citizens purchased the homes, all in ignorance of the deep-seated instability. During the Good Friday earthquake of March 27, 1964, homes at Turnagain Heights toppled and flowed downhill in a slipping quagmire that caused millions of dollars of damage. Ironically, new homes were later built atop the same quick clays—perhaps demonstrating that no mistake is so bad that it cannot be repeated.

In contrast, an impressive study that revealed the benefits of geological site evaluations was conducted in 1969 by the City of Los Angeles Department of Building and Safety. It examined the history of damage to buildings from slope failure over a 40-year period. The enlightening revelation of the study was *that when both competent soils engineering and geologic analyses were required and when professionals were required by law to certify their work, the failure percentages were diminished from 10 percent before 1952 to 0.15 percent between 1963 and 1969.* The resulting reduction in repair costs provided savings many times the costs of the geological investigations of the sites.

PROGRESSIVE DECREASE IN LOSSES DUE TO FOUNDATION AND SLOPE FAILURES WITHIN THE CITY OF LOS ANGELES

Status - Pre 1952	Status - 1952-1962	Status - 1963-1969
No grading code, no soils engineering or engineering geology	Improved grading code, soils engineering required, very limited geology required but without formal professional status or legal responsibility for geologists	Updated grading codes; soils engineering and engineering geology required for both design and construction. Design engineers, soils engineers and geologists achieve professional status and assume legal responsibility.
10, 000 construction sites	27,000 construction sites	11,000 construction sites
$3,300,000 geotechnical damage at 1040 sites	$2,767,000 geotechnical damage at 350 sites	$80,000 geotechnical damage at 17 sites
Average loss of $330.00 per site per number produced	Average loss of $100.00 per site per number produced	Average loss of $7.00 per site per number produced
$3,173.00 averageloss to damaged site	$7,905.00 averageloss to damaged site	$4,705.00 averageloss to damaged site
Failure rate of sites built - 10.4%	Failure rate of sites built - 1.3 %	Failure rate per sites built 0.15 %

As geological input is required, losses due to geologic hazards decrease markedly. (modified from Slosson, 1969)

SUMMARY of PART 1

Geologic hazards annually take more than 100,000 lives and wrench billions of dollars from the world's economy. Such hazards can be divided into hazards that result dominantly from particular earth materials or from particular earth processes. Most of these losses are avoidable, provided that the public at large makes use of state-of-art geologic knowledge in planning and development. It has been demonstrated repeatedly that involvement of professional geologists can minimize hazards and reduce losses. A public largely ignorant of geology cannot usually perceive the need for geologists in many environmental, engineering or even domestic projects. Currently, most of our public is uneducated about geology, partly because few schools require any geology and partly because there is a lack of rigor in qualifications to teach earth science. This results in a populace prone to making expensive mistakes, particularly in the area of public policy.

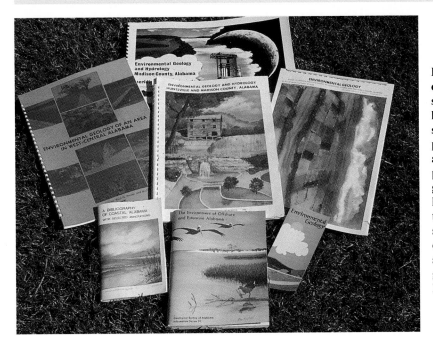

Education is one of the most effective ways of preparing to deal successfully with geologic hazards. Every state geological survey produces useful publications, distributes maps, and answers inquiries by the public. Unfortunately, lack of good earth science education leaves many citizens unaware of the resources that their geological surveys provide. Readers are encouraged to contact their state survey through the addresses given in Appendix A. (photo by Paul Moser)

References for Additional Reading on Geologic Hazards

The literature of geologic hazards falls primarily under two indexed subfields of geology: *environmental geology* and *engineering geology,* although some flood hazards may also be found under the subfield *hydrology.* Books (those titles in italics) and other references are listed that provide broad coverage of geologic hazards. References that focus on particular hazards follow each chapter in this booklet. Those marked with an "E" are considered as particularly suitable for students and teachers involved with pre-college courses.

American Society of Civil Engineers, 1974, *Analysis and Design in Geotechnical Engineering*: New York, Amer. Soc. Civil Engrs.

American Society of Civil Engineers, 1976, *Liquefaction Problems in Geotechnical Engineering*: New York, Amer. Soc. Civil Engrs.

American Society of Foundation Engineers, 1975 - Ongoing, **Case History Series**: ASFE/ The Association of Engineering Firms Practicing in the Geosciences, 811 Colesville Road Suite G 106, Silver Spring, MD, 20910. A series of case studies arranged

in terms of background, problems and outcomes, and lessons learned in brief one-page two-sided formats.

Attwell, P., and Farmer, I., 1976, *Principles of Engineering Geology*: New York, Methuen.

Bennison, A. P., and others (eds.), 1972, **Tulsa's Physical Environment**: Tulsa Geol. Society Digest, v. 37. Tulsa Geol. Soc., Suite 116, Midco Bldg., Tulsa, OK, 74103.

Bilodeau, S. W., Van Buskirk, D., and Bilodeau, W. L., 1987, **Geology of Boulder, Colorado, United States**

of America: Bull. Assoc. of Engrg. Geologists, v. 24, pp. 289 - 332. The Bulletin of the Association of Engineering Geologists occasionally features the environmental and engineering geologic aspects of major cities. This citation is one example.

Bolt, B. A., Horn, W. L., Macdonald, G. A., and Scott, R. F., 1977, *Geological Hazards* [E]: New York, Springer-Verlag.

Bowen, F. G., 1984, *Geology in Engineering*: New York, Elsevier.

Bryant, E. A., 1991, *Natural Hazards*: New York, Cambridge University Press.

Burton, I., Kates, R. W., and White, G. F., 1978, *The Environment as Hazard*: New York, Oxford Univ. Press.

Coates, D. R., 1981, *Environmental Geology*: New York, John Wiley.

Coates, D. R., 1985, *Geology and Society*: New York, Chapman and Hall.

Cornell, J., 1976, *The Great International Disaster Book* [E]: New York, Charles Scribner's Sons, Pocket Books.

Dapples, E. C., 1973, *Basic Geology for Science and Engineering*: Melbourne, FL., Krieger Pub.

Costa, J. E., and Baker, V. R., 1981, *Surficial Geology - Building with the Earth*: New York, John Wiley.

Dennen, W. H., and Moore, B. R., 1986, *Geology and Engineering*: Dubuque, IA, Wm. C. Brown.

Dodd, K., Fuller, H. K., and Clarke, P. F., 1989, **Guide to Obtaining USGS Information** [E]: U.S. Geol. Survey Circular 900. Our federal geological survey serves more than just other geologists. This free circular tells how to access their vast storehouse of information and how to order many of the USGS publications. Write Books and Open-File Reports Section, USGS, Federal Center, Box 25425, Denver, CO 80225.

El-Sabk, M. I., and Marty, T. C. (eds.), 1988, *Natural and Man-Made Hazards* : Dordrecht, Netherlands, Reidel.

Fang, H. Y., 1986, *Environmental Geotechnology*: Bethlehem, PA, Envo Pub.

Farmer, I., 1983, *Engineering Behavior of Rocks* (2nd. ed.): London, Chapman and Hall.

Federal Emergency Management Agency (FEMA), 1991, **Are you ready? Your guide to disaster preparedness** [E]: FEMA, Publications Dept., P. O. Box 70274, Washington, DC, 20224.

Federal Emergency Management Agency (FEMA), 1991, **How to help children after a disaster: A guidebook for teachers** [E]: FEMA Earthquake Education Program, 500 C Street S.W., Washington, DC 20472, (202) 646-2812.

Finkl, C. W. (ed.), 1984, *The Encyclopedia of Applied Geology* [E]: New York, Van Nostrand Reinhold.

Flawn, P. T., 1970, *Environmental Geology*: New York, Harper & Row.

Foster, H. D., 1980, *Disaster Mitigation for Planners: The Preservation of Life and Property*: New York, Springer-Verlag.

Frazier, K., 1979, *The Violent Face of Nature: Severe Phenomena and Natural Disasters* [E]: William Morrow.

Freedman, J. L. (ed.), 1977, **"Lots" of Danger - Property Buyers Guide to Land Hazards of Southwestern Pennsylvania** [E]: Pittsburgh Geol. Soc., 85 p. This is a model publication that serves property owners and prospective property owners of southwestern Pennsylvania.

Galster, R. W., 1989, **Engineering geology in Washington**: WA Div. of Geology and Earth Resources Bull. 78, v. I and v. II, 1234 p.

Gerla, P. J., and Jehn-Dellaport, T., 1989, **Environmental impact assessment for commercial real estate transfers**: Bull. Assoc. Engrg. Geologists, v. 26, pp. 531 - 540.

Gregory, K. J., and Walling, D. E., 1987, *Human Activity and Environmental Processes*: New York, John Wiley.

Griggs, G. B., and Gilchrist, J. A., 1983, *Geologic Hazards, Resources, and Environmental Planning* (2nd. ed.): Belmont, CA, Wadsworth.

Haney, D. C., Mankin, C. J., and Kottlowski, 1990, **Geologic mapping: a critical need for the nation**: Washington Concentrates, Amer. Mining Congress, June 29, 1990.

Hanna, J. A., 1991, *Disaster Planning for Health Care Facilities*: Canadian Hospital Assoc., 17 York St. Suite 100, Ottawa, Ontario, Canada, K1N 9J6, 273 p.

Harris, S. L., 1990, *Agents of Chaos* [E]: Missoula, MT, Mountain Press.

Harvey, J. C., 1983, *Geology for Geotechnical Engineers*: New York, Cambridge Univ. Press.

Hays, W. W., (ed.), 1981, **Facing geologic and hydrologic hazards** E: U.S. Geol. Survey Prof. Paper 1240-B.

Henderson, R., Heath, E. G., and Leighton, F. B., 1973, **What land use planners need from geologists**: in *Geology, Seismicity, and Environmental Impact*: Assoc. Engrg. Geologists Spec. Pub., Los Angeles, CA, pp. 37 - 43.

Howard, A. D., and Remson, I., 1978, *Geology in Environmental Planning*: New York, McGraw-Hill.

Hunt, R. E., 1984, *Geotechnical Engineering Practice*: New York, McGraw-Hill.

Hunt, R. E., 1984, *Geotechnical Engineering Investigation Manual*: New York, McGraw-Hill.

Johnson, R. B., and DeGraff, J. V., 1988, *Principles of Engineering Geology*: New York, John Wiley.

Kehew, A. E., 1988, *General Geology for Engineers*: Englewood Cliffs, NJ, Prentice-Hall.

Keller, E. A., 1985, *Environmental Geology* (5th ed.) E: Columbus, OH, Charles E. Merrill.

Krynine, D. P., and Judd, W. P., 1957, *Principles of Engineering Geology and Geotechnics*: New York, McGraw-Hill.

Legget, R. F., 1973, *Cities and Geology*: New York, McGraw-Hill.

Legget, R. F., and Hatheway, A. W., 1988, *Geology and Engineering* (3rd ed.): New York, McGraw-Hill.

Legget, R. F., and Karrow, P. F., 1982, *Handbook of Geology in Civil Engineering*: New York, McGraw-Hill.

Lundgren, L., 1986, *Environmental Geology*: Englewood Cliffs, NJ, Prentice-Hall.

Lykes, R. S., 1990, **Are you ready for disaster? A corporate guide for preparedness and response**: Manufacturers' Alliance for Productivity and Innovation, 1200 18th St. N.W., Washington, DC 20036.

McAlpin, J., 1985, **Engineering geology at the local government level: planning, review, and enforcement**: Bull. Assoc. Engrg. Geologists, v. 22, p. 315 - 327.

McHarg, I. L., 1969, *Design with Nature* E: New York Natural History Press.

Mclean, A. C., and Gribble, C. D., 1988, *Geology for Civil Engineers* (2nd ed.): London, Unwin-Hyman.

Matthewson, C. C., 1981, *Engineering Geology*: Columbus, OH, Charles E. Merrill.

Mileti, D. S., 1975, *Natural Hazard Warning Systems in the U.S.* : Natural Hazards Research and Applications Information Center, Univ. Colorado at Boulder.

Milnes, A. G., 1985, *Geology and Radwaste*: London, Academic Press.

Montgomery, C. W., 1985, *Environmental Geology* E: Dubuque, IA, Wm. C. Brown.

National Geographic, 1986, **When the earth moves** E: Natl. Geog., May,, pp. 638 - 654.

National Research Council, 1987, **Confronting natural disasters** E: NRC/NAS/NAE Advisory Committee on DNHR, 2101 Constitution Ave. NW, Washington, D. C. 20418. 60 p.

Natural Hazards Research and Applications Information Center, 1975 - present, **Natural Hazards Observer** E: Natural Hazards Research and Applications Information Center, Univ. CO, Boulder - a free bimonthly periodical featuring news, editorials and notices of newly published resources.

Neel, H. H., 1988, **The history of the registration of geologists in California**: Part 1, The Professional Geologist, September, 1988, pp. 3-5 ; Part 2, **History of the registration of geologists in California, the sequel**: The Professional Geologist, January, 1989, p. 5.

Palm, R. I., 1990, **Natural Hazards: An Integrative Framework for Research and Planning**: Baltimore, MD, Johns Hopkins University Press.

Peck, D. L., 1991, **Natural hazards and public perception: earth scientists can make the difference** E: Geotimes, v. 36, n. 5, p. 5.

Petak, W., and Atkinson, A., 1982, *Natural Hazard Risk Assessment and Public Policy; Anticipating the Unexpected*: New York, Springer-Verlag.

Pipkin, B. W., and Proctor, R. J.,(eds.), 1992, **Engineering Geology Practice in Southern California**: Assoc. Engrg. Geologists Spec. Pub., Belmont, CA, Star Publishers, 779 p.

Pitts, J. A., 1986, *Manual of Geology for Civil Engineers*: New York, Halsted Pub.

Rahn, P. H., 1986, *Engineering Geology - An Environmental Approach*: New York, Elsevier.

Roberts, A., 1982, *Applied Geotechnology: a Text for Students and Engineers on Rock Excavation and Related Topics*: Elmsford, NY, Pergamon.

Scheidegger, A. E., 1975, *Physical Aspects of Natural Catastrophes*: New York, Elsevier.

Schuirman, G., and Slosson, J. E., 1992, *Forensic Engineering*: New York, Academic Press.

Sinha, D. K. (ed.), 1990, **Natural disaster reduction for the nineties: perspectives, aspects and strategies**: International Journal Services, Rabindra Pally, P. O. Prafulla Kanan, Calcutta, 700 - 059 India, 750 p.

Slosson, J. E., 1969, **The role of engineering geology in urban planning**: in Governor's Conference on Environmental Geology: Colorado Geol. Survey Spec. Pub. n. 1, pp. 8 - 15.

Smith, K., 1992, *Environmental Hazards*: New York, Routledge, Chapman Hall, Inc.

Smith, J. V., 1985, **Protection of the human race against natural hazards (asteroids, comets, volcanoes, earthquakes)**: Geology, v. 13, pp. 675 - 678.

Spangle, W., and Associates, and others, 1976, **Earth science information in land-use planning: guidelines for earth scientists and planners**: U.S. Geol. Survey Circular 721.

Steinbrugge, K. V., 1982, *Earthquakes, Volcanoes, and Tsunamis, Anatomy of Hazards*: New York, Skandia America Group.

Tank, R. W., (ed.), 1983, *Environmental Geology; Text and Readings* (3rd ed.) E: New York, Oxford Univ. Press.

Tufty, B., 1969, *1001 Questions Answered About Earthquakes, Avalanches, Floods and Other Natural Disasters* E: New York, Dover Pub.

United States Geological Survey, 1968 - present, **Earthquakes and Volcanoes** E: A magazine that combines news reporting with journal articles. It is published bimonthly and is designed for both generalized and specialized readers. USGS, Denver Federal Center, Bldg. 41, Box 25425, Denver, CO 80225.

Utah Geological Survey, 1991, Places with Hazards: A **Teacher's Handbook on Natural Hazards in Utah for Secondary Earth Science Classes, Geologic Hazards Lecture Set** E: UT Geol. Survey, 2363 Foothill Drive, Salt Lake City, UT 84109-1491, (801) 267-7970.

Varnes, D. J., 1974, **The logic of geologic maps, with reference to their interpretation and use for engineering purposes**: U.S. Geol. Survey Prof. Paper 837.

Way, D. S., 1978, *Terrain Analysis: A Guide to Site Selection Using Aerial Photographic Interpretation*: McGraw-Hill Community Development Series, New York, McGraw-Hill.

Wermund, E. G., 1974, **Approaches to Environmental Geology - a Colloquium and Workshop**: Austin, TX, Texas Bureau Econ. Geol.

White, G. F., 1974, *Natural Hazards: Local, National, Global* E: New York, Oxford Univ. Press.

Whittow, J., 1979, *Disasters: The Anatomy of Environmental Hazards*: Univ. Georgia Press.

Wiggins, J. H., Slosson, J. E., and Krohn, J., 1978, **Natural hazards: earthquake, landslide, expansive soil loss models**: Natl. Sci. Foundation, NTIS, PB-294686/AS.

Williams, P. J., 1982, *The Surface of the Earth - an Introduction to Geotechnical Science*: New York, Longman.

Young, R. N., 1983, *Geological Environment and Soil Properties*: New York, Amer. Soc. Civil Engrs.

Zaruba, Q., and Mencl, Y., 1976, *Engineering Geology*: New York, Elsevier.

Zeckhauser, R. J., and Vicusi, W. K., 1990, **Risk within reason**: Science, v. 248, pp. 559 - 563.

Videotapes on General Geologic Hazards

No single videotape covers all geologic hazards discussed in this book. The tapes below include several geologic disasters. Some include weather disasters and human-caused disasters.

Disasters of the 20th Century: Release pending, Educational Video Network, 1401 19th St. Huntsville, TX 77340, (409) 295-5767. Call company to learn details of contents.

Geologic Hazards Maps of San Mateo County, California: 1987, 13 minutes, U.S. Geol. Survey. Available on loan from U.S. Geol. Survey Library, Special Collections, MS 955, 345 Middlefield Road, Menlo Park, CA 94025, (415) 329-5009. Although focused on one geographic area, this video can illustrate the uses of hazards maps to any audience.

Infinite Voyage - Living with Disaster E: 1990, 58 minutes, WQED Enterprises, 4802 5th Ave., Pittsburgh, PA 15213, (412) 622-1307.

Myths and Realities of Natural Disasters: 1989, 25 minutes Pan American Health Organization. Available on loan from U.S. Geol. Survey Library, Special Collections, MS 955, 345 Middlefield Road, Menlo Park, CA 94025, (415) 329-5009.

Nature's Fury: A Decade of Disasters: 1989, 60 minutes. Features geological and meteorological disasters. MPI Home Video 15825 Rob Roy Drive, Oak Forest, IL 60452, (800) 323-0442.

Pan American Health Organization Disaster Compilation: 1989, 64 minutes, features earthquake and volcanic disasters in the southern hemisphere; Available on loan from U.S. Geol. Survey Library, Special Collections, MS 955, 345 Middlefield Road, Menlo Park, CA 94025, (415) 329-5009.

Solar System Roulette: Consequences of Large Impact Events for Life on Earth: 1988, 105 minutes, U.S. Geol. Survey. Explains consequences of collision of our planet with an asteroid. U.S. Geol. Survey Library, Special Collections, MS 955, 345 Middlefield Road, Menlo Park, CA 94025, (415) 329-5009.

Slide Sets on Geologic Hazards

Sets of 35 mm slides are very useful to teachers. Illustrations in this book are available on slides from AIPG. Suppliers with extensive collections include the following:

Earthquake Engineering Research Institute, 499 14th St. Suite 320, Oakland, CA 94612-1902, (510) 451-0905.

Geophoto Publishing Company, P. O. Box 1960, Orem, UT 84059, (801) 226-4009.

National Oceanic and Atmospheric Admin. National Geophysical Data Center, 325 Broadway, Boulder, CO 80303-3328, (303) 497-6277.

United States Geological Survey Photographic Library, MS 914, P.O. Box 25046, Federal Center, Denver, CO 80225-0046 (303) 236-1010. This source also supplies photographs of hazards on digital disk for computers (DDS n. 8 by J. K. McGregor, 1992).

Geologists see both the beauty and the power of natural processes as well as the destructive aftermath that takes place when human construction and development conflict with geologic processes. Here, a geologist uses a probe to sample lava underlying the thin crust on which he stands. (photo from USGS Hawaii Volcano Observatory)

Part II - Hazards from Geological Materials

Reducing hazards from geological materials may be the costliest of all environmental projects that the public may bear through the 21st Century. Some dangers are real; some dangers appear to be more imagined than real. Citizens and elected representatives should ask: "What is the current evidence that massive expenditures are really needed to remedy these alleged hazards?" and "What benefits will result from such expenditures?"

The common minerals that most of us encounter daily in soils and rocks are not harmful, but readers who are general science and earth science teachers along with their students may encounter some of the less common ore minerals that contain arsenic, mercury, or other toxic elements. Substances that are seldom encountered outside a mineralogy laboratory do not produce significant loss of life or economic losses, and further coverage of toxic minerals is beyond the scope of this book. A source to consult about working safely with minerals in school is "Classroom dangers of toxic minerals" by J. H. Puffer in the 1979 issue of *Journal of Geological Education* (v. 27, pp. 150 - 153). Minerals and rocks are natural, but just because a substance is "natural" does not necessarily mean it is wholesome.

Regional distribution of natural chemicals in drinking water and locally grown food is related to the geology of the local area. Chemical substances that weather from rocks enter soils and natural waters. They are then ingested in locally produced foods and drinking water. Many substances are necessary nutrients. Some are beneficial when ingested in trace amounts, but become toxic when ingested in larger doses. Common calcium, sulfate, sodium, and less common substances such as zinc, iodine, fluorine and selenium have been shown to have effects on health. Work over recent decades confirms several links between regional geology and environmental health. Laymen interested in this topic are referred to the chapter "The Geologic Aspects of Environmental Health" in E. A. Keller's *Environmental Geology*; (1988, New York, Merrill Publishers) and those with more training in science may choose *Environmental Geochemistry in Health and Disease,* published as Memoir 123 of the Geological Society of America (3300 Penrose Place, Boulder, CO 80301).

Hereafter, we discuss only those geological materials that produce widespread and significant costs to life or to the economy. The geological materials we detail here include reactive minerals, asbestos, and toxic gasses—primarily radon.

Asbestos and radon are now frequent topics in newspapers and popular magazines. A decade ago, these materials were never mentioned in books on geologic hazards, but today the estimated costs for abating these substances in the United States alone could dwarf the costs of all other geologic hazards combined. Estimates include about 100 billion dollars for asbestos remediation and even larger amounts to bring indoor content of radon gas in American homes down to currently recommended levels. Despite the regulatory mandates that triggered such massive expenditures, the benefits to health that these dollars will actually produce remains very open to question.

REACTIVE MINERALS

Some hazards result because certain **minerals** (earth materials with distinctive crystal structure and chemical composition) have properties that change radically during the geological process of **weathering.**

Weathering processes produce chemical and physical changes in all materials exposed at the planet's surface. These changes constitute the natural "aging process" that manifests in deterioration of structures. Examples of damages from weathering are gradual weakening of bridge supports; corrosion and collapse of utility pipes, drainage pipes and tunnels; or cracking of pavement. Weathering constitutes a severe economic liability only when it reduces the life spans of structures below those for which they were designed. However, some weathering processes that involve special minerals are rapid enough to produce dangers to human health and safety. Such hazards include swelling soils, expansive aggregates and acid drainage. These cost the nation billions of dollars each year.

Swelling Soils

Soil, in its simplest definition, consists of unconsolidated earth material that overlies bedrock. It is as vital to life on earth as is water. Soils consist primarily of minerals, but they are much more than weathered bedrock; they are alive with bacteria, algae, fungi, insects, and other tiny organisms as well as the larger familiar plants and animals. These organisms produce important amounts of organic matter, so soils end up being mixtures of clay minerals, quartz and other minerals, along with organic matter, water and living organisms. Soils differ in composition, grain size, amounts of organic constituents, water content and engineering characteristics.

Swelling soils (or **expansive soils**) are those that increase substantially in volume when water is present. They cause over 2 billion dollars in damage annually to highways and buildings in the United States. Swelling soils are common and some occur in every state. Three mineral groups can cause swelling soils.

1. Expandable clay minerals. The most common cause of swelling soils is expandable clay minerals. Clay minerals result from ordinary chemical weathering of common rocks. The constituents of clay minerals—usually silica, with alumina, or magnesia and a little potassium and sodium—are arranged in sheets or sandwich-like structures. Members of one particular clay mineral group (**smectites**) have a powerful attraction for water

Undulation and heaving slabs distinguish this sidewalk near Dallas, Texas, as built upon swelling soils. (photo by Edward Nuhfer)

molecules between the sheets. When a clayey soil has a high percentage of the smectites, it absorbs water and expands or swells. The tiny clay particles may expand by up to 20 times their dry volume, and the bulk soil often increases in volume by about 20% to 50%. (Soils that undergo volume increases above as little as 3% are considered problem soils.) Pressures exerted can easily exceed over 5 tons per square foot, and pressures as high as 10 tons per square foot have been measured. Such pressures easily break concrete floors and cause extensive foundation damage.

2. Calcium sulfates (gypsum and anhydrite). During an afternoon in 1954, a farmer north of Moran, Texas, witnessed a distant explosion accompanied by a cloud of dust and debris. Closer inspection revealed that an area about a thousand feet long had erupted

"Popcorn-like" texture of soils at the ground surface characterized by bulges and cracks is a characteristic of soils with swelling clays. These Wyoming soils are full of bentonite, a deposit of swelling clays mined commercially for many uses—from cosmetics to oil well drilling fluids. (photo by Edward Nuhfer)

upwards as much as 20 feet, and the explosion had scattered rock fragments over some distance. This was one of several violent events that have been recorded when large amounts of the mineral anhydrite (calcium sulfate) are converted into gypsum (hydrated calcium sulfate) through contact with water. The conversion of anhydrite to gypsum, like the smectite reaction, is expansive and produces pressures during confinement of up to 700 tons per square foot. Although the reactions seldom produce as rapid or spectacular events as that recorded above, the presence of calcium sulfate minerals in soils renders them expansive, and therefore these soils must be accorded the same cautions as those that contain smectites.

3. Iron sulfides. Black shales are normally rich in iron sulfides. When these sulfides oxidize, the products (sulfuric acid and sulfate minerals) are corrosive. The sulfate minerals contain much water in their structures, and they occupy a larger volume than the original sulfide. If foundations and pavements are sited without proper design precautions on black shales, these concrete structures will experience rapid deterioration and heaving.

Fine-grained soils that lie on slopes and that are rich in swelling clays are particularly susceptible to creeping and slumping (see also section on landslides). Because of the type of clay mineral and the open fabric arrangement of the tiny clay particles, some soils and sediments can change from solids to liquids when triggered by vibration. Such soils, called **quick clays**, can flow quickly and with devastating consequences. Structures built without proper design on unstable soils soon suffer foundation cracking, sticking doors and windows, and out-of-plumb walls.

Swelling soils can be dealt with successfully, and if structures must be

Heaving of swelling soils has damaged this Texas home, causing separation near the roof. (photo by Edward Nuhfer)

Stresses exerted by swelling soils have caused this block wall surrounding a condominium complex to tilt and break. (photo by Edward Nuhfer)

Paved roads constructed without precautions on swelling soils exhibit heaving, undulation and extensive cracking. (photo by Edward Nuhfer)

located on swelling soils, methods of preparing the foundation are available. Some swelling soils can be stabilized by treatment with lime or other chemicals. These chemicals will increase the strength of soils by placing calcium or potassium ions in the parts of the clay mineral layers that would normally be entered by water. The soil thereafter has less tendency to absorb water. Other methods of treatment include excavating the swelling soils and replacing them with more stable fill material, or installing drainage controls that keep excess water away from sensitive foundations and maintain the natural level of soil moisture. Engineering remedies include placing structures on piers that are anchored below the depth of swelling, and formulating special types of flexible pavement that can withstand some heave and flexure without cracking.

Homeowners in affected regions should be certain that their insurance policies cover damages from swelling soils. In the Front Range region of Colorado, a 1980 study by the Homeowners Warranty Insurance Program of Colorado revealed that a high percentage of claims there occur as a result of swelling soils.

Swelling soils may be troublesome, but swelling properties of some rocks and soils prove useful. The more noteworthy commercial material is **bentonite**, a soft rock rich in swelling clays. Bentonites originate when volcanic ash is altered over geologic time. When properly applied, bentonite serves as moisture seals around foundations, as sealing liners in landfills and waste disposal areas, and as sealants for man-made ponds and reservoirs.

When the following steps are taken prior to construction, losses due to reactive soils are mostly preventable.

1. **Consult soil and geologic maps (where available), so as to anticipate the nature of materials likely to occur at the site.**
2. **Sample the site in an adequate manner to insure that thickness, depth and distribution of all pertinent materials are known.**
3. **Test the soils to determine their physical characteristics.**
4. **Design structures in accord with the soil conditions indicated by testing.**
5. **Build according to design specifications.**
6. **Educate the building owners or occupants about the soil situation, and instruct them in how to care for the structure through maintaining proper drainage and incorporating appropriate landscaping plans.**

No discussion intended for the layman about problem soils would be complete without the mention of **quicksand**. Novelists and movie script writers have conveniently invoked quicksand for sucking down horrified victims. These grisly portrayals are

An uplifting experience that will not be appreciated! LEFT - All is well in this newly built home until water from drains, lawn sprinklers, leaking sewers or water mains soaks swelling soil beneath foundation. RIGHT - With time, expanding soils exert several tons per square foot of pressure on foundation and shallow pilings. Without remedial measures, the house will actually deform out-of-plumb and shatter masonry and windows. Remedies vary from mere maintenance that keeps drainage away from the house to expensive reconstruction of foundations. Prior site planning that takes geology into account is always preferable to dealing with problems after a structure is built.

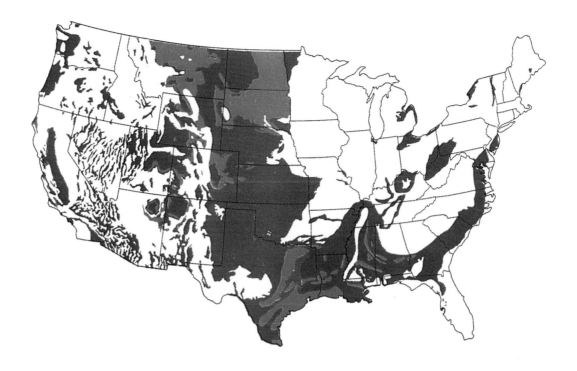

Distribution of swelling soils within the conterminous United States. Areas in red are most abundant in swelling soils, followed by areas in blue. Uncolored areas are not devoid of swelling soils. There are many small local occurrences that are not shown. (from Hays, 1981, USGS Prof. Paper 1240-B)

more ballyhoo than fact. Quicksand occurs where groundwater flows upward through loose sand toward the ground surface and often forms a pond where bubbling springs rise from a sand bottom. The force of the water moving upward pushes the grains of sand apart and prevents the normal grain-to-grain cohesion that gives sands their expected strength. Quicksand is more a condition of sand than a characteristic of sand. Objects placed on quicksand can sink through it much like sinking through water. Quicksand is essentially a hazard comparable to stepping unwittingly into a pond or lake. Just as when one falls into water, panicked thrashing about may tire a victim at some position where the face is covered and may prove fatal. In comparison to other hazards noted in this book, fatalities and economic costs attributable to quicksand are trivial. In engineering practice, diversion of groundwater to eliminate upward will return the sand to a condition capable of providing normal support.

Reactive Aggregates in Concrete

Aggregates consist of sand, gravel or crushed stone, and they are used in a variety of construction projects. After fossil fuels (oil and gas), aggregates constitute the most important economic deposits of earth materials. Finding good sources of aggregate poses a challenge in many areas of the nation. In some developed areas of the United States, most of the easily found higher quality aggregates have been depleted. Some earth materials, when used as concrete aggregates, react with the Portland cement through expansive reactions that cause accelerated aging and premature failure of the resulting concretes. Such materials are called **reactive aggregates**. Reactive minerals that commonly find their way into aggregates include **clay minerals**. Clays hidden within dolostones (rocks composed primarily of the mineral dolomite—calcium-magnesium carbonate), or within limestones (rocks composed primarily of the mineral calcite—

calcium carbonate) can be troublesome. Other reactive minerals are **micas** (layered silicate minerals), some **feldspars** (alumino-silicate minerals), **opal** (hydrated silica), **chert** (a very fine grained mixture of quartz and opal), and, **pyrite** and **marcasite** (iron sulfides). Natural non-crystalline substances that occasionally produce expansive reactions include **volcanic glasses** and **diatomaceous earth** (an earth material that consists of the silica shells of one-celled algae called diatoms). Ignorance about the nature of the aggregate produces expensive mistakes in construction of short-lived highways, bridges and sidewalks. When reactive materials are known to be present, special additives can be placed in the concrete mixture to insure longer life. A key to success lies in knowing which minerals are present before the concrete is made.

Map-cracking in this concrete reveals an expansive reaction between the aggregate and the cement within the concrete. Soon the finished surface will spall away and complete deterioration will follow. (photo by Edward Nuhfer)

Acid Drainage - A Consequence of the Sulfide Oxidation Reaction

The same oxidation of iron sulfides that produces soil expansion causes widespread damage to streams and lakes in the form of *acid drainage*. Acid drainage (often called "acid mine drainage" because of its frequent occurrence at coal mines) occurs when sulfide minerals, particularly pyrite (iron sulfide - FeS_2) and marcasite (another iron sulfide - FeS_2), react with air and water to produce the sulfuric acid and iron sulfate minerals. Iron sulfide minerals are widely distributed. Those most likely to produce acid drainage occur in waste rock from mines, in coal, and in black shales. The sulfate minerals oxidize further to yield a rusty-red iron hydroxide sludge and sulfuric acid. An overall expression of the chemical reaction is:

$$4FeS_2 + 14H_2O + 15O_2 \longrightarrow 4Fe(OH)_3 + 8H_2SO_4$$
which means
Pyrite plus **water** plus **oxygen** from the air makes **iron hydroxide** and **sulfuric acid.**

When this reaction occurs, the sulfuric acid pollutes the water, and reddish iron hydroxide sludges choke streams and reservoirs. The acid waters kill aquatic life and attack man-made structures such as concrete bridge piers, retainer walls, concrete drains, utility and sewer pipes and well casings. Estimates vary between 5,000 and 10,000 linear miles for streams in the United States that have been ruined by acid drainage. The reaction costs mining industries over 1 million dollars a day simply to control it, and cumulative damages have been estimated at between 15 and 50 billion dollars. In nature, the reaction takes place quickly in the presence of the bacterium, *Thiobacillus ferrooxidans*. This species of bacteria derives its energy from the sulfide-oxidation process and serves to speed the reaction above by rates over one hundred times what they would be in bacteria-free conditions. The reaction also produces great quantities of heat and causes problems when coal that contains reactive pyrite is stockpiled or shipped. Natural weathering of rock exposes only a little reactive iron sulfide at a time, and thus the above reaction is not usually a problem until major excavations by humans quickly expose large volumes of sulfide-rich material. Then the reactions proceed quickly and great volumes of acid may form.

Acid drainage from old Appalachian coal mines produced the rust-red sludges in the stream. The acid water corroded the Portland cement - based concrete retainer wall, and bridge supports shown will soon share the same fate. Reclamation and mining practices now minimize acid drainage. Sites like this are rarely caused by modern surface mines. Federal and state abandoned mine lands programs are having a gradual but telling effect on restoring water quality to such streams. (photo circa 1960s from WV Geol. and Economic Survey)

One of nature's water-treatment plants at work. A marsh of cattails, sphagnum moss and jewel weed has established itself below an acid-producing roaster pile left from the processing of lead-zinc ore in the early 1900s in southwest Wisconsin. Wetlands are now recognized as effective in removing toxic metals and other substances from water. Wetlands construction for acid water treatment was pioneered from mining research, and the technology is now being adopted for other types of water treatment as well. (photo by Edward Nuhfer)

Acid drainage occurs where iron sulfide minerals are exposed to air and water in both underground and surface excavations. Damage persists that was begun before acid drainage was understood and could be dealt with. Once the acid formation process establishes at a site, it can be difficult and expensive to control. One method of control is with chemicals such as lime, limestone, sodium hydroxide, or phosphate rock that neutralize acid or inhibit acid production. Another is to use surfactants (compounds such as soaps or detergents) that kill the *Thiobacillus* bacteria by stripping away their outer oily coatings that protect them from the acid. In general, these are costly, temporary measures and not permanent solutions. One promising method is to construct wetlands with special plants such as cattails and *Sphagnum* moss. These aquatic plants can survive in acid water and have a high capacity for removing toxic dissolved metals and sulfate from the water. The acid water is channeled through the constructed wetlands and emerges much cleaner than before, sometimes even clean enough to render further treatment unnecessary. The iron and sulfur are converted back to pyrite and remain in the mud of the wetlands. The best solution, though, is simply not to allow the reaction to become established. In modern surface mines, this is accomplished by mineral extraction that is followed by immediate **reclamation**. In reclamation, the mined or excavated area is graded, drainage controls are installed, topsoil is replaced, and a suitable vegetative cover is established that prevents air and bacteria from reaching the iron sulfides (see p. 21). Waste materials from the mine are not allowed to stand open to air, water and bacteria long enough to generate much acid.

Roles of the Geologist in Coping with Reactive Minerals

In mapping. Geologists are trained to identify earth materials and to know the concepts behind their distribution. Geologists use their training in identification and distribution to quickly evaluate most local sites for reactive minerals. Mapping is probably the most important aspect of both regional planning and local site characterization, and geologists employed in public service by cities, counties, states and the federal government provide an immense service by producing and publishing maps.

In sample studies. Analysis and testing of soil and rock samples overlap between engineering, geology and soil science. Engineering testing usually involves physical tests that tell what will happen when a structure is placed on a given material. Engineering tests are physical and are standardized. They help to deduce the fluid transmission characteristics of soils and the behavior of soils under varying conditions of stress and moisture. Geological testing involves similar physical tests, geophysical tests, and more sophisticated laboratory tests focused on grain size distribution, chemical composition, fabric, and particularly, mineralogy. Geological tests are designed to explain why a soil has particular properties, where such soils are distributed and, in particular, what is likely to happen to a structure such as a tunnel or building as result of changes that may take place in adjoining rocks and soil over long periods of time. Soil scientists deal more with soil as a biological medium for plant growth than do geologists or engineers, and their insights are particularly useful in construction, waste disposal and reclamation projects.

Geologists can help contractors avoid reactive aggregates in concrete by doing a microscopic characterization of prospective aggregates. Geologists who do this work employ a special microscope (called a polarizing microscope because it uses polarized light to observe specimens) that is designed for looking at crystalline materials such as minerals. This study may be done at the site of the pit or quarry where the aggregate is obtained. Technology transfer has given rise to a new field of **concrete petrography** wherein the methods of petrography (the study of rock fabrics, textures and mineral compositions in hand specimens and by polarizing microscopes) are applied to concrete to deduce its integrity, assess quality during curing and application, and learn about reasons for its failure.

In research. Dealing with reactive soils and rocks is an interdisciplinary problem that involves geologists working in conjunction with soil scientists, engineers and sometimes chemists, biologists and environmental scientists. Geologists, particularly those of the United States Bureau of Mines and in those universities and state surveys located in states with extensive coal mining, have done much of the pioneering research that allows prediction about where acid mine drainage will occur before an excavation is begun and how acid drainage can be controlled. Geologists study the processes of rock formation and rock weathering, and this knowledge is useful to help devise methods that work in accord with natural processes to control acid drainage.

Stages of Surface Mine Reclamation

Reclamation restores disturbed lands to a useful purpose and prevents long-term damages, such as acid drainage, that might otherwise result from abandonment. It consists of five stages of activity: (1) drainage control, (2) landform stabilization, (3) revegetation, (4) continued monitoring and (5) return to managed use.

(1) Drainage is continually diverted and controlled from the disturbed area. Proper replacement of waste rock covered by subsoil and then topsoil insures stable slopes and burial of any reactive minerals. This bulldozer lightly compacts the soil as its track leaves cleat marks that parallel the slope and hold seeds and moisture.

(2) Replacement of topsoil is followed by immediate seeding to establish vegetative cover. Here a hydroseeder spreads a mixture of seeds and fertilizer along with a paper mulch. Green color is biodegradable dye that allows the hydroseeder operator to view coverage.

(3) A cover crop of fast-growing rye grass prevents soil erosion and adds organic matter that helps to restore soil quality. Choice of cover crops must be done carefully because suitable cover in one climatic region may be a perennial weed in another. No land use is possible at this delicate stage. Checks on water quality and slope stability verify any need for repairs.

(4) After the cover crop dies back, more permanent perennial grasses and legumes take over and restore this mined area to pasture or meadow. Present use could be limited grazing or for wildlife or recreation. Later, trees might be planted to return this site eventually to forest. Ideally, permanent reclamation vegetation is formulated based on plants native to the local area. Reclamation plans vary and may include restoring a native prairie, returning a site to use as prime farmland, or using a site for building and development.

(photos by Edward Nuhfer)

References for Additional Reading on Reactive Mineral Hazards

Brune, G., 1965, **Anhydrite and gypsum problems in engineering geology**: Bull. Assoc. Engrg. Geologists, v. 3, pp. 26 - 38.

Campbell, D. H., 1986, *Microscopical Examination and Interpretation of Portland Cement and Clinker*: Skokie, IL, Construction Technology Laboratories, Division of Portland Cement Association.

Dougherty, M. T., and Barsotti, N. J., 1972, **Structural damage and potentially expansive sulfide minerals**: Bull. Assoc. of Engrg. Geologists, v. 9, pp. 105 - 125.

Fenner, J. L., Hamberg, D. J., and Nelson, J. D., 1983, *Building on Expansive Soils*: Civil Engineering Dept., Colorado State University, Fort Collins, CO.

Gillott, J. E., 1987, *Clay in Engineering Geology* (2nd ed.): New York, Elsevier.

Gillott, J. E., 1986, **Alkali-reactivity problems with emphasis on Canadian aggregates**: Engineering Geology, v. 23, pp. 29 - 43.

Grattan-Bellew, P. E., and Eden, W. J., 1975, **Concrete deterioration and floor heave due to biogeochemical weathering of underlying shale**: Can. Geotech. Jour., v. 12, pp. 372 - 378.

Hart, S. S., 1974, **Potentially swelling soil and rock in the Front Range corridor: Colorado**: Colorado Geol. Survey, Environmental Geol. n. 7.

Hatheway, A. W., 1992, **Stringfellow Acid Pits, world's first legal hazardous waste disposal site**: in *Engineering Geology Practice in Southern California*, Assoc. Engrg. Geologists Spec. Pub., Belmont, CA, Star Pub. Co., pp. 81 - 117.

Hollingsworth, R., and Grover, E., 1992, **Causes and repair of residential damage in southern California**: in *Engineering Geology Practice in Southern California*, Assoc. Engrg. Geologists Spec. Pub., Belmont, CA, Star Pub. Co., pp. 427 - 441.

Holtz, W. G., and Hart, S. S., 1975, **Home construction on shrinking and swelling soils**: Colorado Geol. Survey Spec. Pub. 11, 18 p.

Huang, S. L., Aughenbaugh, N. B., and Rockaway, J. D., 1986, **Swelling pressure studies of shales**: Intnl. Jour. Rock Mech. Min. Sci. & Geomech. Abstr., v. 23, pp. 371 - 377.

Jochim, C. L., 1981, **Home landscaping and maintenance on swelling soil**: Colorado Geol. Survey Spec. Pub. 14, 31 p.

Jones, D. E., and Holtz, W. G., 1973, **Expansive soils, the hidden disaster**: Civil Engineering, v. 8, pp. 49-51.

Kittrick, J. A., and others, 1979, **Acid sulfate weathering**: Soil Science Society of America, Special Pub. 10, 234 p.

Kleinmann, R. L., 1990, **Bibliography - Constructing wetlands on mined lands (1985-1990)**: Amer. Soc. Surface Mining and Reclamation, Princeton, WV.

Krohn, J. P., and Slosson, J. E., 1980, **Assessment of expansive soils in the United States**: Proceedings, 4th Intnl. Conf. on Expansive Soils: Amer. Soc. Civil Engrs., New York, v. 15, pp. 596 - 608.

Lambe, T. W., 1960, **The character and identification of expansive soils**: Federal Housing Administration Technical Publication 701, Washington, D.C.

Matthewson, C. C., Dobson, B. M., Dyke, D. L., and Lytton, R. L., 1980, **System interaction of expansive soils with light foundations**: Bull. Assoc. of Engrg. Geologists, v. 17, n. 2.

Shelton, D. C., and Prouty, R., 1979, **Nature's building codes, geology and construction in Colorado**: Colorado Geol. Survey Special Publication 12, 72 p.

Snethen, D. (ed.), 1980, **Expansive Soils**: Amer. Soc. Civil Engrs., Conference Proc., 935 p.

Tourtelot, H. A., 1974, **Geologic origin and distribution of swelling clays**: Bull. Assoc. of Engrg. Geologists, v. 11, pp. 259 - 275.

U.S. Bureau of Mines, 1985, **Control of acid mine drainage**: USBM, Info. Circular n. 9027, 61 p.

Van Dine, D. F., and Harrison, C. M., 1982, **Dolostone popouts in asphalt, Kingston, Ontario**: Can. Geotech. Jour., v. 19, pp. 194 - 201.

Velbel, M. A., 1984, **Weathering processes of rock-forming minerals**: in Fleet, M. E. (ed), *Environmental Geochemistry*, Mineralogical Assoc. Canada Short Course Handbook, v. 10, pp. 67 - 111.

Videotape on Reactive Minerals

Pyritic Black Shale Oxidation: 1985, 25 minutes, U.S. Geol. Survey Library Special Collections, MS 955, 345 Middlefield Road, Menlo Park, CA 94025, (415) 329-4009.

ASBESTOS

Abatement of asbestos may cost upwards of 100 billion dollars cumulatively. Over 90 percent of all asbestos used in the U.S. consists of a mineral which current research indicates poses minimal health risk, except under conditions of heavy industrial exposure.

The Substance and Its Uses

Asbestos occurs primarily in metamorphic rocks. "**Asbestos**" was once a loosely used commercial term for fibrous minerals used in heat-resistant fabric. "Asbestos" has a newer meaning as a group of a few fibrous minerals that are specified as health hazards by federal statutes. Asbestos includes two very different mineral groups—sheet minerals and amphiboles.

The sheet mineral group includes **chrysotile** (a hydrated magnesium silicate) which comprises about 95% of asbestos used in commercial and industrial applications. Chrysotile appears under the light microscope as thin needles, but a scanning electron microscope reveals that these fibers are actually made of tightly coiled sheets—much like a roll of gift-wrap-ping paper. Chrysotile occurs in metamorphic rocks which were produced when hot subsurface (hydrothermal) waters reacted with magnesium-rich igneous rocks. Some areas of the world where chrysotile has been commercially mined include Quebec, South Africa, Russia, Italy, Cyprus, Rhodesia and, in the United States, the west flank of the Sierra Nevada Mountains, Arizona, New York and New Jersey.

The asbestos minerals of the amphibole group occur as true needles, not coiled sheets. Those specifically regulated by federal law include **amosite** (also called *brown asbestos* - an iron-magnesium silicate), **crocidolite** (also called *blue asbestos* - a sodium-iron silicate), **anthophyllite** (a magnesium iron silicate), **tremolite** (calcium magnesium silicate), **actinolite** (calcium magnesium iron silicate) and **ferroactino-**

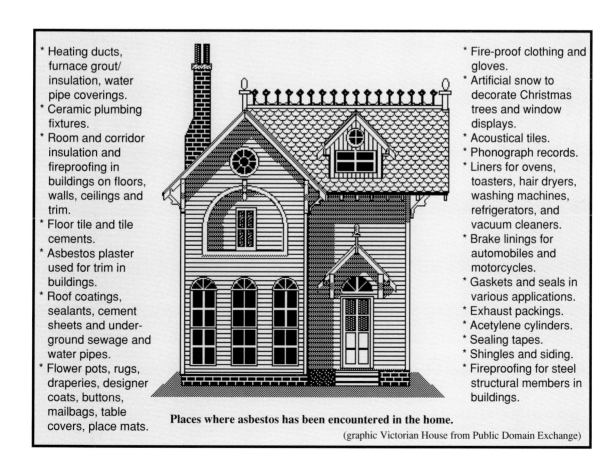

* Heating ducts, furnace grout/insulation, water pipe coverings.
* Ceramic plumbing fixtures.
* Room and corridor insulation and fireproofing in buildings on floors, walls, ceilings and trim.
* Floor tile and tile cements.
* Asbestos plaster used for trim in buildings.
* Roof coatings, sealants, cement sheets and underground sewage and water pipes.
* Flower pots, rugs, draperies, designer coats, buttons, mailbags, table covers, place mats.

* Fire-proof clothing and gloves.
* Artificial snow to decorate Christmas trees and window displays.
* Acoustical tiles.
* Phonograph records.
* Liners for ovens, toasters, hair dryers, washing machines, refrigerators, and vacuum cleaners.
* Brake linings for automobiles and motorcycles.
* Gaskets and seals in various applications.
* Exhaust packings.
* Acetylene cylinders.
* Sealing tapes.
* Shingles and siding.
* Fireproofing for steel structural members in buildings.

Places where asbestos has been encountered in the home.

(graphic Victorian House from Public Domain Exchange)

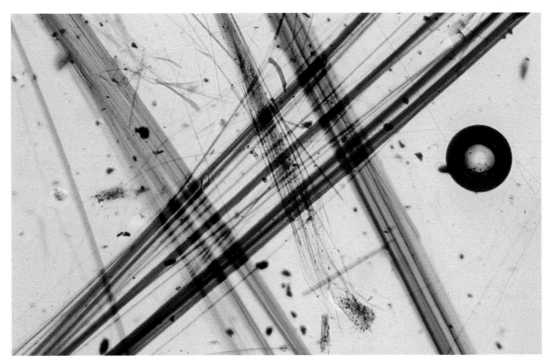

Colorful and deadly, crocidolite ("blue asbestos") fibers magnified 100 times appear in their characteristic blue and green color when seen in the petrographic microscope. Crocidolite, a potent carcinogen, was used in only a small percentage of commercial products. (photo by Janet Blabaum, Highland Geotechnical)

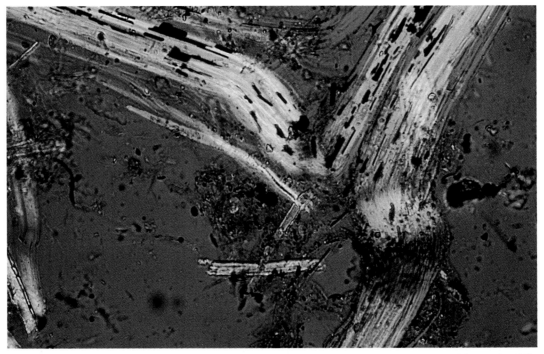

The mineral, chrysotile, magnified here at 100 times, has extensive uses. It is in many homes, offices and public buildings and is the primary substance being removed in abatement actions. It differs completely in its crystal structure from the amphibole asbestos minerals, and casual exposure to chrysotile at low levels poses no presently documented appreciable risk. Yet property owners, school districts and churches spend millions each year to have it removed as though it were the same deadly substance as crocidolite. Grouping chrysotile and crocidolite together as equal hazards results more from government edict than from scientific fact. (photo by Janet Blabaum, Highland Geotechnical)

lite (calcium iron silicate). Together these make up only about 5% of commercial asbestos.

All of these asbestos minerals have a naturally fibrous mode of occurrence and tend to separate easily into minute fibers. The fibers themselves display flexibility, high tensile strength, heat and corrosion resistance, and physical durability. These qualities have made asbestos minerals important to a broad spectrum of industrial and home products.

The Dangers of Asbestos

Exposure to specific kinds of asbestos and asbestos-containing material has been found to cause severe and often fatal lung diseases. To date, asbestos is documented as a health hazard only if it becomes friable (easily torn apart and dispersed) and airborne so that it may be inhaled. Health problems arise because amphibole asbestos fibers cannot be broken down in the lung. Fibers retained in the lung constitute a constant irritant, and the body's reaction over 10 to 40 years eventually produces cancerous cells at the site. Once these cells overcome the body's immune system, rapid mortality usually follows.

Melvin Benarde in his book, *Asbestos, The Hazardous Fiber*, notes that exposure to cigarette smoke has been found to increase the incidence of lung cancers by a factor of 10 to 18 times that of nonsmokers with occupational exposure, and 5 to 9 times that of smokers without occupational exposure. Current (1993) research shows that the best step anyone can take to reduce risk from lung disease is simply to stop smoking. The risk of dying of diseases caused from smoking is about 1 in 5; the risk of dying from asbestos without smoking is about 1 in 100,000—about 1/3 the risk of being killed by lightning.

Demographic studies, such as those carried out in the Thetford area of Quebec, Canada, support the hypothesis that asbestos which is ingested orally does not pose a significant health problem. Even diets that contained 1 percent asbestos (amosite), an astronomically huge dose, produced no enhanced mortality in laboratory rats.

The Controversy About Asbestos

Most of the proof of toxicity to humans centers around the amphibole types of asbestos, particularly crocidolite. Statistics are indeed grim for that mineral.

One study conducted at the Dana-Farber Cancer Institute in Boston, Massachusetts, showed that, of 33 men from one factory who were involved in 1953 in cigarette filter manufacture that utilized crocidolite, 19 had died of asbestos-associated disease by 1990. Crocidolite is considered the most dangerous form of asbestos. In contrast, chrysotile (95% of all asbestos used commercially) has not been clearly implicated as a hazard except in unusually heavy industrial exposures over long periods of time, but it is nevertheless legally defined as a hazardous substance.

It is difficult to gather data from general workers because there is usually no control on what kinds of asbestos individuals have been exposed to. Working groups such as carpenters, laboratory chemists, plumbers, builders, air conditioning and heating duct installers, or residents of asbestos shingle homes—all of whom have lived daily for most of their lives with chrysotile—do not report heightened mortality attributable to asbestos. Those few studies which have been able to discover and evaluate a population (one example is from Thetford, Quebec) exposed to high concentrations of chrysotile (and no other form of asbestos) show no significant enhancement of mortality. The preponderance of current data indicates that working or attending school in a building that contains the common asbestos, chrysotile, poses little risk. This data is in serious conflict with federal policy which defines chrysotile asbestos as a hazardous substance and mandates its abatement in public buildings. If chrysotile is not actually a serious health hazard, then an economic drain on our economy that may extend beyond 100 billion dollars is taking place to abate a material which is not a proven threat to health or longevity.

Misidentification of asbestos minerals is also a chronic problem. Lack of standards that result in misidentification of samples places huge, unwarranted financial burdens on some clients and sometimes leaves the general public at risk. Analysts often consist of graduates from a brief (4 days to one week) short-course, and misidentification becomes more common as poorly trained microscopists enter the profession of asbestos identification. A current (1992) program exists to accredit *laboratories* through test-round samples (through the National Voluntary Laboratory Accreditation Program - NVLAP) but not the *analysts* who perform the identifications. Therefore it is possible to have analysts of both high and low proficiency working in a NVLAP-accredited laboratory. NVLAP test-round samples can receive special attention not received by samples that are routinely

Sign north of Coalinga, Fresno County, California, warns of asbestos dust hazard. The sign was posted because of rock and soil in the area that contains chrysotile. Natural dust in the air contains some asbestos that comes simply from weathering and wind erosion. Oral ingestion of asbestos in food and water apparently poses little danger. (photo by Malcolm Ross, courtesy of USGS)

processed in large numbers, so the passing of periodic test-rounds by participating laboratories does not guarantee reliability. Because reliability in asbestos identification depends so heavily upon the personal skills of individual microscopists, periodic testing for certification of individual analysts, rather than for an entire corporation's or agency's laboratory, seems reasonable. There is currently (1993) no required qualification, testing or review process to certify every asbestos analyst who actually performs the work.

Regulation and Asbestos

Asbestos detection, management, abatement, and disposal are highly regulated. At the federal level, the United States Environmental Protection Agency (EPA) is the organization concerned with protection of the environment and occupants of school buildings. The health and safety of workers in the private sector is the concern of the Occupational Safety and Health Administration (OSHA). Further regulation and control occurs at the state level.

The Asbestos Hazard Emergency Response Act (AHERA) became effective December 14, 1987. This first phase of legislation mandated specific asbestos management procedures for all schools. The second phase, the Asbestos School Hazard Abatement Reauthorization Act (ASHARA), became effective November 28, 1992, and extends to other public buildings. These acts have produced a sudden demand for an entirely new group of asbestos specialists including asbestos analysts and asbestos abatement workers. AHERA also spurred a growing cognizance of legal liabilities (and resulting lawsuits) within the asbestos mining and manufacturing industry. This impacted manufacturers of asbestos-containing materials (ACMs), building contractors, construction companies or other employers who may unknowingly (or knowingly) expose their employees to airborne asbestos fibers.

Current (1993) policy by EPA mandates that both the amphibole and the chrysotile forms of asbestos be treated as identical hazards. This means that liability extends to owners of buildings containing asbestos, to real estate agents selling such buildings, to banks and lending institutions issuing loans for purchasing those buildings, and to purchasers of land upon which asbestos (or other hazardous materials) may be present in building materials. Homeowners who have asbestos inside their homes will, in many states, have difficulty selling their home without first abating the asbestos. Those involved in ownership or transfer of land where some asbestos may have been buried or dumped are similarly vulnerable. *At present (1993) these legal liabilities exist regardless of whether the asbestos present is benign chrysotile or one of the dangerous amphibole types.* Potential liabilities have spurred the development of an asbestos abatement industry which includes building inspection and sampling in order to minimize the cost of doing unnecessary building renovation, avert future liabilities, and prevent investments in property that may require major clean-up.

Roles of the Geologist in Asbestos Abatement

In identification. Because of their unique education in mineralogy and laboratory techniques, geologists should assume the lead role in the identification of asbestos. True asbestos consists of minerals, and only professionals who have substantial formal education in mineralogy and experience in determinative methods for minerals should perform identification work. It is common for unskilled analysts to mistake cellulose wood fiber for chrysotile, or the benign calcium silicate mineral, wollastonite ($CaSiO_3$), for the regulated amphiboles, actinolite and tremolite.

A few other fibrous minerals may yet be added to the list of materials implicated in lung disease. One zeolite (a group of silicate minerals that contain water in their crystal structures), erionite, has been recently implicated in lung disease in Turkey. However, the worry that all fibrous minerals may be serious health hazards appears groundless. Only a few minerals are hazardous, and it is important that they be clearly distinguished and not confused with the much more abundant and diverse group of benign substances.

In education. Laymen are unfamiliar with the risks of asbestos and they are unable to distinguish asbestos from other fibers or between the various mineral types of asbestos. Secondary schools should provide information about asbestos as part of the "rock and mineral" section of earth science courses, and students should be familiar with what kinds of materials may contain asbestos. Geology programs at

the university level should be aware of the need for skilled optical mineralogists in asbestos monitoring and abatement and be prepared to respond to the market needs. Colleges can prepare graduates for asbestos work by providing special course work in advanced microscopic techniques, asbestos analysis, and microscopy of man-made and earth-related materials for their students. These courses would also provide excellent electives for students who are entering the environmental, waste disposal or industrial hygiene fields.

In developing public policy. Government policies that mandate remediation and abatement should be based only upon the well-reviewed scientific evidence of the health risks and not on interests of those who may benefit financially or politically from growth of an abatement industry. Asbestos abatement has developed quickly into a multi-billion dollar business. Abatement is expensive, and businesses, homeowners, churches and school districts can be bankrupted by it. Large sums of money have been spent in abating chrysotile, which is probably a benign substance (except in unusual occupational settings that are beyond 20 fibers per cubic centimeter of air—about 10 times that of even present exposures experienced in modern asbestos mines.) For perspective, it should also be added here that even quartz, the most common earth material and the main constituent of beach sand, is clearly implicated as the cause of a disease (silicosis) when inhaled as dust in unusual quantities over considerable time, such as might occur in heavy occupational exposures as the result of not wearing protective equipment.

The difficult decisions about what actually demands abatement must be based on information provided by experts with competence, ethics and no conflicts of interest. Geologists who are specialists in mineralogy can serve as team members with health professionals to ensure that studies that link a disease with a mineral make that link with a very specific, correctly identified mineral. In 1991, 2,900 people died simply from choking on food or ingested objects. The fact that a huge abatement industry, along with a massive regulatory component of government, has sprung up to control an asbestos "hazard" which probably causes less than 100 deaths each year requires serious examination of priorities and current public policy. All asbestos is not the same, and the most common variety seems to pose little actual threat to health or longevity. The asbestos "hazard" appears at time of this writing (1993) to have been overrated beyond reason.

References for Additional Reading on Asbestos

Benarde, M. A., (ed.) 1990, *Asbestos, The Hazardous Fiber*: Boca Raton, FL, CRC Press. This is a very thorough book. Benarde's Chapter 4 on adverse health effects is recommended reading for anyone involved in asbestos legislation and remediation.

Croke, K., Mensah, E., Fabian, R., and Tolley, G., 1989, **Asbestos in buildings: effects on residential and commercial real estate values**: The Environmental Professional, v. 11, pp. 256 - 263.

Cullen, M. R., 1987, **Controversies in asbestos-related cancer**: Occup. Medicine State of the Art reviews, v. 2, p. 259.

Deer, W. A., Howie, R. A., and Zussman, J., 1982, *An Introduction to the Rock Forming Minerals*: Longman Group Ltd., England.

McCrone, W. C., 1970, **Identification of asbestos fibers by microscopical dispersion staining**: Microscope, v. 18, p. 1.

McCrone, W. C., 1987, *Asbestos Identification*: Chicago, IL, McCrone Research Institute.

McCrone, W. C., 1989, **Asbestos, twenty years later**: Amer. Environmental Laboratory, Sept., pp. 60 - 65.

McCrone, W. C., and Delly, J. G., 1973 and 1978, *The Particle Atlas* (2nd. ed.): Ann Arbor Science Publishers Inc., Michigan.

Phillips, W. R., and Griffen, D. T., 1981, *Optical Mineralogy - The Nonopaque Minerals*: W. H. Freeman and Co.

Ross, M., 1984, **A survey of asbestos-related disease in trades and mining occupations and in factory and mining communities as a means of predicting health risks of non-occupational exposure to fibrous minerals**: Amer. Society for Testing Materials, Special Technical Publication 834, pp. 51 - 104. This article is recommended reading for anyone involved in asbestos legislation and remediation.

Rutstein, J., 1989, **Asbestos, geology, and asbestology**: The Professional Geologist, Nov., 1989, pp. 7- 11.

Skinner, H. C. W., and Ross, M., and others, 1989, **Fibrous minerals, mining, and disease**: Geol. Soc. Amer. Report of Committee on Geology and Public Policy, 11 p.

Skinner, H. C. W., Ross, M., and Frondel, C., 1988, *Asbestos and other Inorganic Fibrous Materials: Mineralogy, Crystal Chemistry and Health Effects*: New York, Oxford Univ. Press.

Veblen, D. R., (ed.), **Amphiboles and other hydrous pyriboles**: Washington DC, Mineralogical Soc. Amer. Spec. Pub. 9A. Chapter 6 by Malcolm Ross on geological occurrences and health hazards of amphibole and serpentine asbestos is particularly pertinent.

World Health Organization, 1986, **Asbestos and other natural mineral fibers**: Environmental Health Criteria, n. 53, Geneva, Switzerland, World Health Organization.

Zoltai, T., 1978, **History of asbestos-related mineralogical terminology**: Natl. Bur. Standards Spec. Pub. 506.

Videotapes on Asbestos

Asbestos: 1978, 27 minutes, U.S. Natl. Institute for Occupational Safety and Health, National Audiovisual Center, National Archives and Records Administration, Customer Service Section PZ, 8700 Edgeworth Drive, Capitol Heights, MD 20743-3701, (301) 763-1896.

Asbestos: 1979, 41 minutes, Marshfield Regional Video Network, 1000 N. Oak Ave., Marshfield, WI 54449-5777, (800) 782-8581.

Asbestos Safety: 1988, 20 minutes, International Film Bureau 332 South Michigan Avenue, Chicago, IL 60604-4382, (312) 427-4545.

Asbestos: A Lethal Legacy: 1984, 57 minutes, Time-Life Video, 1271 Avenue of the Americas, New York, NY 10020 (219) 484-5940.

Asbestos - Playing it Safe: 1985, 37 minutes, National Audiovisual Center, National Archives and Records Administration, Customer Service Section PZ, 8700 Edgeworth Drive, Capitol Heights, MD 20743-3701, (301) 763-1896.

Asbestos: The Manageable Hazard: 1988, 99 minutes, Educational Video Network, 1401 19th St. Huntsville, TX 77340, (409) 295-5767.

Dangers of Asbestos in Our Environment: Separating Fact from Fiction: 1986, 70 minutes, U.S. Geol. Survey Library Special Collections, MS 955, 345 Middlefield Road, Menlo Park, CA 94025, (415) 329-5009. Geologist Malcolm Ross reviews the conflicts between epidemiological studies and the safe record of public health.

RADON and OTHER HAZARDOUS GASSES

Natural gasses are geological hazards that have caused much recent concern. Radon is unique among gas hazards because it is radioactive, its toxic effects in amounts usually found indoors are obvious only after a long period of time, and its effects are not yet well assessed. Although radiation is doubtless damaging to the cells of living organisms, there is no such thing as a "radiation-free" environment on this planet. What actually constitutes a radon level we can live with as an acceptable health risk is one of the most heated controversies of all current environmental debates. At stake is the health risk for millions of people if low levels are serious hazards, or the needless drain of many billions of dollars from the national economy for remediation if risks are negligible.

Recognizing the Radon Problem

The annual dose of radiation we receive comes from many sources. In addition to radioactivity from soil and rock, we receive radiation from diagnostic medical X-rays, from devices such as color televisions, computer screens and smoke detectors, from the sun and other cosmic sources, and from radiation inside our own bodies that enters with food and nutrients (in the form of potassium-40 and carbon-14). It has been estimated that about 40% of the average American's dose of radiation comes from indoor radon.

1984 marked the beginning of the recognition of radon, an invisible, odorless, radioactive gas, as a

major geologic hazard. In that year a worker at a nuclear power plant in Pennsylvania repeatedly set off the alarms used to detect employees' exposure to radiation at the plant. Intensive investigation finally revealed that the source of the worker's exposure was not his place of employment, but instead was his own home! The unusual accumulation in the home came from natural radon released from the soils and rock beneath the foundation, and this natural, radioactive gas provided constant, dangerous, radiation exposures for the employee and his family. The soils and rocks were not a uranium ore deposit; instead, the rocks were a **mylonite,** a rock type that is produced in fault zones where the rock is sheared and ground together. Mylonites are less common than other rocks, but they

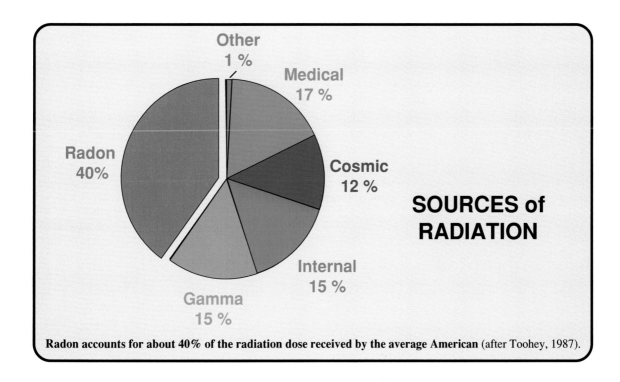

Radon accounts for about 40% of the radiation dose received by the average American (after Toohey, 1987).

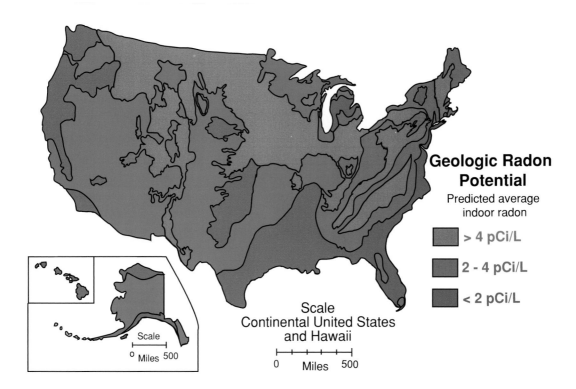

Geologic Radon Potential

Predicted average indoor radon

> 4 pCi/L

2 - 4 pCi/L

< 2 pCi/L

Scale
Continental United States
and Hawaii

0   Miles   500

Scale

0 Miles 500

Map of general radon potential in the United States. Radon concentrations are reported in the United States in picocuries (pronounced peek-o-curees) per liter of air (pCi/L). One picocurie-per-liter is about the level of radiation produced by the decay of two radon atoms in a liter of air over the course of one minute. This map is a very condensed rendition of the September, 1992, version of the *Radon Potential Map of the United States* by L. C. S. Gundersen and others in the USGS Branch of Sedimentary Processes, Denver, CO, and from the U.S. Environmental Protection Agency, Washington, D.C. This map should not be used as a substitute for actual testing.

are certainly not rare. An obvious question was, *"How many other homes might be similarly affected?"* Subsequent follow-up studies over several years now confirm that radon gas is a natural contaminant in virtually every state. This revelation may not have occurred for many years had it not been for the intense monitoring of employees by the nuclear industry.

Most homes and buildings do not have hazardous concentrations of radon. Yet owners should realize that awareness of potential radon hazards is growing, and future regulation may assign responsibility for disclosure of indoor radon levels to the seller. In some areas of the nation, a building is not marketable without an indoor radon survey.

Radiation from Geological Materials

Radiation is produced when unstable forms (radioactive isotopes) of a few chemical elements "decay." Decay is a process wherein radioactive atoms release both energy and mass. Release of energy occurs as emission of high energy radiation (gamma

rays). Mass is lost when very small heavy and light particles (alpha particles and beta particles, respectively) are shot out of the atom at high velocities like tiny bullets.

Isotopes are forms of a chemical element that differ from one another by weight. Some isotopes are radioactive; others are stable and never decay. Isotopes are distinguished in writing by presenting the name or symbol of the chemical element along with a number which denotes the atomic weight. Thus the radioactive isotope of carbon that weighs 14 units can be denoted as carbon-14 or as ^{14}C, and the stable isotope of carbon, ^{12}C that weighs 12 units can also be written as carbon-12 . ^{14}C forms naturally in the atmosphere.

Low-level radiation occurs in virtually all geological materials. In fact, natural low-level radiation has long been recognized, and its measurement has been used for decades as a useful means to distinguish different rock types in drilled wells. Potassium-40 is the most common geological radiation source and occurs in high levels in potassium-rich rocks such as granites, gneisses, slates, some schists, many shales and sandstones, in most types of glacial deposits, and in special potash salt deposits formed by evaporation of sea water. Potassium-40 decays in a single step that releases only gamma rays and produces harmless stable daughter products, calcium-40 and argon-40. Potassium-40 is not considered to be a health hazard.

Most of the remaining natural radiation come from three other isotopes: uranium-238, uranium-235 and thorium-232. In terms of radon, the important isotope is uranium-238. Uranium-238 decays in a series of steps that eventually changes uranium-238 into stable lead-206. **Radon** gas (radon-222 to be more precise) is a radioactive isotope produced during

34 STATES -- HOW THEY RANKED in the STATE/EPA INDOOR RADON SURVEY

State	Average Concentration pCi/L	% greater than 4 pCi/L	Rank
Iowa	8.8	71.1	1
North Dakota	7	60.7	2
Nebraska	5.5	53.5	3
Minnesota	4.8	45.4	4
Colorado	5.2	41.5	5
Pennsylvania	7.7	40.5	6
Maine	4.1	29.9	7
Ohio	4.3	29	8
Indiana	3.7	28.5	9
Wisconsin	3.4	26.6	10
Wyoming	3.6	26.2	11
Massachusetts	3.4	22.7	12
Kansas	3.1	22.5	13
New Mexico	3.1	21.8	14
Rhode Island	3.2	20.6	15
Idaho	3.5	19.3	16
Connecticut	2.9	18.5	17
Kentucky	2.7	17.1	18
Missouri	2.6	17	19
Vermont	2.5	15.9	20
Tennessee	2.7	15.8	21
West Virginia	2.6	15.7	22
Michigan	2.1	11.7	23
Nevada	2	10.2	24
Alaska	1.7	7.7	25
Georgia	1.8	7.5	26
North Carolina	1.4	6.7	27
Arizona	1.6	6.5	28
Alabama	1.8	6.4	29
South Carolina	1.1	3.7	30
Oklahoma	1.1	3.3	31
California	0.9	2.4	32
Louisiana	0.5	0.8	33
Hawaii	0.1	0.4	34

This list is an arrangement of data from Gundersen et al., 1991, *Preliminary Radon Potential Map of the United States*, USGS, Denver, CO. Data from other states are still being compiled. One pCi/L (picocurie per liter) is about the level of radiation produced by the decay of two radon atoms in a liter of air over the course of one minute.

one of these intermediate steps of decay of uranium-238 on its way to becoming lead-206.

Relationship between Indoor Radon and Geological Materials

Mylonites are now known to be very concentrated sources for radon gas. Uranium is also enriched in granites, gneisses, schists, slates, some sandstones and some glacial deposits. Uranium is highly concentrated within black shales deposited in marine environments and in rocks used as commercial phosphate deposits.

Low content of uranium in the bedrock beneath a structure favors low radon in that structure, but the character of the bedrock is not always a foolproof indicator. Limestones and dolostones are normally low in uranium, but they can weather to leave behind insoluble clay-soils that are rich in radioactive minerals. As a result, homes situated in limestone-derived soils can be high in radon even though the unweathered bedrock is low in uranium. This is particularly true in humid or temperate areas, such as the northern and eastern U.S., where weathering builds thick soils. Caverns in limestones can also accumulate radon, primarily because they contain floors of clay muds derived from weathering of the surrounding limestones. Fracture fillings within limestones and dolostones can contain uranium mineralization brought into the fractures at an earlier time by groundwater. Coals are usually not high in radioactive elements when deposited, but the black shales that constitute roof and floor rocks of coal seams, particularly of coals that were deposited in brackish water near marine coasts, may be high in uranium. The numerous fractures in coal (called cleats) can accumulate this radon. Elsewhere, particularly in low-grade coals (lignites), ground water may add large amounts of uranium to these coals after they are deposited and make them sources of radon. In summary, even houses sited on "clean" rocks may exhibit high radon readings if soil-forming conditions are favorable to concentrating the uranium-bearing minerals in the soil.

Radon-222 has a short half-life (time for 50% of a given amount to decay—in this case 3.8 days), which allows it to remain a toxic, radioactive gas for less than a month. About 75% of radon produced at a given time decays in about one week after its formation. These constraints mean that radon must come either from uranium within a very immediate source, or there must be conduits available for very rapid migration from below. Such conduits might be open fractures, caves, old mines, or open well bores. Most radon contamination occurs as leakage from soil and bedrock into basement foundations. Sometimes, but rarely, construction materials made from certain kinds of rock may be a source of radon, and sometimes, but rarely, water supplied by private domestic wells may be a source where radon is carried into the home dissolved in the water. There everyday activities such as showering, flushing, heating or boiling of this water release the dissolved radon into the atmosphere of the building's interior. A factor which may increase indoor radon concentrations is the use of tighter, more energy-efficient construction that greatly reduces the draftiness associated with older buildings.

Remediation, except in cases of very high concentrations of radon, can be simple. Keeping radon gas out of basements is an exercise similar to keeping a basement dry. Caulking along joints of basement floors, sealing sumps with a tight-fitting plug, or coating porous walls with a sealer can be very effective in reducing radon content. Low amounts may also be brought down to acceptable levels simply by getting additional ventilation into the building. Opening basement windows and using the fan of the central heating and air system or installing a basement window fan to bring in fresh air are helpful measures, although in most climates they could be considered as only temporary seasonal remedies. In a few cases, a more complex system (sub-slab suction) may be required to flush soil gas from beneath the foundation floor.

Why Radon is a Hazard

Radon is a hazard because it decays quickly to yield a radioactive solid (Polonium-218) which lodges permanently in the lungs. The solid then begins a rapid decay cycle that releases alpha and beta particles inside the lung within a matter of minutes. The result is damage to lung cells that may give rise to lung cancer. Ordinary concentrations of radon in the atmosphere are unavoidable and likely do not pose any danger. The gas becomes a serious threat when high concentrations build up within poorly ventilated enclosures. It is particularly dangerous to smokers who are exposed to high concentrations.

Radon Measurements

Radon concentrations are reported in the United States in **picocuries** per liter of air (pCi/L). One picocurie-per-liter is about the level of radiation produced by the decay of two radon atoms within a one liter volume over the course of one minute. The average level of outdoor radon is about 0.2 pCi/L and the average indoor level is about 1.5 pCi/L or 5 times the outdoor levels. At present, the EPA calls concentrations above 4 pCi/L "action level" concentrations and recommends remedial action when radon content is above that level.

Homeowners and managers of public buildings can perform rapid short-term measurements with inexpensive test kits. These are exposed to the building's atmosphere and are then sealed and mailed to a laboratory for prompt analyses. Test kits commonly include charcoal cannister kits and alpha-track kits. These may be purchased at many hardware stores, and the cost of the kit should include the analysis.

The inexpensive charcoal cannister kits are used to monitor for only short-term periods (one to four days) and therefore they provide a convenient means for a quick evaluation. However, a four-day survey represents only a little over 1% of the year. Results from just a single short-term study should not serve as the sole basis for remedial action. A few short-term tests through the seasons will give a more realistic picture of the degree of hazard. An unusually high result should lead quickly to more precise evaluation.

Alpha track detectors are also inexpensive and can be deployed through an entire year. They require at least 3 months' exposure to obtain good data. These kits should be placed initially in those areas of the home that are likely to receive radon from external sources (such as in the bathroom where radon might enter through a domestic water source) and in living areas where radon may be concentrated by reduced circulation (such as a basement; crawl spaces don't qualify as living areas). Because radon is a heavy gas, it may be concentrated more at lower levels of the house. However, foundations constructed with hollow materials, such as some types of concrete block, can divert the radon to the first floor rather than to the basement.

Indoor radon concentrations vary markedly through the year in accord with weather changes. Maximum readings should be expected to occur during the time of year of minimum ventilation. This is usually winter, when the building is operated to conserve heat loss and when snow and ice prevent easy escape of radon from soils into the atmosphere.

COMPARATIVE RISK CHART for RADON LEVELS

Radon Level pCi/L	*Estimated Fatal Lung Cancers/1000*	*Comparable Exposure Levels*	*Comparable Risk Estimate*
200	440 - 770	1,000 times average outdoor level	More than 60 times non-smoker risk
100	270 - 630	100 times average indoor level	Four pack/day smoker or 20,000 chest X-rays/yr
40	120 - 380	100 times average outdoor level	Two pack/day smoker
20	60 - 210		
10	30 - 120	10 times average indoor level	One pack/day smoker
4	13 - 50	10 times average outdoor level	Five times non-smoker risk
2	7 - 30		
1	3 - 13	Average indoor level	Non-smoker risk of fatal lung cancer
0.2	1 - 3	Average outdoor level	20 chest X-rays/yr

EPA recommends action be taken if indoor radon levels exceed 4 pCi/L, which is 10 times the average outdoor level. Some EPA representatives believe the action level should be lowered to 2 pCi/L; other scientists dissent and claim the risks estimated in this chart are already much too high for low levels of radon. The action level in European countries is set at 10 pCi/L. Note that this chart is only one estimate; it is not based upon any scientific result derived from a study of a large population meeting the listed radiation criteria. (from U.S. Environmental Protection Agency)

The Radon Controversy

Some scientists hotly contest the need for widespread concern and expensive remediation. Disagreement comes because assessing the radon hazard is very difficult at this time. To assess the degree of hazard clearly, scientists must be able to attribute to the hazard the specific fatalities that result from it within a large population. The case for radon is especially troublesome because (1) radon produces lethal consequences only after many years of exposure and has only recently become recognized as a hazard and, (2) lung cancer, the terminal disease produced by radon, is produced by many other lung irritants as well, the greatest of which is smoking and not the least of which may be passive inhalation of smoke. To use the mortality rate for lung cancers directly, scientists need to distinguish specifically the lung cancers that are caused by radon. At time of this writing, that data is just not available for a sufficient population to directly assess the radon risk.

At present, evidence that low concentrations of radon in homes may pose significant risk must come from two indirect observations. The main indication of potential danger comes from known populations of miners exposed to radon in uranium mines. These workers, particularly *the workers who smoke as well as suffer occupational exposure* to radon, do have a significantly increased frequency of lung cancer. There is an undeniable risk for smokers at these levels of exposure. In contrast, another line of evidence which shows no significant risk lies in recent demographic studies which have tried to relate average life span over an area to regional concentrations of geological background radiation. These fail to support any link between regional radiation levels and expected longevity. In fact, North Dakota, which has high background radiation and some very high radon levels, is the state with the greatest longevity.

Problems arise when such indirect evidence becomes the basis for policy. First, the population of miners who received high doses of radiation from both radon gas *and* mineral dust is not representative of the populace that receives only low doses of radon gas at home. Radon concentrations such as those found in uranium mines and in the home of the nuclear plant worker in Pennsylvania are rare occurrences, and using these exceptions as the basis to develop policy for the general populace may lead to unwise mandates and needless terror. In contrast, the regional background radiation studies do not directly address the indoor radon concentrated in specific homes for specific individuals, and thus these regional studies may lead to an interpretation that induces false security.

In summary, concentrations of radon in a home can be inexpensively monitored and measured. Once a level has been established in pCi/L, the risks of the actual likelihood of contracting lung cancer, as estimated by the United States EPA, can be obtained from the risk table on radon levels (see page 33). Remember that the table is based only upon indirect evidence. If it is correct, then indoor radon should produce about 20,000 fatalities in the U.S. each year.

Other Toxic Gasses

Although radon has been a frequent topic of the media in the late 1980s and early 1990s, there are other natural gasses that sometimes pose deadly hazards under special conditions. About 1,000 people a year in the U.S. die through accidental poisoning by gas; many of these poisonings are due to **methane** used as "natural gas" in home heating and cooking. Residents who are not miners or drillers by profession, and who do not live with the special conditions listed below, will not likely be affected.

Methane, **carbon monoxide** and **carbon dioxide** are gasses that were particularly dreaded by coal miners prior to modern design, monitoring and ventilation of mines. The gasses were colloquially dubbed "fire-damp" or "choke-damp" in reference to the deaths of miners by fires, explosions and suffocation. These are not simply hazards of the distant past; 200 miners died in 1992 in Ankara, Turkey, in a methane explosion.

Hydrogen sulfide, a natural gas associated in lethal concentrations with some petroleum deposits, is even more toxic than the "cyanide" gas used in executions. The human body can sense hydrogen sulfide gas by its unpleasant "rotten egg odor" in quantities of less than a few parts per million in air. The gas is still dreaded by oil drillers, and whole drill crews have been killed instantly when this "sour gas" belched from a well onto a drill floor.

All gasses have the ability to migrate into shallow openings such as pore space in soils or rocks or into man-made openings such as wells, mines and tunnels, shallow sewers, septic tanks, utility conduits, drains or basements. Where seeps of these gasses occur naturally, their presence is evident by phenomena such as foul odors or "burning springs," and therefore

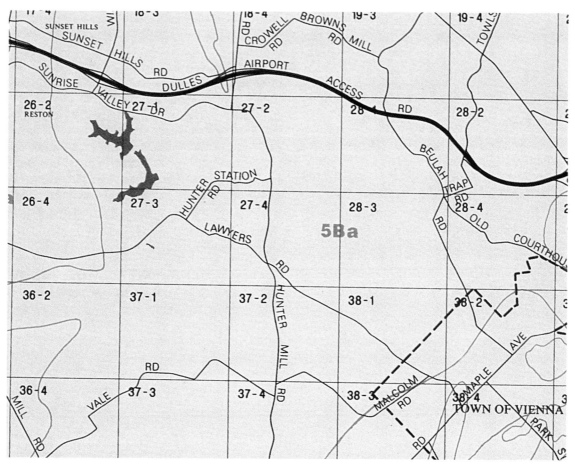

Portion of radon map from USGS Map Folio 2047, Fairfax County, VA. Radon-risk areas labeled and outlined in red ink are keyed to a text which accompanies this map. Such detailed maps are now not common in the U.S., but may become more so as result of 1992 funding for the National Geologic Mapping Act of 1992 (H. R. 2763).

the area is avoided for residence. Some danger occurs when development occurs over old mine workings or old leaking well casings. When gasses reach sufficient concentrations in developed areas, dangers arise from the potential for combustion (methane), explosion (methane), toxic inhalation (hydrogen sulfide) or suffocation (carbon dioxide and nitrogen). Methane gas from gas mains or sewers may leak and migrate through underground openings over a large area and explode with fatal consequences. Such a methane explosion occurred in Guadalajara, Mexico, on April 22, 1992, and left nearly 200 dead.

Gasses can also be released during earthquakes. Broken gas and sewer mains are obvious gas sources, but gasses can also be released with mud and sand boils and from ruptured cover over waste sites.

Volcanoes (see section this book, p. 54) are well known for release of toxic and nauseous gasses that include sulfurous and chloride acid vapors. In Cameroon in 1986, over 1,700 people as well as wildlife and farm animals perished beneath a plume of carbon dioxide that belched forth from beneath a 200-meter-deep lake located within a volcanic cone.

Underground fires in coal seams, abandoned coal mines and spoil piles can perpetually release foul-smelling and health-damaging fumes on unfortunate residents nearby. These fumes consist of sulfurous gasses and hydrocarbons with an asphalt odor that are released and distilled from the coal and associated organic-rich roof and floor rocks.

Finally, man's disposal of wastes, particularly organic wastes and trash into the geological environment in "land fills," can often be a source of hazardous gasses. The same microorganisms that are responsible for converting natural organic matter into methane in swamps and marshes are also responsible for converting man-made organic wastes in landfills to that same gas. In instances where careless land use planning occurred, structures built over old land fills accumulated methane within basements, sewers and utility conduits with disastrous consequences of fire and explosion. Production of methane gas at waste disposal sites is so prolific, that it can at times serve as a useful local source of fuel.

Roles of the Geologist in Reduction of Gas Hazards

In mapping. Geologists can tell from simply looking at a geologic map where a number of areas of risk are likely to be located. The ability to make this interpretation comes from formal university training obtained in a number of courses and from field experience. This same training permits geologists to map deposits, both at the surface and at depth, in areas that have not been previously mapped, and to interpret older maps and reports in the light of newer, state-of-the-art knowledge.

In public service. As evidenced from this entire booklet, sites for new buildings should be evaluated by a qualified geologist before construction or design plans are begun. Often the state geological survey can provide help of a general nature with maps that outline those areas that are underlain by bedrock of known or probable elevated concentrations of uranium. Aeroradioactivity maps, maps of surface radiation made from readings taken in low-flying airplanes, have been produced by the USGS for some areas. The state survey will likely have these maps available for review. The state surveys should also know about particular ground water sources that may be high in radon. As of 1993, the Branch of Sedimentary Processes at the USGS in Denver completed a map of the radon potential of the United States. The map is published with an accompanying booklet for each state.

In research. As result of the recently recognized radon problem, geologists have learned surprising facts about the types of geologic conditions that lead to increased radon in structures, and about how radon becomes enriched in soil, groundwater and rock. New work will reveal more, and the data provided by geologists will likely lead to a more precise statement about actual dangers of radon to homeowners.

SUMMARY of PART II

Widespread education is the most significant step that can be taken against hazards from geological materials. However, some individuals teaching earth science, physical geography, physical geology and introductory geology have never themselves taken formal courses in mineralogy, petrology or soils. Property owners are the main victims of economic losses, where swelling soils or inappropriate construction materials can wreak havoc with structures. Safeguards there include procuring good information about the nature of the site from a professional geologist, and obtaining appropriate insurance to cover possibility of loss.

Radon and asbestos are two topics that are frequently in the national media. Massive amounts of money are already being spent to remedy these hazards, and some estimates to remediate these exceed the combined costs of all geological hazards. State-of-the-art knowledge about these hazards seems to be unknown or misunderstood by policy makers and journalists. The public remains ill-informed without realizing the substance behind the controversies that surround asbestos and radon. While some segments of the populace suffer needless fear and unwarranted financial loss, others are oblivious to real dangers. Massive regulatory actions that are not based upon solid science may be some of the most expensive blunders of this century.

References for Additional Reading on Radon and other Gasses
"E" Denotes references particularly suitable for educators.

Abelson, P. H., 1990, **Uncertainties about health effects of radon** E: Science, v. 250, p. 353.

Adams, J. A. S., and Lowder, W. M. (eds.), 1964, *The Natural Radiation Environment*: University of Chicago Press.

Association of Bay Area Governments, 1991, **Toxic gas releases in earthquakes: existing programs, sources, and mitigation strategies**: ABAG Metro Center, P.O. Box 2050, Oakland, CA 95604.

Brookins, D. G., 1990, *The Indoor Radon Problem* E: New York, Columbia University Press.

Cabarrubias, J., 1992, **Methane gas hazard in Fairfax District, Los Angeles**: in *Engineering Geology Practice in Southern California*, Assoc. Engrg. Geologists Spec. Pub., Belmont, CA, Star Pub Co., pp. 131 - 143.

Cohen, B., 1989, *Radon - A Homeowner's Guide to Detection and Control*: New York, Avon Books.

Environmental Protection Agency, 1986, **A citizens' guide to radon, what it is and what to do about it** E: U.S. EPA., OPA-86-004.

Environmental Protection Agency, 1985, **Nationwide occurrence of radon and other natural radioactivity in public water supplies**: U.S. EPA., 520/5-85/008.

Environmental Protection Agency, 1986, **Radon reduction methods, a homeowners guide** E: U.S. EPA., OPA-86-005.

Environmental Protection Agency, 1986, **Radon reduction techniques for detached houses - technical guidance**: U.S. EPA., 625/5-86/019.

Environmental Protection Agency, 1991, **International symposium on radon and radon reduction technology**: Proceedings papers in 5 volumes. U.S. EPA, Air and Energy Environmental Research Laboratory, Research Triangle Park, NC 27711.

Gates, A. E., and Gundersen, L. C. (eds.), 1993, **Geologic controls on radon**: Geol. Soc. Amer. Spec. Paper 271, in press.

Graves, B., (ed.), 1987, *Radon in Groundwater*: Chelsea, MI, Lewis Publishers. (Produced from the conference of the National Water Well Association and the U.S. EPA; also available from Natl. Ground Water Assoc., Dublin, OH).

Gundersen, L. C. S., 1992, **Hidden Hazards of radon - scanning the country for problem locations** E: Earth, November, pp. 54 - 61.

Gundersen, L. C. S., and others, 1991, **Preliminary radon potential map of the United States**: U.S. Geol. Survey, Denver, CO, in press.

Horton, T. R., 1985, **Nationwide occurrence of radon and other natural radioactivity in public water supplies**: U.S. EPA., 520/5-85-008, 708 p.

Lafavore, M., 1987, *Radon: the Invisible Threat*: Emmaus, PA, Rodale Press.

Mafoske, W. J., and Edelstein, M. R., 1988, *Radon and the Environment*: Park Ridge, NJ, Noyes Pub.

Morrow, R. (ed.), 1989, *The Radon Industry Directory*: P.O. Box 25551, Alexandria, VA 22313, Radon Press Inc.

Nazaroff, W. W., and Nero, A. V., Jr. (eds.), 1987, *Radon and Its Decay Products in Indoor Air*: New York, Wiley.

National Council on Radiation Protection and Measurements, 1975, **Natural background radiation in the United States**: NCRP, Rept. 45, Bethesda, MD, 163 p.

National Council on Radiation Protection and Measurements, 1984, **Exposures from the uranium series with emphasis on radon and its daughters**: NCRP, Rept. 77, Bethesda, MD, 132 p.

National Council on Radiation Protection and Measurements, 1984, **Evaluation of occupational and environmental exposures to radon and radon daughters in the United States**: NCRP, Rept. 78, Bethesda, MD, 204 p.

Nero, A. V., Jr., 1985, **The indoor radon story**: Technology Review, v. 89, p. 28 - 31; and p. 336- 340.

Schumann, R. R., Gundersen, L. C. S., and Tanner, A. B., 1993, **Geology and occurrence of radon**: in *Radon; Measurement, Prevalence, and Control*, Amer. Soc. for Testing Materials ASTM MNL 15.

Tanner, A. B., 1986, **Indoor radon and its sources in the ground**: U.S. Geol. Survey Open File Rept. 86-222, 5 p.

Toohey, R. E., 1987, **Radon *vs.* lung cancer: New study weighs the risks**: Logos, Argonne Natl. Laboratory, v. 5, pp. 7 - 11.

Videotapes on Radon and Other Gasses

H$_2$S: The Unexpected - How to Work Safely Around Hydrogen Sulfide: undated, 28 minutes, Gulf Publishing Co. Video Publishing, 3301 Allen Parkway, Houston, TX 77019-1896, (713) 529-4301. A safety film that focuses on dealing with hydrogen sulfide (H$_2$S) as a hazard at well sites.

Radon: 1989, 26 minutes, Films for the Humanities and Sciences, 743 Alexander Road, Princeton, NJ 08540, (609) 452-1128. Possible health implications and methods homeowners can use to detect radon and minimize its concentrations in the living area.

Radon - a Homeowners Guide E: 1989, 25 minutes, Atlas Video, 4915 St. Elmo Ave., Suite 305, Bethesda, MD 20814, (301) 907-0030.

Part III - Hazards From Geological Processes

Part III contains chapters on earthquakes, volcanoes, landslides, subsidence, floods and coastal hazards that result from the dynamic processes that characterize our planet. Each chapter details distribution of the hazard, the nature of the hazard through deep time, methods of measuring or quantifying the severity of a hazard where applicable, dangers posed by the hazard, methods of reducing losses from the hazard, and the role of geologists in mitigating the hazards. Every chapter ends with an extensive list of references for further information, including lists of available videos on specific hazards.

EARTHQUAKES

In densely populated areas that have taken no precautions through building codes, single earthquakes have taken more than 100,000 lives within less time than it will take you to read this page. Since 1884, there have been over 30 major earthquakes within the United States that have produced significant financial loss and loss of life. The 1989 Loma Prieta earthquake alone produced over 6 billion dollars in damage. Loss is minimized through land use zoning and engineering design that take geology into account. The eastern and midwestern U.S. are not exempt from earthquake hazards; some of the most powerful earthquakes in the continent have occurred there.

Former five-story communications building in Spitak, Armenia. This failure is typical of buildings constructed without adequate ties between floors and walls. During vibration, the floors collapse through standing walls and leave no open space where victims might survive. Hospitals in this area were constructed in the same way, and their collapse killed a large part of the medical personnel. The Armenian earthquake left 25,000 dead, 15,000 injured and over half a million homeless. Losses were more than 14 billion U.S. dollars. (photo by C. J. Langer, USGS)

Earthquake Severity and Magnitude

The power suddenly released during a major earthquake produces a terrifying experience. This power is described in terms of its magnitude and its intensity. The Alaskan quake of 1964 (magnitude 9.2) released as much energy as would 25 thousand atomic bombs of the size that destroyed Hiroshima in 1945.

The **Richter Magnitude Scale**, devised in 1934 by the late Dr. Charles F. Richter at California Institute of Technology, expresses the calculated energy released by an earthquake. The Richter magnitude is based on a logarithmic scale with each whole number step on the scale representing a tenfold increase in seismic wave trace amplitude. A magnitude of 1 on the Richter scale represents the energy released in detonation of about 6 ounces of TNT, whereas a quake with a magnitude of 8 represents energy equivalent to that released by an explosion of over 6 million tons of TNT. Earthquakes that register above 7 are considered to be "major" earthquakes; those above 8 are termed "great" quakes.

Another scale, the **Mercalli Intensity Scale** developed in 1902 by the Italian geologist Giuseppe Mercalli, employs observations of an earthquake's effects on man-made structures, and is a more easily understood expression of severity to the non-scientist. Mercalli's scale, as modified in 1931, is expressed by Roman numerals "I" through "XII." A "I" is rarely felt; a "V" is easily felt, with small objects such as vases overturning or falling from shelves. A "XII" results in extreme damage to nearly all structures.

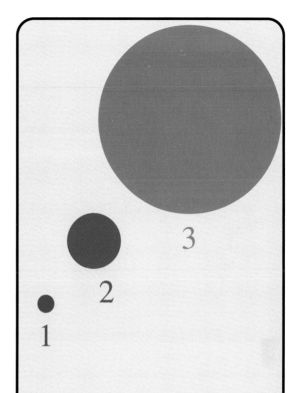

Small numbers mean a big difference on the Richter scale. Each integer on the scale indicates a quake producing an *amplitude* 10 times as large as the quake described by the next lower digit. *Energy* released increases about 40-fold between integers. Circle *areas* above show the scale of logarithmic growth of amplitudes for Richter magnitudes 1-3. To show a magnitude of 10 at this same scale would require a sheet of paper nearly 500 feet (150 meters) wide.

EARTHQUAKE RATING SCALES COMPARED IN TERMS OF ENERGY RELEASED AND DAMAGE OBSERVED

RICHTER MAGNITUDE	MERCALLI INTENSITY	EQUIVALENT ENERGY in WEIGHTS of TNT	WITNESSED OBSERVATIONS	
up to 3	I - II	less than 400 lbs	barely noticeable	
3 - 4	II- III	up to 6 tons	feels like vibration of nearby truck	
>4 - 5	IV - V	up to 200 tons	small objects upset, sleepers awaken	Modified from Petak and Atkisson (1982) and Earthquake Information Bulletin (1974, Sept.- Oct.)
>5 - 6	VI - VII	up to 6, 270 tons	difficult to stand; damage to masonry	
>6 - 7	VII - VIII	up to 100,000 tons	general panic; some walls fall	
>7 - 8	IX - XI	up to 6, 270,000 tons	wholesale destruction, large landslides	
8 - 9	XI - XII	up to 200,000,000 tons	total damage; waves seen on ground surface	

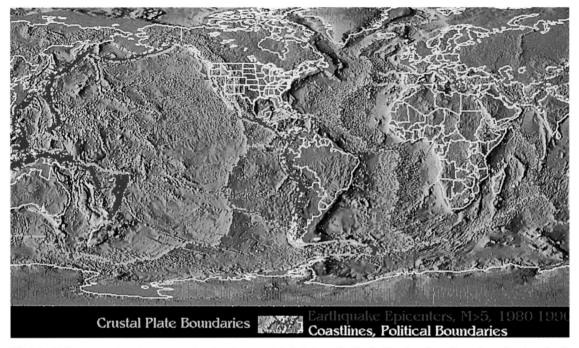

Crustal Plate Boundaries   Earthquake Epicenters, M>5, 1980-1990
Coastlines, Political Boundaries

World relief map produced on computer showing crustal plate boundaries (yellow) and earthquake epicenters (red) for large earthquakes from 1980 through 1990. (image produced by National Geophysical Data Center)

Distribution of Earthquakes

We know that the crust of the planet is not a continuous skin, but instead it is like a completed jigsaw puzzle, with the actual pieces of crust termed **plates**. Unlike a jigsaw puzzle's pieces, the plates move. Plate movement is driven by motion within the deeper portion of the earth (the mantle) that supports the crust. The plates move only at about the rate at which your fingernails grow, but tremendous energy is required to move such immense masses of rock at all.

Over deep time, the motion is not smooth and steady. Instead, the motion is jerky, with the plates jamming up against each other for a while, until stress builds sufficiently to break the locking friction, and motion proceeds with a rapid snap. **Earthquake** is the term for an event when the ground trembles and shakes during the snapping release of the accumulated stress. Major stresses along plate boundaries produce numerous fractures along which the movement repeatedly occurs. Such fractures are termed **faults**, and faults along which motion has been perceived in historic time are termed **active faults**. Almost all earthquakes occur from the process of natural stress being released along large faults. However, in a few rare instances, minor earthquakes have been produced by human activities such as injection

A bird's-eye view shows the San Andreas fault of California as a linear gash dividing the Carizzo Plain (left) from the Temblor Range. (photo by R. E. Wallace, USGS)

WORLD'S MAJOR DISASTROUS EARTHQUAKES

YEAR	RICHTER MAGNITUDE	LOCATION	APPROXIMATE DEATHS
365	unknown	Crete and Greece	50,000
526	unknown	Syria Area	250,000
893	unknown	India	180,000
1138	unknown	Syria	100,000
1293	unknown	Japan	30,000
1455	unknown	Italy	40,000
1556	unknown	Shaanxi, China	830,000
1667	unknown	Caucasia	80,000
1693	unknown	Sicily	60,000
1737	unknown	Calcutta, India	300,000
1755	8.7	Lisbon, Portugal	60,000
1783	unknown	Italy	50,000
1797	unknown	Ecuador	41,000
1868	unknown	Ecuador and Colombia	70,000
1908	7.5	Southern Italy	58,000
1915	7.5	Central Italy	32,000
1920	8.6	Kansu, China	200,000
1923	8.3	Yokohama, Japan	103,000
1927	8.3	Nan-Shan, China	200,000
1932	7.6	Kansou, China	70,000
1935	7.5	Northern India	60,000
1939	7.8	Chile	40,000
1939	7.9	Erzincan, Turkey	23,000
1949	7.3	Pelileo, Ecuador	6,000
1960	5.8	Agadir, Morocco	12,000
1970	7.7	Chimbote, Peru	67,000
1976	8.0	Tangshan, China	242,000
1976	7.5	Guatemala	23,000
1978	7.7	Northeast Iran	25,000
1985	8.1	Mexico City, Mexico	9,500
1988	6.8	Armenia	25,000
1990	7.7	Northwest Iran	40,000

Casualties given here on fatalities include associated fires, landslides, and tsunamis. Data comes primarily from Gere and Shah, 1984, *Terra Non Firma* **and Office of Foreign Disaster Assistance, 1992,** *Disaster History.*

of fluids underground near Denver, Colorado, in 1962 or by filling of large reservoirs, such as at Koyna Reservoir in India in 1967. In these cases, human-induced stress causes rock to move along **joints** (natural fractures in the rock which have experienced no prior offset movement) and quakes are the result.

Earthquake Occurrence and the Concept of Deep Time

Earthquakes are one of the few geologic hazards that seldom produce sufficient warning to permit evacuation or relocation. The major problems in dealing with earthquakes lie in their anticipation and prediction. If earthquakes occurred periodically at regular time intervals, then they would be easy to predict. Unfortunately, earthquakes don't occur with regularity. Where earthquakes occur frequently, such as in California and Japan, they are easy to anticipate (i.e., we know that one or more will occur within the next few years), but they are not possible to predict (i.e., no one knows on what day or even year that they will occur.)

In the midwestern and eastern United States, earthquakes are not associated with plate boundaries, but instead occur along deep faults within the North American plate. These faults are apparently tightly locked because tremors are infrequent. When energy is not released in a series of frequent tremors, this energy builds over time until huge amounts are released in a single earthquake. Such earthquakes are noted for their size and destructive power, and because they occur infrequently, from once every few decades to perhaps centuries, they are difficult to anticipate, much less predict.

The realm of our planet's crust is active, and the million or so earthquakes that occur within it each year testify to its dynamic nature. Over 99% of these million quakes pose no danger, and are only known through the responses they produce in the sensitive instruments of seismologists. Yet, over 100 earthquakes occur each year that are capable of doing severe damage.

Dangers from Earthquakes

Strangely, the release of all of this power beneath the surface of the planet poses little *direct* danger to an individual. Humans are not "shaken to death" by earthquakes, and film depictions that show struggling, terrified victims falling into bottomless fiery chasms are portrayals with entertainment as their sole redeeming value.

The greatest dangers come from the interaction between earthquake vibrations and man's own structures. The dangers of being crushed in a falling building, getting burned in fires that burst from ruptured gas mains or fuel tanks, being swept away and drowned in a flood from a burst reservoir, or getting buried beneath quake-induced landslides are very real. About every 20 years a single earthquake occurs that takes over 100,000 lives. One earthquake in China in 1556 killed over three-quarters of a million people.

The hazard arising from a particular earthquake will depend in part on its location and severity. When rock under stress ruptures, the violent adjustment sends shock waves radiating outward from around the rupture point or **focus** (usually several kilometers deep). To an observer on the ground, the shock wave vibrations move as ripples, much as ripples radiate outward in circles when a rock is tossed into a body of still water. The **epicenter** is the point on the ground surface directly above the point of origin or focus. In general, the vibrations will be felt less strongly the farther an observer is from the epicenter.

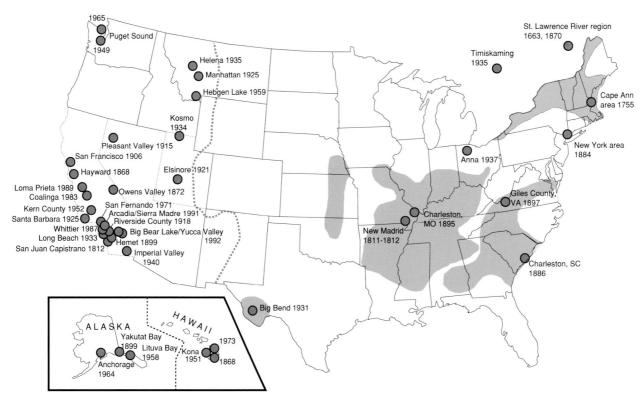

Earthquakes in United States and nearby Canada that have caused notable damage. Shaded zones show high-risk areas for earthquake damage in eastern and midwestern U.S. Most of western U.S. to left of dashed line running from New Mexico through Montana is high-risk area. The 1992 Big-Bear Lake/Yucca Valley quake caused little dollar damage or loss of life, but is listed because of severe surface cracking that fortunately occurred in a rural area. (map updated from Hays, 1980, USGS Prof. Paper 1114, with shading added based on various seismic-risk maps)

42

SELECTED EARTHQUAKES IN THE UNITED STATES

YEAR	NEAREST CITY / EPICENTER	RICHTER MAGNITUDE	NUMBER OF DEATHS - COMMENTS
1755	Boston, / Cape Ann, MA	6	buildings damaged
1811 - 12	Memphis, TN / New Madrid, MO	7.8	8 in 3 separate quakes
1812	San Juan Capistrano mission/ San Gabriel, CA	7	40 - roof of church caved in
1857	Los Angeles/ Ft. Tejon, CA	8.0	1 - San Andreas Fault
1865	San Francisco, CA	6.3	? - Severe damage
1868	San Jose, CA	7.0	30 - Hayward Fault
1872	Bishop, CA / Lone Pine, CA	8.0	27 - Sierra Nevada Fault
1886	Charleston, SC	6.8	100 - Liquefaction of soils
1906	San Francisco, CA	8.0	700 - Liquefaction of soils
1925	Santa Barbara, CA	6.3	13 - Unnamed offshore fault
1933	Long Beach, CA	6.3	120 - inspired codes for construction of schools
1934	Salt Lake City/Kosmo, UT	6.6	0 - Wasatch Fault System
1940	Brawley/ Imperial Valley, CA	7.1	8 - An area of frequent quakes
1949	Seattle,/ Puget Sound, WA	7.1	8 - Area of occasional quakes
1952	Bakersfield/ Kern County, CA	7.7	12 - White Wolf Fault
1954	Reno/Dixie Valley, NV	7.1	0 - Epicenter in rural area
1959	Bozeman/ Hebgen Lake, MT	7.3	28 - In landslide caused by quake
1964	Anchorage/ Prince William Sound, AK	9.2	131 by tsunami and landslides; tsunami kills 11 in CA
1971	Los Angeles/San Fernando Valley, CA	6.4	65 - buildings and highway bridges collapse
1975	Kalapana, Hawaii	7.2	2 - tsunami damage
1983	Coalinga, CA	6.5	1 - older buildings destroyed
1987	Whittier, CA	5.9	8 - 358 million dollars damage
1989	San Francisco - Oakland / Loma Prieta, CA	7.1	62 - Most in overpass collapse; over $6 billion damage
1991	Arcadia/Sierra Madre, CA	6	2 - $ 18 million dollars damage
1992	Yucca Valley & Big Bear Lake, CA	7.4 & 6.5	2 - over 170 injured. Extensive ground cracking in remote area.

(data from Bolt and others, 1977; Gere and Shah, 1984; and the National Oceanic and Atmospheric Administration.)

1886 Photograph of the Charleston, South Carolina, earthquake along East Bay Street. Because of infrequency with which major quakes occur away from plate boundaries, many property owners do not realize they are at risk and have no insurance against earthquake damage.
(photo by J. K. Hillers; from USGS Photo Library, Denver, CO)

Tsunami damage high above the coastline is revealed by shattered trees near the edge of this Alaskan shoreline cliff. This tsunami was generated by the 1964 earthquake near Anchorage. (photo from USGS photo library, Denver, CO)

Earthquakes cause damage in four ways.

1. **Ground shaking.** Ground shaking is generally the most severe direct cause of damage. Crowded public buildings that cannot be evacuated quickly, such as churches, schools and hospitals, may collapse during ground shaking and result in major loss of life. One example is the collapse of the Veterans' Hospital in Sylmar, California, in 1971 that killed 45 people.

2. **Surface rupture.** Surface rupture is the horizontal or vertical displacement of the ground surface along a narrow fault zone. While affecting a much smaller area compared to ground shaking, it can severely damage structures located adjacent to faults. Damage from surface rupture was particularly severe in the 1971 San Fernando earthquake in California.

3. **Ground failure.** Ground failure is an indirect cause of damage, but it may be widespread and produce some of the most devastating losses of life. Fissures (open fractures) may develop in certain soils during major quakes due to ground shaking, but most are shallow. Chances of being "swallowed" by one, as

displayed in the film portrayals of *Shogun* or *Clan of the Cave Bear,* are about on par with the odds of a vegetarian choking to death on a bone. Extreme dangers, however, do result when a quake produces landslides and mudflows. Then, burial alive is a real possibility. The vibration of an earthquake causes sensitive soils to flow. Some even liquefy as the soil grains collapse together, and water is released from microscopic pores. Structures built on sensitive soils collapse and sink. Quake-induced landslides in China during 1920 killed about 100,000 people.

4. **Tsunamis.** Tsunamis are ocean waves produced by earthquakes, volcanic eruptions or major landslides (see chapter on coastal hazards). These may sweep ashore, causing damage at points thousands of kilometers from the earthquake epicenter. Similar waves can also be produced within enclosed or restricted bodies of water such as lakes and reservoirs. Damage can be severe where the waves move forward up the shoreline or overtop dams, allowing downstream areas to be inundated. At Valdez, Alaska, 81 lives were lost in 1964 as result of the tsunami produced by an earthquake.

Reducing Earthquake Damage

Worldwide, on the average, 10,000 people die each year from earthquakes. It is anticipated that a major northern California earthquake, in or near San Francisco, will produce several thousand deaths and over 40 billion dollars in damage. An insurance coalition termed "The Earthquake Project" estimates that insurance losses for a major quake, including fires following the quake, workers' compensation and general liability, would surpass 50 billion dollars for losses along the Newport-Inglewood fault in southern California. The Loma Prieta earthquake produced over 6 billion dollars in damage, but *insured property damage accounted for only 16% of this loss.* It is obvious that many property owners were not insured against this hazard. Another large earthquake in the Midwest, Northeast or Carolina coast, where neither comparable earthquake building codes nor disaster plans exist, would likely be even more devastating.

It is possible to significantly reduce the damages to structures and loss of life through the following:

1. **requiring buildings to be placed a specific distance from known active faults**
2. **restricting land use in areas underlain by soils prone to landsliding or settling**
3. **enforcing stringent requirements for sites and design**
4. **incorporating construction designs that withstand ground shaking**
5. **strengthening of existing structures to withstand ground shaking**
6. **encouraging effective damage reduction through fiscal planning**
7. **adjusting insurance rates to encourage remodeling to limit damage**
8. **providing tax incentives for land uses that are compatible with existing hazards**
9. **educating the public to protect themselves and their property.**

A casualty to ground shaking, an Armenian stone masonry church lies in ruins in the wake of the 1988 earthquake. High unsupported roofs in such public structures are responsible for large loss of life at a single site. (photo by C. J. Langer, USGS)

Ground cracking in Guatemala earthquake in 1976. (photo from USGS photo library, Denver, CO)

Railway in Guatemala offset by surface rupture. (photo from USGS photo library, Denver, CO)

Roles of the Geologist in Reduction of Earthquake Hazards

In regional monitoring. Geologists are involved at both the regional and the local levels. At the regional level, geologists monitor earthquakes through a world-wide network of seismic stations that are linked to central information banks via computer. When a quake occurs anywhere in the world, its intensity, depth and location of its epicenter are immediately calculated and recorded in the information bank. This information can then be used to determine if an earthquake is the likely cause of a specific disaster such as a landslide or a collapsed structure. Furthermore, this seismic network allows identification of particularly large quakes that may produce tsunamis and provides warning time for preparation and evacuation of dwellers along coastal areas who would otherwise be unaware of their pending fate.

In public service. In conjunction with historic records, seismic information is used to compile maps of geological conditions that favor earthquakes and earthquake damage. Regional seismic risk maps have been compiled for the entire United States. Other more detailed maps are being developed for local areas. State and federal geological surveys provide publications on earthquakes that range from educational brochures for children to technical papers intended for use by professional engineers.

In engineering applications. Engineering structures that are earthquake-resistant require accurate site mapping of the geology underlying the structure. Geologists are trained to identify and to map the distribution of earth materials. They apply this knowledge at the local level in the mapping, sampling and testing of foundation materials for works of construction, zoning, land use management and risk assessment. Geology is of paramount importance to engineering and architecture in any setting, but especially so in earthquake country. Even when engineering design and construction are of the highest quality, a structure may instantly fail with fatal consequences if the geological conditions have been ignored or incorrectly evaluated. States that have frequent earthquakes usually require that geologists perform the geological investigation. Many professional geologists are employed by engineering firms or as independent consultants to such firms.

Landslide of nearly 4000 cubic yards of material rests at base of cliff near Fort Funston, California, after the Loma Prieta earthquake of 1989. Such slides often block transportation routes and prevent rescue and evacuation. (photo by D. M. Peterson, USGS)

In research. Earthquake prediction comprises a particularly fascinating and active field of geological research. Eventual development of a reliable earthquake prediction model will be a major milestone in scientific achievement. To date, only a few quakes have been predicted such as at Blue Mountain Lake, New York, and Hsing-t'ai, China. Although accurate prediction of earthquakes is not yet possible, the present state of knowledge allows geologists to delineate most areas where earthquakes can be anticipated to occur within the next several decades.

In education. In California, where earthquakes are repeatedly evident, the public has a real desire to know about earthquakes. "Are You Prepared for the Next Big Earthquake?" was a colorful magazine-style insert that recently was placed in 2.4 million newspapers in the San Francisco area. It was produced by the U.S. Geological Survey and printed through funding from the American Red Cross and United Way. The public response was extraordinary and resulted in over 700,000 requests for additional copies within a few weeks of the publication's release.

Citizens in many parts of the country who live in endangered areas are largely unaware of the nature of the risks they face. Complacency results there because of long time intervals between major earthquakes. Only a small percentage of property owners outside California have earthquake insurance, and most structures are not designed to be earthquake-resistant. Geologic hazards are not covered in most earth science courses, and few students take any earth science in schools. In terms of earthquake literacy, citizens of most areas of the nation outside California are not aware of earthquake dangers, do not plan or design for the next inevitable earthquake, and are generally unprepared to deal with this hazard.

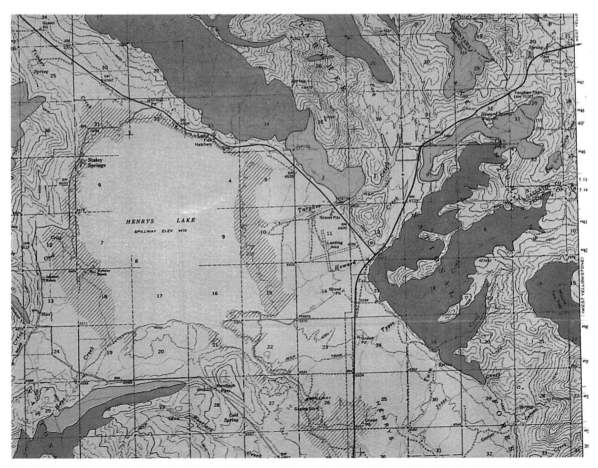

Special maps that emphasize geologic hazards are one of the geologists' major contributions to planners and engineers. Above is a portion of such a map constructed by the USGS for the Henrys Lake area of Montana. This map shows areas of earthquake- related hazards that may be avoided. Red and orange reveal areas where earthquake tremors are likely to trigger landslides. Hachured blue around the edge of the reservoir delineates land that may be inundated by waves generated in the reservoir by an earthquake. The United States currently lags behind other nations in providing such detailed maps for public use.

Collapsed building in the Marina District of San Francisco during the 1989 Loma Prieta Earthquake. This area was filled with sand and waste materials from the 1906 earthquake. Such fill liquefies and flows under vibration; structures such as these should never have been built on such material in earthquake country. Nine people died in fires and building collapse in this district. As in 1906, fires could not be fought with city water because shifting, liquefying ground shattered water mains. (photo from NOAA by D. Perkins, USGS)

References for Additional Reading on Earthquakes

"E" Denotes references particularly suitable for educators.

American Geophysical Union, 1993, **Earthquake Curriculum Package** E: AGU, 2000 Florida Avenue, N.W., Washington, DC 20009, (202) 462-6900. The exercises for grades 7-12 now being field tested in 1993 will be generally available in 1994.

American Red Cross, 1984, **Safety and survival in an earthquake** E: Los Angeles, American Red Cross.

American Society of Civil Engineers., 1976, *Liquefaction Problems in Geotechnical Engineering*: New York, Amer. Soc. Civil Engrs.

Arkansas Earthquake Preparedness Program, 1990, **Home and family earthquake preparation guidebook**: P. O. Box 758, Conway, AR, 72032.

Atkinson, W., 1989, *The Next New Madrid Earthquake - A Survival Guide for the Midwest* E: Carbondale, IL, Southern IL Univ. Press, 210 p.

Asada, T., (ed.), 1982, *Earthquake Prediction Techniques: Their Application in Japan*: Univ. Tokyo press.

Bay Area Regional Earthquake Preparedness Project, 1989, **Home buyers guide to earthquake hazards** E: BAREPP, Metro Center, 101 8th St., Suite 152, Oakland, CA 94607, 13 p.

Beavers, J. E., (ed.), 1981, *Earthquakes and Earthquake Engineering: Eastern United States*: Ann Arbor, MI, Ann Arbor Science Pub. 2 vols.

Berlin, G. L., 1980, *Earthquakes and the Urban Environment*: Boca Raton, FL, CRC Press, 3 vol.

Bertero, V. V., (ed.), 1989, **Lessons learned from the 1985 Mexico earthquake**: Earthquake Engineering Research Institute, 6431 Fairmount Ave. Suite 7, El Cerrito, CA 94530-3624.

Bolt, B. A., 1980, **Earthquakes and volcanoes** E: Readings from Scientific American, San Francisco, CA, W. H. Freeman.

Bolt, B. A., 1988, *Earthquakes* E (2nd ed.) : New York, Freeman, Cooper & Co.

Bolt, B. A., Horn, W. L., Macdonald, G. A., and Scott, R. F., 1977, *Geological Hazards* E: New York, Springer-Verlag.

California Division of Mines and Geology, 1982, **Earthquake planning scenario for a magnitude 8.3 earthquake on the San Andreas Fault in the San Francisco Bay area**: Sacramento, CA, CDMG Special Pub. n. 62 (see also Special Pub. n. 60 for Southern California area).

California Seismic Safety Commission, 1992, **Architectural Practice and Earthquake Hazards**: CA-SSC, 1900 K St., Suite 100, Sacramento, CA 95814.

California Seismic Safety Commission, 1992, **The Homeowner's Guide to Earthquake Safety** E: CA-SSC, 1900 K St., Suite 100, Sacramento, CA 95814.

Canby, T. Y., 1973, **California's San Andreas Fault** E: National Geographic, Jan, 1973, pp. 38 - 53.

Cluff, L. S., 1983, **The impact of tectonics on the siting of critical facilities**: EOS, Trans. Amer. Geophysical Union, v. 64, p. 860.

Cohen, D., Menuez, D., and Tussy, R. G. (eds.), 1990, *Fifteen Seconds: The Great California Earthquake of 1989* E: Covelo, CA, Island Press. Extensive collection of photos.

Coulter, H. W., and Migliaccio, R. R., 1966, **Effects of the earthquake of March 27, 1964, at Valdez, Alaska**: U.S. Geol. Survey Prof. Paper 542-C, 36 p.

Dunbar, P. K., Lockridge, P. A., and Whiteside, L. S., 1992, **Catalog of Significant Earthquakes, 2150 B.C. - 1991 A. D.**: Boulder, CO, NOAA Natl. Geophysical Data Center, 260 p.

Earthquake Engineering Research Center, 1991 - 1992, **Loma Prieta clearinghouse catalog** E: EERC, 1301 South 46th St., Richmond, CA 94804-4698. Four issues through October, 1992, that are bibliographies of articles, slides, videos, photos and data from the Loma Prieta earthquake.

Earthquake Engineering Research Institute, 1989, **Annotated bibliography for urban and regional planners interested in reducing earthquake hazards**: EERI, 499 14th Street, Suite 320, Oakland, CA 94612, (510) 451-0905, 4 p.

Eckel E., and others, 1970, **The Alaska earthquake, March 27, 1964, lessons and conclusions** E: U.S. Geol. Survey Prof. Paper 546, 57 p.

Eiby, G. A., 1980, *Earthquakes* E: New York, Van Nostrand Reinhold.

Engholm, C., 1989, *The Armenian Earthquake* E: San Diego, CA, Lucent Books, World Disaster Series. Written in children's book format in narrative style.

Enserch Engineering and Construction, 1989, **Catastrophic earthquake: the federal response... a simulation of Washington's reaction to the inevitable Eastern U.S. earthquake**: Enserch E & C, 1025 Connecticut Ave. N.W., Suite 1014, Washington, DC 20036, 62 p.

Evans, D. M., 1966, **Man-made earthquakes in Denver** E: Geotimes, v. 10, pp. 11 - 18.

Federal Emergency Management Agency, 1985, **The home builder's guide for earthquake design** E: Washington, Government Printing Office.

Gere, J. M., and Shah, H. C., 1984, *Terra Non Firma* E: New York, W. H. Freeman.

Goter, S., 1990, **World Seismicity 1979-1988** E: Earthquake Information Center, U.S. Geol. Surv., Box 25046, Federal Center MS 967, Denver, CO, 80225. Beautiful large wall-sized poster-map that is as much a work of art as a technical or reference display.

Gupta, H. K., and Rastogi, B. K., 1976, *Dams and earthquakes*: New York, Elsevier.

Hamilton, R. M., 1980, **Quakes along the Mississippi** E: Natural History, v. 89, pp. 70 - 75.

Hamilton, R., and Johnson, A., 1990, **Tecumseh's prophecy: preparing for the next New Madrid earthquake** E: U.S. Geol. Survey Circular 1066.

Hansen, G., and Condon, E., 1989, *Denial of Disaster: The Untold Story and Photographs of the San Francisco Earthquake and Fire of 1906* E: San Francisco, Cameron and Co.

Hauksson, E., 1992, **Seismicity, faults and earthquake potential in Los Angeles**: in *Engineering Geology Practice in Southern California,* Assoc. Engrg. Geologists Spec. Pub., Belmont, CA, Star Pub. Co., pp. 167 - 179.

House, J., and Steffens, B., 1989, *The San Francisco Earthquake* E: San Diego, CA, Lucent Books, World Disaster Series. Written in children's book format in narrative style.

Iacopi, R., 1982, *Earthquake Country* [E] (revised ed.): Menlo Park, CA, A Sunset Book, Lane Books.

Jahns, R. H., Page, B. M., and Howard, A. D., 1978, **Earthquakes and the environment**: in *Geology and Environmental Planning*, A. D. Howard and I. Remson (eds.), New York, McGraw-Hill, pp. 209 - 245.

Kimball, V., 1992, *Earthquake Ready: The Complete Preparedness Guide* (updated ed.) [E]: Malibu, CA, Roundtable Pub.

Krinitzsky, E. L., and Slemmons, D. B.,(eds.), **Neotectonics in earthquake evaluation**: Geol. Soc. Amer. Reviews in Engineering Geol. 8., 160 p.

Lecomte, E., 1989, **Earthquakes and the insurance industry**: Natural Hazards Observer, Univ. CO, Boulder, CO, v. 15, n. 2, pp. 1-2.

Lindh, A. G., 1990, **Earthquake prediction: the seismic cycle pursued**: Nature, v. 348, pp. 580-581.

Litan, R. E., 1991, **A national earthquake mitigation and insurance plan: response to market failures**: The Earthquake Project, Ten Winthrop Square, Boston, MA 02110 (617) 423-4620. Worthy reading—an argument for a national earthquake insurance program based on economics.

Lomnitz, C., 1974, *Global Tectonics and Earthquake Risk*: New York, Elsevier.

National Research Council, Panel on Regional Networks, 1990, *Assessing the Nation's Earthquakes*: Washington, DC, National Academy Press.

Nichols, D. R., and Buchanan - Banks, J. M., 1974, **Seismic hazards and land - use planning**: U.S. Geol. Survey Circular 690, 33 p.

Nuttli, O., 1973, **The Mississippi Valley Earthquake of 1811 and 1812**: Bull. Seism. Soc. Amer., v. 63, pp. 227 - 248.

Nuttli, O. W., Bollinger, G. A., and Herrmann, R. B., 1986,, **The 1886 Charleston, South Carolina, Earthquake—A 1986 Perspective** [E]: U.S. Geol. Survey Circular 985, 52 p.

Olson, R. S., Podesta, B., and Nigg, J. M., 1989, *The Politics of Earthquake Prediction*: Princeton Univ. Press.

Pakiser, Louis C., 1990, **Earthquakes** [E]: One of series, "Popular Publications of the U.S. Geol. Survey" Obtain from Books and Open-File Reports Section, U.S. Geol. Survey, Denver, CO 80225, 20 p.

Perkins, D. M., 1974, **Seismic risk maps**: Earthquake Info. Bull. U.S. Geol. Survey v. 6, n. 6, pp. 10 - 15.

Pitak, W. J., 1982, *Natural Hazard Risk Assessment and Public Policy: Anticipating the Unexpected*: New York, Springer-Verlag.

Plafker, G., and Galloway, J. P., 1989, **Lessons learned from the Loma Prieta, California, Earthquake of October 17, 1989** [E]: U.S. Geol. Surv. Circular 1045.

Press, F., 1975, **Earthquake prediction**: Scientific American, v. 232, pp. 14 -23.

Richter, C. F., 1958, *Elementary seismology*: New York, W. H. Freeman.

Rikitakr, T., 1983, *Earthquake forecasting and warning*: London, Reidel.

Ross, K. E., 1989, **Bibliography of earthquake education materials** [E]: Natl. Center for Earthquake Engineering Research, SUNY Buffalo, Red Jacket Quadrangle, Buffalo, NY 14261, 70 p.

Ross, K. E., 1992, **Issues in earthquake education** [E]: Buffalo, NY 14261, Natl. Center for Earthquake Engineering Research, SUNY at Buffalo, 150 p.

Saucier, R. T., 1991, **Geoarcheological evidence of strong prehistoric earthquakes in the New Madrid (Missouri) Seismic Zone**: Geology, v. 19, pp. 296-298.

Schnell, M. L., and Herd, D. G., (eds.), 1984, **National earthquake hazards reduction program: Report to the United States Congress**: U.S. Geol. Survey Circular 918.

Seismic Loss Analysis Committee, 1990, **Metropolitan Boston area earthquake loss study: Loss Analysis Committee report and recommendations**: Massachusetts Civil Defense Agency and Office of Emergency Preparedness, 400 Worcester Rd., P.O. Box 1496, Framingham, MA 01701.

Sieh, K., and Jahns, R. H., 1984, **Holocene activity of the San Andreas Fault at Wallace Creek, CA**: Geol. Soc. Amer. Bull., v. 95, pp. 883 - 896.

Simkin T., and others, 1989, **This Dynamic Planet - World Map of Volcanoes, Earthquakes and Plate Tectonics** [E]: Smithsonian Institution, NHB-MS 109, Washington, DC 20560. Attractive wall-sized map compiled by the Smithsonian Institution and the U.S. Geological Survey. Excellent educational display.

Simpson, D. W., and Richards, P. G., (eds.), 1981, **Earthquake prediction**: American Geophysical Union, Washington, DC, (51 papers).

Slemmons, D. B., 1977, **State-of-the-art for assessing earthquake hazards in the United States; Report 6, Faults and earthquake magnitudes**: Misc. Paper S-73-1, U.S. Army Waterways Experiment Station, Vicksburg, MS 39180.

Snider, F. G., 1990, **Eastern U.S. Earthquakes: Assessing the Hazard** E: Geotimes, v. 35, n. 11, pp. 13 - 15.

Soren, D., 1988, **The day the world ended at Kourion** E: National Geographic, July, 1988, pp. 30 - 53 (details of the earthquake at Crete in 365 A. D.).

Walker, B., and others, 1982, *Earthquake* E: Alexandria, VA, Time Life Books (well written and spectacularly illustrated).

Wallace, R. E., (ed.), 1990, **The San Andreas Fault System, California**: U.S. Geol. Survey Prof. Paper 1515. Detailed text and beautiful full-page color photos.

Ward, P. L., 1990, **The next big earthquake in the bay area may come sooner than you think: Are you prepared?** E: 24 -page earthquake preparedness guide for San Francisco Bay area delivered as a newspaper supplement. Over 3 million were distributed. Available from USGS, 345 Middlefield Road, Menlo Park, CA 94025, (415) 329-5009.

Ward, P. L., and Page, R. A., 1990, **The Loma Prieta Earthquake of October 17, 1989** E: U.S. Geol. Survey Pamphlet, 16 p. Contains excellent 4 - page annotated bibliography of particular use to planners and managers.

Ward, S. N., 1992, **Synthetic quakes model for long-term prediction**: Geotimes, July, 1992, pp. 18 - 20.

Wilson, R. C., 1991, **The Loma Prieta Quake, What One City Learned**: Washington, DC, International City Management Assoc., 64 p.

Yanev, P., 1991, *Peace of Mind in Earthquake country: How to Save Your House and Your Life* (2nd ed.) E: San Francisco, Chronicle Books.

Ziony, J. I., (ed.), 1985, **Evaluating earthquake hazards in the Los Angeles region**: U.S. Geol. Survey Prof. Paper 1360, (16 papers).

Videotapes on Earthquakes

A Predictable Disaster E: 1976, 32 minutes, Time-Life Video, 1271 Avenue of the Americas, New York, NY 10020, (219) 484-5940.

Aftershocks of the Loma Prieta Earthquake - Computer Animations: 1990, 23 minutes, U.S. Geol. Survey, Library, Special Collections, MS 955, 345 Middlefield Road, Menlo Park, CA 94025, (415) 329-5009.

Approach to the Prediction of Earthquakes E: 1971, 27 minutes, American Educational Films, 3807 Dickerson Road, Nashville, TN 37207, (800) 822-5678.

Are you ready? E: 1984, 84 minutes, U.S. Geol. Survey Library, Special Collections, MS 955, 345 Middlefield Road, Menlo Park, CA 94025, (415) 329-5009. A taping of experts concerning earthquake characteristics.

Born of Fire: 1983, 60 minutes, Vestron Video, P.O. Box 576, Itasca, IL 60143, (800) 523-5503. Video Produced by National Geographic. A documentary on volcanos in rift areas but focuses also on earthquakes.

Earthquake: Tapes made available to insurance industry on effects to the economy by earthquakes. Washington Independent Productions, Inc., 400 North Capitol Street N. W., Suite 183, Washington, DC 20001, (202) 638-3400.

Earthquake! E: 1988, Disaster in Los Angeles, Finley-Holiday Corp., P.O. Box 619, Whittier, CA 90608, (213) 945-3325. Provides actual footage on 1987 Whittier earthquake.

Earthquake Awareness and Risk Reduction in Utah E: 1992, 25 minutes, Utah Geological Survey, 2363 Foothill Drive, Salt Lake City, UT 84109-1491, (801) 581-6831.

Earthquake Country E: 1987, 52 minutes, Channel Four Television, United Kingdom, Available on loan from U.S. Geol. Survey Library Special Collections, MS 955, 345 Middlefield Road, Menlo Park, CA 94025, (415) 329-5009.

Earthquake Do's and Don't's E: 1987, 11 minutes, Natl. Safety Council, Film Communicators, 108 Wilmot Road, Deerfield, IL 60015-5196.

Earthquake Emergency Procedures E: 1985, 27 minutes, Southwestern Pub. Co., 5101 Madison Road, Cincinnati, OH 45227, (513) 271-8811.

Earthquake Risk to the Central U.S. E: 1988, 9 minutes, Federal Emergency Management Agency program, U.S. Geol. Survey, Library, Special Collections, MS 955, 345 Middlefield Road, Menlo Park, CA 94025, (415) 329-5009. A portrayal of the risks of a modern earthquake in the Mississippi Valley similar to the major 1811 - 1812 quake.

Earthquakes E: 1977, 29 minutes, Dallas County Community College District, Center for Telecom-munications, 4343 N Hwy. 67, Mesquite, TX 75150-2095, (214) 324-7988. Features the 1964 Alaska Earthquake and the San Andreas Fault in California.

Earthquakes E: 1990, Corporation for Public Broadcast-ing, Annenberg - CPB Project, 901 E St. Washing-ton, DC 20004-2006, (800) 532-7637.

Earthquakes E: 1990, 60 minutes, NOVA, Vestron Video, P.O. Box 576, Itasca, IL 60143, (800) 523-5503.

Earthquakes and Moving Continents: 1987, 25 minutes, Educational Activities Inc., 1937 Grand Avenue, Baldwin, NY 11510, (516) 223-4466.

Earthquakes: Exploring Earth's Restless Crust E: 1987, 22 minutes, American Educational Films, 3807 Dickerson Road, Nashville, TN 37207, (800) 822-5678.

Earthquakes: Prediction and Monitoring E: 1989, 26 minutes, Films for the Humanities and Sciences, 743 Alexander Road, Princeton, NJ 08540, (609) 452-1128.

Earthquakes: Seismology at Work E: 1989, 25 minutes, Media Guild, 11722 Sorento Valley Road, Suite E, San Diego, CA 92121, (619) 755-9191.

Earth's Interior and Plate Tectonics E: 1984, Gulf Publishing Co., 3301 Allen Parkway, P.O. Box 3881, Houston, TX 72001, (713) 529-5928. Produced by Phillips Petroleum Co.

Effects of Earthquakes on Building Contents: A Visual Experience: 1991, 8 minutes, Loma Prieta Clearinghouse Project, EERC, 1301 South 46th Street, Richmond, CA 94804-4698, (415) 231-9401.

H.E.L.P. Hands-on Earthquake Learning Package E: 1984, 17 minutes, Environmental Volunteers. Elementary students use models and puzzles to illustrate hazards that include liquefaction and earthquake damage. Available on loan from U.S. Geol. Survey Library Special Collections, MS 955, 345 Middlefield Road, Menlo Park, CA 94025, (415) 329-5009.

How to Prepare for Earthquakes: 1992, 8 minutes, Earthquake Video Distribution Manager, Advocate Films, 555 Bryant St. Box 263, Palo Alto, CA 94301 (408) 244 - 9489.

Italy's 1000 Earthquakes E: 1975, 10 minutes, Journal Films, 930 Pitnet Ave., Evanston, IL 60202, (800) 323-5448. Focuses on Anacona, Italy, where persistent earthquakes have caused over 800 million dollars in damages.

Iran Earthquake and **Iran Earthquake Relief**: 1990, 60 minutes each, ABC Nightlines, MPI Home Video, 15825 Rob Roy Drive, Oak Forest, IL 60452, (800) 323-0442.

EERI Loma Prieta Earthquake Briefing: 1990, 57 minutes, Earthquake Engineering Research Institute, 6431 Fairmount Ave. Suite 7, El Cerrito, CA 94530-3524, (510) 525-3668.

Loma Prieta Earthquake of October, 1989 E: 1989, 60 minutes, *and* **Loma Prieta Earthquake of October, 1989 - Overview** E: 1989, 10 minutes, Earthquake Engineering Research Institute, 499 14th Street, Suite 320, Oakland, CA, 94612 (510) 451-0905. Available on loan from U.S. Geol. Survey Library Special Collections, MS 955, 345 Middle-field Road, Menlo Park, CA 94025, (415) 329-5009.

Mapping Earthquakes: 1989, 36 minutes, Narration and lecture by Dr. Bruce Bolt on mapping location and size of earthquakes. Dr. Bruce Bolt, Dept. of Geology and Geophysics, University of California at Berkeley, CA, 94720. Available on loan from U.S. Geol. Survey Library Special Collections, MS 955, 345 Middlefield Road, Menlo Park, CA 94025, (415) 329-5009.

Mexico Earthquake - September 19, 1985 E: 1985, 20 minutes, National Audiovisual Center, National Archives and Records Administration, Customer Service Section PZ, 8700 Edgeworth Drive, Capitol Heights, MD 20743-3701, (301) 763-1896. or Instructional Video, P. O. Box 21, Maumee, OH 43537. Produced by U.S. Geol. Survey.

Our Active Earth E: 1985, 25 minutes, The Film Library, 3450 Wilshire Blvd., Number 700, Los Angeles, CA 90010-2215, (800) 421-9585. Produced by National Safety Council.

Outlasting the Quakes E, 1975, 4 minutes, American Educational Films, 3807 Dickerson Road, Nashville, TN 37207, (800) 822-5678.

Predictable Disaster E: 1988, 60 minutes, Vestron Video, P.O. Box 576, Itasca, IL 60143, (800) 523-5503.

San Francisco Earthquake: 1990, release pending, Educational Video Network, 1401 19th St. Huntsville, TX 77340, (409) 295-5767.

Subject to Change...E: 1988, 18 minutes, PACBELL, Available on loan from U.S. Geol. Survey Library Special Collections, MS 955, 345 Middlefield Road, Menlo Park, CA 94025, (415) 329-5009.

Restless Earth - The Earthquake E: 1972, 26 minutes, Indiana University Audiovisual Center, Bloomington, IN 47405-5901, (812) 335-8087.

Soil and Structure Response to Earthquakes: 1979, Earthquake Engineering Research Institute, 499 14th Street, Suite 320, Oakland, CA 94612, (510) 451-0905. 4 lectures in B&W, each 2 hours, sold as set.

Subject to Change E: 1988, 17 minutes, U.S. Geol. Survey, Library, Special Collections, MS 955, 345 Middlefield Road, Menlo Park, CA 94025, (415) 329-5009. (A tape targeted at teachers, planners and laymen about earthquake hazards).

Surviving the Big One - How to Prepare for a Major Earthquake E: 1989, 58 minutes, KCET Home Video, P.O. Box 310, San Fernando, CA 91341, (800) 228-5238. A comprehensive, detailed guide to earthquake preparedness. Available on loan from U.S. Geol. Survey Library Special Collections, MS 955, 345 Middlefield Road, Menlo Park, CA 94025, (415) 329-5009.

The Alaska Earthquake E, 1966, 20 minutes, National Archives and Records Administration, Customer Service Section PZ, 8700 Edgeworth Drive, Capitol Heights, MD, 20743-3701, (301) 763-1896. Produced by U.S. Geol. Survey. Available on loan from U.S. Geol. Survey Library Special Collections, MS 955, 345 Middlefield Road, Menlo Park, CA 95025, (415) 329-5009.

The Earthquake Connection E: 1988, 44 minutes, Films Incorporated Video, 5547 North Ravenswood Ave., Chicago, IL 60640-1199, (800) 323-4222, ext. 43.

The Great San Francisco Earthquake E: 1989, 60 minutes, PBS Video American Experience Series, 1320 Braddock Place, Alexandria, VA 22314-1698, (800) 424-7693. Rare footage of the 1906 earthquake and recovery of the city over 3 years.

The San Francisco Earthquake E: 1989, 60 minutes, MPI Home Video, 15825 Rob Roy Drive, Oak Forest, IL 60452, (800) 323-0442. Footage of the Loma Prieta earthquake of 1989, produced by ABC News.

The Great Quake of '89 E: 1989, 60 minutes, A laserdisc presentation set up for APPLE and MACINTOSH computers. Voyageur Co., 1351 Pacific Coast Highway, Santa Monica, CA 90401, (800) 446-2001.

The Quake of '89: A Final Warning? E: 1990, BBC, Osborn Court, Olney Buckinghamshire, MK 46 4AG United Kingdom, Phone 0234-711198 or 713390. Produced for BBC Horizon Series. Available on loan from U.S. Geol. Survey Library Special Collections, MS 955, 345 Middlefield Road, Menlo Park, CA 94025, (415) 329-5009.

The Armenian Earthquake E: 1989, 60 minutes, Earthquake Engineering Research Institute, 499 14th Street, Suite 320, Oakland, CA 94612, (510) 451-0905.

The Parkfield Earthquake Prediction Experiment: The Emergency Response: 1988, 5 minutes, U.S. Geol. Survey. Available on loan from U.S. Geol. Survey Library Special Collections, MS 955, 345 Middlefield Road, Menlo Park, CA 94025, (415) 329-5009.

Tomorrow's Quake E: 1983, 16 minutes, American Educational Films, 3807 Dickerson Road, Nashville, TN 37207, (800) 822-5678.

Tomorrow's Quake, Earthquake Prediction E: 1977, American Educational Films, 3807 Dickerson Road, Nashville, TN 37207, (800) 822-5678.

To Predict and Control Earthquakes E: 1985, 20 minutes, The Cinema Guild, 1697 Broadway, Room 802, New York, NY 10019, (212) 246-5522.

Warning: Earthquake E: 1976, 24 minutes, Britannica Films, 310 South Michigan Ave., Chicago, IL 60604 (800) 621-3900. Call for current prices. Occasional special sale prices on videos are given.

We Aren't Asking For the Moon: 1986, 58 minutes, Icarus Films, 200 Park Avenue South, Suite 1319, NY, NY 10003, (212) 674-3375. Film focuses on the economic effects of the 1985 Mexico City Earthquake, particularly on garment industry.

When the Bay Area Quakes E: 1990, 20 minutes, U.S. Geol. Survey. Available on loan from U.S. Geol. Survey Library Special Collections, MS 955, 345 Middlefield Road, Menlo Park, CA 94025, (415) 329-5009.

When the Earth Quakes: 1990, 28 minutes, National Geographic, 17th and M Streets, NW, Washington, DC 20036, (800) 368-2728.

VOLCANOES

Disasters produced by volcanic hazards are not frequent, but they are devastating. In some densely populated developing countries, volcanoes are a serious threat. Major eruptions can affect global climates for at least a year or two after the actual volcanic event. Only a fraction of the world's volcanoes have been studied in detail.

Volcanic Occurrences

Few things excite the imagination so much as the exclamation, "Volcano!" The very word brings to mind thunderous explosions, rivers of fiery orange lava and images of smoking destruction. The actual capability for destruction is not overrated—volcanic eruptions are one of the most devastating of all geologic hazards. There are about 700 potentially dangerous volcanoes in the world, and about 50 eruptions occur each year worldwide. The United States is the third most volcanically active country in the world. Here, 58 volcanoes have erupted over 470 times since just 1700 A. D. Only Japan and Indonesia have had more eruptions.

The Aleutian Islands of Alaska contain the largest number of U.S. volcanoes—more than 40 volcanoes that have erupted historically. The island of Hawaii consists of 5 volcanoes, 2 of which have been consistently active with about 100 major eruptions between them since the early 1800s. Haleakala volcano, on Maui, northwest of Hawaii, erupted in 1790. Within the conterminous United States, 11 peaks of the Cascade Range, which runs from northern California through Oregon and Washington, have histories that are replete with eruptions; 6 of these peaks have erupted within historic time.

About 80% of the earth's volcanoes occur near **subduction boundaries** or **island-arc** trenches. Subduction boundaries occur where denser, oceanic crustal plates (made primarily of the black, fine-grained igneous rock, basalt) are slowly but relentlessly shoved beneath less dense, continental plates (made primarily of the light-colored coarse-grained igneous rock, granite). Island-arc trenches are similar, in that subduction of a basaltic oceanic plate occurs, but the plate is pushed beneath another slab of oceanic plate which has been jammed up against the side of a

Schematic showing cross-section of the crust with (from left to right) island arc with subduction zone, hot spot, mid-ocean ridge rift (divergent) zone, subduction zone beneath continental plate and continental rift-valley zone. Actual analogs from left to right are: ISLAND ARC - Japan and Philippines; HOT SPOT - Hawaii; MID-OCEAN RIDGE - Pacific Rise and Mid-Atlantic Ridge; SUBDUCTION ZONE (beneath CONTINENTAL PLATE) - Cascade Mountains of western U.S.; CONTINENTAL RIFT VALLEY - present East African Rift. (from Simkin and others, 1989, *This Dynamic Planet - World Map of Volcanoes, Earthquakes and Plate Tectonics*, by Smithsonian Institution and U.S. Geological Survey; art work by James Caldwell)

The Pacific "Ring of Fire" with yellow showing plate boundaries and red depicting epicenters of earthquakes of Richter magnitude 5 or above. The Ring of Fire derives its name from numerous volcanoes that are located along the plate boundaries. Most earthquakes and volcanoes are associated geographically along plate boundaries, but earthquakes do not cause volcanoes, and most earthquakes are not caused by volcanoes. (Relief-globe image produced on computer by Dr. Peter Sloss, NOAA National Geophysical Data Center, Boulder, Colorado)

continental plate. Subduction of oceanic plates occurs around the circumference of most of the Pacific Ocean, an area that is so replete with volcanic eruptions that it is has been called "the Ring of Fire" by generations of geologists. Volcanoes in the Cascade Range of the northwestern United States and along the Aleutian Islands of Alaska occur along subduction boundaries, whereas those in Japan and the Philippines occur along island arcs.

About another 15% occur at **divergent zones,** where two distinct plates are slowly being separated from one another. The border zone where such separation begins is called a **rift** area. An example of a divergence zone is along the Mid-Atlantic Ridge, where the North American Plate and the Eurasian Plate are separating at a few centimeters-per-year. Here, submarine volcanoes beneath the mid Atlantic Ocean occur as magma enters the rift left by separation. The exposed volcanoes of Iceland, such as Surtsey, are simply surface expressions of this same type of volcanism, where the molten rock ejected by volcanoes has built land above sea level. Divergence can also begin within an existing plate, gradually rifting the plate apart, and sometimes succeeding in completely separating it into two distinct plates. The Malpai lava flows of New Mexico, which are only a few thousand years old, probably erupted when the Rio Grande Rift

was briefly active within North America. Some volcanoes associated with this rifting are near major cities such as Albuquerque, New Mexico, but these are now thought to be extinct. Finally, a very few areas of volcanic activity appear within plates and are not related to plate boundaries. These are attributed to **hot spots**—areas below the crust that have enough heat to produce surface volcanism through the plate. The Hawaiian Islands, near the center of the Pacific Plate, and Yellowstone Park, within the North American Plate, are examples of volcanism associated with hot spots.

Volcanism and the Concept of Deep Time

Although volcanoes are violent hazards, time between eruptions is often great, particularly in comparison to historic events. Like the sleeping, fire-breathing dragons of lore and fable, many volcanoes lie silent for centuries, until the terrifying moments when they reawaken with life-threatening eruptions. If you were to ask, "Why do people live next to volcanoes?" one answer would be "Because volcanoes provide some of the richest soils for agriculture, and because dense populations, like those of Japan and the Philippines, desperately need all available living space." Elsewhere, where pressures dictated by agricultural needs and living space are not so critical, such as in the Cascade Mountains of the United States, the answer would be "Because volcanic terrain is beautiful! It is some of the most desirable of all terrain for residence." A question more pertinent to volcanic hazards, "Why do volcanic eruptions produce such heavy casualties?" is answered ultimately with "Because volcanoes lie dormant for centuries between eruptions, and long periods of inactivity bring a false sense of security to residents who often fail to evacuate the area in time."

If humans lived for several hundred years, their perceptions about volcanic hazards would be much clearer. A lifetime view shows constancy and changelessness, but a deeper time view shows an area characterized by violence and catastrophic change. Mount Pinatubo in the Philippines awoke in 1991, after over 600 years of inactivity. El Chichón in Mexico was assumed to be an extinct volcano, perhaps because no geologist had studied it in enough detail to see evidence that proved otherwise. Its eruption in 1982 killed over 1800 people. When about ten thousand years of history of eruptions in the Cascade Mountains are

Fine ash roars upward from the throat of Mount St. Helens as it erupts in May of 1980. (photo by D. A. Swanson, USGS)

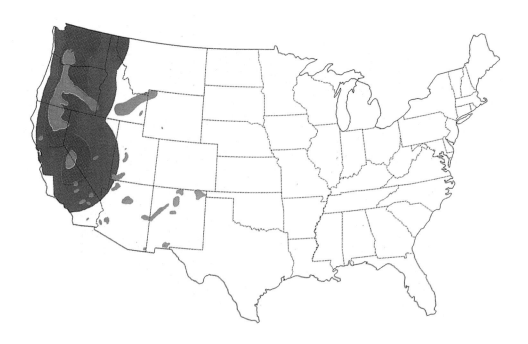

Map of potential volcanic hazards within conterminous United States. Severity of risk decreases from red to green to blue. (compiled by Donal Mullineaux of the USGS and reproduced from Hays, 1981, USGS Prof. Paper 1240-B)

compressed through computer simulation onto about 10 seconds of film, a map view that includes northern California, Oregon and Washington resembles the staccato series of flashes and explosions of an ignited string of firecrackers.

Geologists have much more success with forecasting volcanic eruptions than with predicting earthquakes. The task is simplified because volcanoes just do not occur outside the well-known volcanic habitats of plate boundaries and hot spots. Yet, classifying volcanoes as "extinct" is risky business since thousands of years may elapse between eruptions. Geological events that are separated by such amounts of time are never easy to predict. When an eruption is imminent, warnings usually occur a few weeks to a few days before an eruption. The most common warning is a series of earthquakes of increasing magnitude and frequency. Special tremors called **harmonic tremors** show that magma is moving upward, and these tremors may be detected on modern seismographs. Topographic changes, usually bulges, may occur on some volcanic peaks as a result of the stress that is building from below. Such changes in shape can be detected by sensitive surveying instruments and by instruments deployed at the volcano that show slight changes in tilt of the ground surface (**tiltmeters**). Although some volcanoes have erupted without warning, modern sensitive instruments make it easier to see the warning signals given by volcanoes. As these methods become more refined and more frequently applied, deaths caused by "surprise" eruptions can be decreased because more time for evacuation becomes available. To make use of this technology, governments may sponsor monitoring programs so that scientific personnel are available and instruments can be deployed. One of the most critical actions any government can take is to actually heed geologists' warnings and take action to clear residents from an area in *danger*.

GLOBAL HISTORIC VOLCANIC ERUPTIONS, VOLCANIC EXPLOSIVITY INDEX (VEI) AND APPROXIMATE CASUALTIES

YEAR	VOLCANO	VEI	LOCATION (AGENT of MORTALITY)	CASUALTIES
1628 B.C.	Santorini	6	Greece (explosion, tsunami)	unknown
79	Vesuvius	5	Pompeii & Herculaneum (pyroclastic flow)	3,360
1631	Vesuvius	4	Naples & Resina (pyroclastic flows)	3,500
1783	Skaptar (Laki)	4	Iceland (tephra and starvation)	9,500
1792	Unzen	2	Kyushu, Japan(avalanche and tsunami from eruption-related earthquake)	15,000
1815	Tambora	7	Indonesia (tephra, tsunami and starvation)	92,000[a]
1822	Galunggung	4	Indonesia (pyroclastic flows and mudflows)	4,000
1883	Krakatau	6	Indonesia (tsunami)	36,400
1902	Pelée	4	Martinique (pyroclastic flows in 2 eruptions. First produced 28,000 deaths)	29,000
1902	Santa Maria	6	Guatemala (pyroclastic flows)	6,000
1919	Kelut	4	Java (mudflows)	5,110
1951	Lamington	4	New Guinea (debris avalanche, pyroclastic flows)	2,942
1977	Nyiragongo	1	Tanzania (lava flows from burst wall of lava lake flood valley at up to 100 km/hr)	less than 100
1980	Mt. St. Helens	5	Washington (lateral blast, debris avalanche and mudflows)	57
1982	El Chichón	4	Mexico (pyroclastic flows)	1877
1985	Nevado del Ruiz	3	Colombia (mud flows)	23,000
1986	Nyos	NA	Cameroon (CO_2 gas cloud)	1,746[b]
1990	Kelut	4	Java, Indonesia (tephra)	32
1991	Unzen	2?	Shimabara, Japan (pyroclastic flows)	38
1991	Pinatubo	5	Luzon, Philippines (tephra collapses roofs; disease in evacuation camps)	932
1993	Mayon	NA[c]	Mayon, Philippines	60[c]

[a] 70,000 deaths from famine due to crop destruction   [c] Eruption began at the time this book went to press
[b] cold gas cloud erupted from beneath lake in old volcano

Data from Barberi et al. (1990); Smithsonian Institution, written communication (1991), and Office of Foreign Disaster Assistance, *Disaster History* (1992)

In a display of dazzling beauty and power, red-hot lava and white-hot lightning dance together in the night sky in the eruption of Galunggung, Indonesia. Lightning bolts are common products of eruptions, but they are seldom caught in still photographs. (photo by Ruska Hadian, Volcanological Survey of Indonesia)

A tragic example where officials did not heed warnings took place at the November 13, 1985, eruption of Nevado del Ruiz, Colombia. Over 20,000 people died after the heat produced by the eruption melted glacial ice and sent hot mudflows (lahars) racing through narrow river canyons and out onto the alluvial plain where the city of Armero lay sleeping. Warning signs of an eruption had been noted in 1984, and by summer of 1985 an extensive seismic monitoring network had been deployed. Yet government officials failed to recognize the degree of danger, the communication network between scientists and officials failed, and the local city government of Armero took no action. Some survivors recounted the mayor as having a radio conversation in which he expressed there was little danger—moments before he too was swept away in the mudflow! Others recalled authority figures counseling people simply to go back inside their houses and remain calm. A simple order to evacuate to higher ground would have saved thousands of lives. In contrast, no chances were taken in the 1991 eruption of Mt. Pinatubo in the Philippines. Clark Air Base, and nearby villages were evacuated as result of authorities' heeding the early warning provided by geologists. Loss of life was minimized, even though the eruption was one of the largest in historic time.

Explosivity of Volcanoes

Volcanoes obtain most of their devastating, explosive force from a very innocuous material—water. Water confined at several times its boiling temperature exerts enormous pressure as superheated steam. When the confining seal of rock above wet magma fails, immense pressure that can shatter cubic miles of solid rock into tiny fragments is released in a few moments of explosive violence. Geologists have used several scales through which to express and compare the energies released during different historic explosions. The current convention is with a number expressing the **Volcanic Explosivity Index** (VEI) rating. This rating, devised by C. G. Newhall of the U.S. Geological Survey, is based upon measurements of the volume of ejecta (the rock and ash blown out of the volcano), the height of the cloud column, and other observations. On the VEI scale, 1 is small and 5 is very large. The scale continues to 8 but no eruption in the last 10,000 years has been assigned a VEI of 8. Historically, the greatest eruption recorded (VEI of 7) was Tambora, Indonesia, in 1815 where an estimated 36 cubic miles (147 km^3) of material was ejected (Mt. St. Helens ejected 1.5 cubic miles or about 6 km^3).

Single eruptions can affect the entire planet. The 1815 explosion of Tambora released the energy of about 10,000 atomic bombs of the size used in World War II. The encircling ash layer and release of sulfurous gasses increased the albedo of the planet and dropped the world average temperature 2 °F for 2 years. Snows were recorded in New England, even in July and August, and 1816 became known as the "year without summer." Elsewhere the low temperatures resulted in crop failures and even famine in a few areas. Less drastic global cooling in 1992 followed Pinatubo's eruption that took place in summer of 1991.

Mudflow engulfs garage on the North Fork of the Toutle River after the May 18, 1980, eruption of Mount St. Helens. (photo by Lynn Topinka, Cascades Volcano Observatory)

Weyerhaeuser logging company bus caught in mudflow. Mudflows covered roads and poured through homes during the 1980 Mount St. Helens eruption. Melted snow pack provided most of the water needed to bring the mudflows into inhabited areas and pristine streams. (photo by Lynn Topinka, Cascades Volcano Observatory)

Dragline dredges St. Helens' volcanic mud from channel of North Fork of the Toutle River in an attempt to restore a navigable channel and prevent downstream sedimentation. (photo by Lynn Topinka, Cascades Volcano Observatory)

Heavy ash-laden steaming cloud (pyroclastic flow) rushes down the side of Mount St. Helens. The only defense against such flows lies in not being there. (photo by G. Coyler, Cascades Volcano Observatory)

Dangers of Volcanoes

Although glowing lava comes to mind when we hear the word "volcano," lava ranks low in danger to life. A list of hazards associated with volcanoes follows.

1. Mudflows (lahars) and debris avalanches. "Lahar" is a term that originated in Indonesia where these flows caused thousands of deaths. Lahars may be hot or cold and are generated when water is supplied by rain, or when massive amounts of glacial ice or snow on a volcanic peak melt rapidly from heat released during an eruption. As this water moves downslope, it initially incorporates large amounts of volcanic ash and soil, and then eventually large boulders and trees. Most mudflows follow the established drainage network of stream valleys. Flows can reach great distances beyond the actual volcano. The prehistoric Osceola mudflow extended 60 miles (96 km) from Mt. Rainier, Washington. Mudflows can move at close to 30 miles per hour (up to 50 km/hr), which is much faster than a human can run. They crush, bury or carry away everything in their path.

Lahars killed between 20,000 and 24,000 residents in 1985 when Nevado del Ruiz erupted in Colombia. Over 200 homes were destroyed by mudflows along the Toutle River when Mount St. Helens erupted in 1980. In Japan, an elaborate system of sensors has been used in some up-valley areas where mudflows are likely to start. There, officials can learn early about movement and warn people down-valley.

The May 18, 1980, eruption of Mount St. Helens produced debris avalanches and mudflows that destroyed Spirit Lake and filled the basin with mud and debris. The avalanche established a large debris dam that created a new impoundment. The new Spirit Lake was 200 feet deep, and its new bottom was close to the surface elevation of the former lake. New Spirit Lake held over 350 million cubic yards of water. Had this dam failed, towns downstream would have been swept away beneath a wall of water over 150 feet high. Because there was no way to stabilize this dam, a tunnel was drilled through a bedrock ridge at a cost of over 13 million dollars to drain Spirit Lake waters into nearby Coldwater Lake. (Coldwater Lake was another lake created in 1980 when a mudflow dammed Coldwater Creek. However, this natural dam was thick and solid. It required only construction of a concrete spillway to insure its permanence.)

Seepage of contaminants from decaying rubble and vegetation may also cause pollution of springs and streams that flow from the new deposits. The waters of Spirit Lake were heavily contaminated with harmful microorganisms after the May 18, 1980, St. Helens eruption.

Years after mudflows occur, debris still chokes stream channels and causes extensive sedimentation far below the actual extent of the flows. Extensive dredging of waterways miles away from Mount St. Helens was necessitated as streams carried debris onward from the mudflows that had penetrated upper regions of drainage basins. Major sediment retention dams had to be built to prevent further downstream fouling.

2. Pyroclastic flows (including glowing avalanches and hot gas releases). **Pyroclastic** is a term that is used to describe rock debris produced during an explosive eruption. When explosive eruptions occur, volcanic gasses mix with air, water and pyroclastic debris to form heavy gas-and-ash-charged clouds. These clouds may travel downslope at over 200 miles per hour to cover areas of more than a hundred square miles near the volcano. In the Windward Islands southeast of Puerto Rico, more than 30,000 people were killed at Martinique in 1902 when a pyroclastic flow from Mt. Pelée, glowing red-hot at about 800° C, swept over the town of St. Pierre. In moments every structure was smashed and simultaneously incinerated; almost every living creature perished.

Some pyroclastic flows are cooler but are still lethal even without heat. The ash is so concentrated within the cloud that suffocation takes place; lungs simply cannot handle such concentrations of dust. The amount of ash debris in these clouds gives them a dense consistency more akin to water than to air. Their density coupled with their speed gives these clouds the impacting force of a jackhammer and the abrasive power of a sandblaster. Buildings and structures are crushed and shattered; trees are blown away from their stumps and their bark and limbs

Looking deceptively like a newly fallen snow, deposits of white volcanic ash like this blanketed thousands of square miles down-wind of Mount St. Helens. (photo from USGS photo library, Denver, CO)

Volcanic ash seen under the polarizing microscope magnified 140 times. Dark grains are glass with black, hard magnetite; bright grains are plagioclase feldspar; grains with a hint of color are the minerals hornblende and diopside. The hardness of this material makes ash devastating to machinery because it grinds into all moving parts that it contacts. Sample is from the smaller May 25, 1980, eruption of Mount St. Helens. (photo by Edward Nuhfer)

61

Glowing orange, hot, viscous lava creeps from a fissure and will slowly cover the area. Observer stands on black basaltic rock formed from earlier, perhaps prehistoric, lava flows. This flow is not dangerous to the observer in the foreground, but flows can cause devastating economic damage as they encroach over highways, structures and residences. (photo from USGS Hawaiian Volcano Observatory)

stripped away in a violent abrasive storm of sharp rock fragments. Violent electrical storms may also occur within the clouds, even some distance down-wind, and the lightning bolts can start additional fires.

Although steam is the primary gas within volcanic clouds, acidic carbon dioxide, carbon monoxide, hydrogen chloride, and sulfurous oxides may also occur in lethal concentrations. Pockets of poison gasses that occur around volcanic vents prove lethal to animals or hikers that may wander into them before the danger is realized. Eruptions of gasses may prove lethal even when they are cool. In Cameroon, in 1986, over 1700 fatalities occurred when a plume of cool carbon dioxide burst from the bottom of Lake Nyos, which was located within a volcanic cone.

3. Tephra deposits. Tephra refers to pyroclastic debris which is blasted into the atmosphere during eruptions. Very fine-grained tephra is called **ash**. When violent eruptions discharge tephra high into the air, ash may fall on areas hundreds of miles downwind, and fine dust may even circle the planet and remain for years in the atmosphere. Air-fall deposits several tens of feet thick may accumulate on the immediate leeward side of the volcano. Ash removal is a serious economic

problem, and even deposits of less than an inch (a few mm) are devastating to a town. In the town of Moses Lake, WA (population of about 11,000), the May 18, 1980, eruption of Mount St. Helens required removal of 230,000 cubic meters of ash. The Washington Department of Transportation reported that over

A far more deadly volcanic hazard than the lava above, Lake Nyos, housed in its volcanic crater in Cameroon, stood muddy and full of debris several days after carbon dioxide gas belched from beneath the lake bottom and killed over 1700 people. (photo by Michelle Tuttle, USGS)

540,000 metric tons of Mount St. Helens ash was removed from state highways.

Ash clouds endanger aircraft that may enter them because the ash can destroy an aircraft engine in moments. A commercial jet carrying over 200 passengers encountered an ash plume from Alaska's Redoubt Volcano on December 15, 1989. The engines failed and the plane fell over 12,000 feet before the pilot could restart the engines. A tragedy was avoided by the narrowest of margins, and the plane suffered millions of dollars in damage. Redoubt's eruption caused about 100 million dollars in damages.

In addition to the short-term problems of lung irritation associated with the fine dusty ash, long-term problems continue until it is removed. An ash fall is similar to a snowfall in that it must be removed in order for a community to return to a normal life, but this "snowfall" doesn't melt! Instead, it must be painstakingly cleaned up and trucked away to a fill area. The ash consists of very fine but very hard particles of glass and even harder minerals. The hardness of the material allows it to damage all moving parts, and its small size permits the particles to gain access to virtually every piece of machinery—automobile engines, electrical generators, motors in heating and air conditioning units, lawn mowers, electrical appliances, computers, clocks; anything with moving parts is subject to premature wear and damage. If you can imagine the effects of pouring finely ground glass into the moving parts of your favorite appliance, computer or motor vehicle, then you can conceive of the economic burden on residents whose homes and businesses receive an ash fall. Residents of Anchorage, Alaska, experienced this first-hand in 1992 with the eruption of Mt. Spurr.

Huge trees lie aligned like the quills on a porcupine's back. Researchers learned that such blow-downs of timber resulted from the force of heavy, ash-laden clouds that followed the contour of the land and flattened the forests they passed across. (photo from USGS Cascades Volcano Observatory)

Shattered tree trunk at right testifies to the blasting power of eruptions that push heavy ash-laden clouds. (photo by N. Banks, USGS)

POTENTIALLY HAZARDOUS VOLCANOES IN THE CONTERMINOUS UNITED STATES

SITE	DATES of MOST RECENT ERUPTIONS	GENERAL FREQUENCY OF MAJOR ERUPTIONS
Cascade Volcanoes		
Mt. Adams, WA	more than 3500 years ago	once per 5000 years (?)
Mt. Baker, WA	1870 - steaming in 1975	once per century
Mt. Hood, OR	1730, 1859, 1865, 1907	once per 4000 years
Mt. Lassen, CA	1914-1921	once per century (?)
Mt. Rainier, WA	1820 (?), 1879, 1882	once per 500 years
Mt. Shasta, CA	1786	once per 800 years
Mt. St. Helens, WA	1844, 1857, 1980-1986	once per century
Mono Craters, CA	1340	once per 1000 years (?)
Some other sites of recent major volcanism		*Nearest Cities*
Craters of the Moon, ID	1200 B. C.	Pocatello & Idaho Falls, ID
Inyo Craters, CA	1400 years ago	Mammoth Lakes, CA
Sunset Crater, AZ	1200 years ago	Flagstaff, AZ
Bandera Field lava flows, NM	1000 years ago	Grants, NM
Yellowstone, WY	about 70,000 years ago	Cody, WY; Bozeman, MT

(data from Harris, 1980, and USGS. General frequencies are useful for comparison but not prediction because eruptions do not occur at regular intervals. Frequencies with "?" are based on data that too insufficient to be much more than order-of-magnitude approximations.)

4. Lava flows. Lava is a term for magma that erupts from volcanic cones or fissures and flows like a fluid out upon the earth's surface. Lava flows pose little hazard to life because they follow pathways dictated by topography. Because their downslope courses are known beforehand, there is usually plenty of time for evacuation. At times, dams and channels are constructed that successfully divert lava away from homes and other structures. In Iceland, special hoses were used to pump seawater onto the front of a slowly advancing flow. This solidified the lava and successfully stopped the flow from advancing onto the harbor area of Vestmannaeyjar.

Fluid lava flows usually accompany gentle types of eruptions such as those often filmed in Hawaii Volcanoes National Park. These fluid eruptions are spectacular, but usually affect only small areas at a given eruption and are preceded by seismic tremors that provide warning and allow evacuation. The most dangerous volcanoes are explosive eruptions or those that release pyroclastic flows such as Mount St. Helens, Washington, and Mount Unzen, Japan. These explosive eruptions are lethal over large areas, but they are seldom are associated with fluid lava.

Roles of the Geologist in Reducing Volcanic Hazards

In monitoring, prediction and hazard-assessment. Geologists are the major professionals at the first line of defense, which is prediction. Monitoring has occurred for years at the Hawaiian Volcano Observatory. The eruption of Mt. St. Helens in 1980 led to the establishment of the Cascades Volcano Observatory and to the constant monitoring for earthquakes beneath those volcanos that are judged to be most likely to erupt. Established by the U.S. Geological Survey, the Observatory's crew of 50 scientists conducts active and ongoing research to determine potential volcanic activity. Seismic warnings provided by volcanic earthquakes were particularly useful in minimizing the loss of life in 1980 at Mt. St. Helens, Washington. The information gained since has allowed predictions of the smaller eruptions that have taken place since May 18, 1980.

Research scientists from universities and state geological surveys are also involved in studies of prediction. Some notable advances have already been

Mount Pinatubo in June of 1991 in the Philippines was one of the largest eruptions of the 20th Century. It destroyed Clark Air Base and displaced thousands of Filipino citizens. However, warning followed by evacuations greatly minimized loss of life. Immense amounts of ash were released, and ash blankets the nearby terrain. The ash cloud sent into the upper atmosphere should contribute to red sunsets and lowered global temperatures for about two years after the eruption. (photo by USGS Cascades Volcano Observatory)

Sensitive instruments, like this tiltmeter, help to provide warnings that prevent loss of life from volcanic hazards. Instruments can help geologists keep watch on areas of concern, some of which are listed in the table on the facing page. (photo by J. C. Ratte from USGS photo library)

made in the science of prediction, which, under ideal conditions, can sometimes provide at least a day's warning before a specific volcano erupts. University of Buffalo researchers were successful in using a computer model to predict the April 16, 1991, eruption of Mount Colima, Mexico. Prediction, however, is presently far from foolproof. Eruptions, such as the January, 1993, eruption of Galagos volcano in Columbia that killed at least five volcanologists, have occurred without any detected precursory warning.

Hazard assessment involves estimating how large an eruption will be, whether it is likely to be explosive, and what the effects of an eruption could be. Assessments are made by reconstructing the eruptive history of the volcano, interpreting the origin of eruptive deposits, dating the deposits to provide a chronology of past eruptions, and mapping deposits to determine what areas could be affected by eruptions in the future. The product of these studies will usually be a report with an accompanying map. The map can be used for zoning plans and for determining evacuation routes and access restriction.

In USGS Bulletin 1383-C by Dwight Crandell and Donal Mullineaux, published in 1978, the general direction of the main ash plume and the pathways of mudflows as deduced from studies of older deposits proved remarkably accurate for forecasting the effects of the 1980 eruption of Mount St. Helens. Only the distance of the blast-effect and the reach of pyroclastic flows to the north, northeast and northwest were underestimated, primarily because no two eruptions are exactly alike, and the 1980 eruption extended further in these directions than had previous eruptions. At least 15 nations, including the U.S., now have volcanic-hazards assessments and hazards zonation maps for one or more of their volcanos. However, of about 600 volcanoes in the world that are probably active, only a small fraction have been studied in detail. There has been far too little commitment of research to these particular hazards.

In engineering and environmental evaluation. Another role of geologists involves the engineering geology that is required in redeveloping an area after an eruption has occurred. Duties include recognizing areas that may be prone to destruction by lahars, evaluating stability of natural dams, and providing geotechnical data for reconstruction and remediation.

In education. Although geologists can produce hazards maps and reports, individuals must have sufficient geological education in order to make good use of this information. Forbidding development of population centers in areas of risk is not usually the desirable solution because volcanic terrain is beautiful and, except during the brief periods punctuated by violent eruptions, volcanism creates truly desirable areas in which to live. To live in such terrain without tragedy, the populace should be prepared for those punctuated periods through acquiring awareness of the hazard and acceptance that an eruption may someday occur. A thorough understanding of volcanic events and past history of volcanoes is required to assure an appreciation for contingency plans and warning policies. Some California business representatives were outraged in 1982 when geologists recorded earthquakes beneath the Mono Lakes area and warned the public of a possible eruption. The tremors ceased and the eruption did not occur, but the antagonistic response (by those whose very lives might be saved by such warnings) points to insufficient education and to lack of respect for volcanic phenomena.

References for Additional Reading on Volcanoes

"E" denotes references particularly suitable for primary and secondary educators and students.

Barberi, F., and others (International Association of Volcanology and Chemistry of the Earth's Interior, Task Group for International Decade of Hazards Reduction), 1990, **Reducing volcanic disaster in the 1990's**: Bull. Volcanological Society of Japan, v. 35, pp. 80 - 95. Available from U.S. Geol. Surv., Mail Stop 905, Reston, VA 22092.

Berreby, D., 1991, **Barry *versus* the Volcano** E: Discover, June, 1991, pp. 60 - 67. A brief, colorful article on the current research on prediction of volcanic eruptions.

Blong, R. J., 1984, *Volcanic Hazards* E: New York, Academic Press.

Brantley, S. R., 1990, **The eruption of Redoubt Volcano, Alaska, December 14, 1989—August 31, 1990**: U.S. Geol. Survey Circular 1061, 33 p.

Bullard, F. M., 1984, *Volcanoes of the Earth* (2nd ed.): Waukesha, WI, Kalmbach Pub. Co.

Carey, S., Sigurdsson, H., and Mandeville, C., 1992, **Fire and water at Krakatau** E: Earth, v. 1, n. 2. Investigators from University of Rhode Island use field studies for a renewed look at the famous 1883 eruption.

Casadevall, T. J. (ed), 1991, **First international symposium on volcanic ash and aviation safety— program and abstracts**: U.S. Geol. Survey Circular 1065.

Crandell, D. R., and Waldron, H. H., 1956, **A recent volcanic mudflow of exceptional dimensions from Mt. Rainier, Washington**: Amer. Jour. Science, v. 254, pp. 349 - 362.

Crandell, D. R., and Waldron, H. H., 1969, **Volcanic hazards in the Cascade Range**: Proc. Conf. on Geologic Hazards and Public Problems: Office of Emergency Preparedness, Santa Rosa, CA, pp. 5-18.

Crandell, D. R., and Mullineaux, D. R., 1975, **Technique and rationale of volcanic hazards appraisal in the Cascade Range, northwestern United States**: Environ. Geol., v. 1, pp. 23 - 32.

Crandell, D. R., and Mullineaux, D. R., 1978, **Potential hazards from future eruptions of Mt. St. Helens volcano, Washington**: U.S. Geol. Survey Bull. 1383-C, 26 p. (Published prior to the 1980 eruption).

Crandell, D. R., and Mullineaux, D. R., 1980, **Recent eruptive history of Mt. Hood, Oregon, and potential hazards from future eruptions**: U.S. Geol. Survey Bull. 1492, 81 p.

Decker, R. W., Wright, T. L., and Stauffer, P. H., (eds.), 1987, **Volcanism in Hawaii**: U.S. Geol. Survey Prof. Paper 1350, 1667 p.

Decker, R. W., 1978, **State of the art volcano forecasting**: in Geophysical Predictions, Natl. Acad. Sci., Washington, DC, pp. 47 - 57.

Decker, R. W., and Decker, B., 1980, *Volcano Watching* [E]: Hawaii Natural History Assoc.

Decker, R. W., and Decker, B., 1991, *Mountains of Fire —The Nature of Volcanoes*: New York, Cambridge University Press.

Foxworthy, B., and Hill, M., 1982, **Volcanic eruptions of 1980 at Mount St. Helens, the first 100 days** [E]: U.S. Geol. Survey Prof. Paper 1249, 125 p.

Francis, P., 1976, *Volcanoes*: New York, Penguin Books.

Gore, R., 1982, **Mediterranean—Sea of man's fate** [E]: (Vesuvius and other volcanoes) National Geographic, Dec., 1982, pp. 694 - 737.

Harris, S. L., 1980, *Fire and Ice—The Cascade Volcanoes* [E]: Seattle, WA, Pacific Search Press.

Heliker, C., and Wright, T. L., 1991, **Lava flow hazards from Kilauea** [E]: Geotimes, v. 36, n. 5, pp. 16 - 19.

Herd, D. G., 1986, **The 1985 Ruiz Volcano disaster**: EOS, Trans. Amer. Geophysical Union, pp. 457-460.

Hill, D. P., and others, 1991, **Response plans for volcanic hazards in the Long Valley Caldera and Mono Lakes Crater area, California**: U.S. Geol. Survey Open File Report 91-270, 66 p.

Hovey, E. O., 1902, **Observations on the eruption of 1902 of LaSoufriere, St. Vincent, and Mt. Pelée, Martinique**: Amer. Jour. Sci., v. 14, pp. 319 - 358.

Howard, A. D., and Dickinson, W. R., 1978, **Volcanic environments**: in Geology and Environmental Planning, A. D. Howard and I. Remson, (eds.), McGraw - Hill, pp. 246 - 274.

Kerr, R. A., 1988, **Lake Nyos was rigged for disaster**: Science, v. 235, pp. 528 - 529.

Kling, G. W., and others, 1987, **The 1986 Lake Nyos gas disaster in Cameroon, West Africa**: Science, v. 236, pp. 169 - 175.

Lipman, P. W., and Mullineaux, D. R., (eds.), 1981, **The 1980 eruptions on Mt. St Helens, Washington** [E]: U.S. Geol. Survey Prof. Paper 1250, 844 p.

Krafft, M., and Krafft, K., 1975, *Volcano* [E]: New York, Harry N. Abrams. Very readable book for the layperson, with superb color photographs. Written and produced by the late authors shown on the dedication page of this book.

McTaggart, K. C., 1960, **The mobility of nuée ardentes**: Amer. Jour. Sci., v. 258, pp. 369 - 382.

MacDonald, G. A., 1972, *Volcanoes*: Englewood Cliffs, NJ, Prentice-Hall.

MacDonald G. A., Abbott, A. T., and Peterson, F. L., 1983, *Volcanoes in the Sea*: Waukesha, WI, Kalmbach Pub. Co.

Martin, R. C. and Davis, J. F., 1982, **Status of volcanic predictions and emergency response in volcanic hazard zones in California** : Calif. Div. Mines & Geology Special Pub. 63.

Mason, A. C., and Foster, H. L., 1953, **Diversion of lava flows at Oshima, Japan**: Amer. Jour. Sci., v. 251, pp. 249 - 258.

Miller, C. D., 1980, **Potential hazards from future eruptions in the vicinity of Mt. Shasta Volcano, northern California**: U.S. Geol. Survey Bull. 1503.

Miller, C. D., and others., 1982, **Potential hazards from future volcanic eruptions in the Long Valley - Mono Lake area, east central California and southwest Nevada - a preliminary assessment**: U.S. Geol. Survey Circular 877.

Moxham, R. M., 1972, **Thermal surveillance of volcanoes**: in The Surveillance and Prediction of Volcanic Activity, UNESCO, Paris, pp. 103 - 124.

Mullineaux, D. R., 1976, **Preliminary overview map of volcanic hazards in the 48 conterminous United States**: U.S. Geol. Survey Map Folio 786.

National Research Council, 1991, *The Eruption of Nevado del Ruiz Volcano, Colombia, South America, November 13, 1985*: P. O. Box 285, Washington, DC, Natl. Academy Press.

Newell, R. E., and Deepak, A., 1982, **Mount St. Helens eruptions of 1980 - Atmospheric effects and potential climate impact**: Washington, DC, Natl. Aeronautics and Space Administration SP 458.

Peterson, D. W., 1988, **Volcanic hazards and public response**: Jour. Geophysical Res., v. 93, pp. 4161-4170.

Oakeshott, G. B., 1976, *Volcanoes and Earthquakes, Geologic Violence*: New York, McGraw-Hill.

Pellegrino, C., 1991, *Unearthing Atlantis - An Archaeological Odyssey* E: New York, Random House. A superb and readable reconstruction of the eruption in the eastern Mediterranean Sea that produced tsunamis and destroyed the Minoan civilization in 1628 B. C. The myth of Atlantis has this true event as its actual origin.

Pringle, P., 1990, **Mount St. Helens—new link to the past for volcanic stratigraphy** E: Earth Science, v. 43, pp. 18 - 22.

Rittmann, A., and Rittmann, L., 1977, *Volcanoes*: New York, G. P. Putnam's Sons.

Sager, J. W., and Chambers, D. R., 1986, **Design and construction of the Spirit Lake outlet tunnel, Mount St. Helens, WA**: in *Landslide Dams - Processes, Risk, and Mitigation*, R. L. Schuster, (ed.), Amer. Soc. Civil Engrs. Geotechnical Spec. Pub. n. 3, pp. 52 - 58.

Schuster, R. L., 1989, **Engineering geologic effects of the 1980 eruptions of Mount St. Helens**: in *Engineering Geology in Washington*, R. W. Galster, (ed.), WA Div. Geol. and Earth Resources, Bull. 78,, v. II, pp. 1203 - 1228.

Sheets, P. D., and Grayson, D. K., (eds.), 1979, *Volcanic activity and human ecology*: London, Academic Press. (20 papers), 672 p.

Simarski, L., 1992, **Volcanism and climate change**: Amer. Geophys. Union, 2000 Florida Ave. N.W. Washington, DC 20009.

Simkin, T., and others, 1981, *Volcanoes of the World* E: Dowden, Hutchinson and Ross, 233 p.

Stager, C., 1987, **Cameroon's killer lake** E: National Geographic, v. 172, pp. 404 - 420.

Tilling, R. I., 1989, **Volcanic hazards and their mitigation, progress and problems**: Reviews in Geophysics, v. 27, pp. 237 - 269.

Tilling, R. I., (ed.), 1989, *How Volcanoes Work*: Washington, DC, American Geophysical Union.

Tilling, R. I., (ed.), 1989, **Volcanic Hazards - Short Course in Geology: Volume 1**: Washington, DC, American Geophysical Union.

Tilling, R. I., 1987, **Monitoring active volcanoes** E: U.S. Geol. Survey Pamphlet, 13 p.

Time - Life Books, 1982, *Volcano* E: Alexandria, VA, Time - Life Books, Planet Earth Series.

UNESCO, 1972, **The Surveillance and Prediction of Volcanic Activity**: UNESCO, Paris, 166 p.

United Nations Disaster Relief Coordinator, 1976, **Disaster prevention and mitigation: Volume 1, Volcanological aspects**: United Nations, Geneva, 38 p.

Warrick, R. A., 1975, **Volcano hazards in the U.S.**: Monograph NSF-RA-E-75-012, Univ. Colorado, Boulder, CO.

Weintraub, B., 1982, **The disaster of El Chichón** E: National Geographic, Nov., 1982, pp. 654 - 684.

Williams, H., and McBirney, A. R., 1979, *Volcanology*: New York, Freeman, Cooper & Co.

Williams, R. S., and Moore, J. G., 1973, **Iceland chills a lava flow** E: Geotimes, v. 18, pp. 14 - 17.

Wood, C. A., and Kienle, J., 1990, *Volcanoes of North America* E: New York, Cambridge University Press.

Wright, T. L., and Pierson, T. C., 1992, **Living with volcanoes: The U.S. Geological Survey's volcano hazards program** E: U.S. Geol. Survey Circ. 1073.

Videotapes on Volcanoes

Anatomy of a Volcano E: 1981, 57 minutes, Time-Life Video, 1271 Avenue of the Americas, New York, NY 10020, (219) 484-5940. Focuses on Mt. St. Helens.

Days of Destruction: 1973, 27 minutes, Indiana University Audiovisual Center, Bloomington, IN 47405-5901, (812) 335-8087. Icelandic eruption of Eldfell and its effects on populace of the island of Heimay.

Earth: The Restless Planet: 1973, 25 minutes, National Geographic, 17th and M Streets, NW, Washington, DC 20036, (202) 857-7378.

Earth: The Volcanoes: 1969, 10 minutes, Coronet Film and Video, 108 Wilmot Road, Deerfield, IL 60015, (800) 621-2131.

Eruption at the Sea E: 1988, 30 minutes, Káio Productions, P. O. Box 909, Volcano, HI 96785, (808) 967-7166.

Eruption: Mt. St Helens Explodes E: 1980, 25 minutes, Blackhawk Films, 5959 Triumph St., Commerce, CA 90040-1688, (800) 826-2295.

Eruption of a New Shield Volcano: 1987, 48 minutes, JLM Visuals, 1208 Bridge St., Grafton, WI 53204, (414) 377-7775.

Eruptive Phenomena of Kilauea's East Rift Zone: 1987, 43 minutes, Káio Productions, P. O. Box 909, Volcano, HI 96785, (808) 967-7166.

Forge of Vulcan: 1979, 18 minutes, National Audiovisual Center, National Archives and Records Administration, Customer Service Section PZ, 8700 Edgeworth Drive, Capitol Heights, MD 20743-3701, (301) 763-1896. Focus on the Katmai eruption in Alaska in 1912.

Hawaii Volcanoes National Park: 1987, 9.5 minutes, National Park Service, Available on loan from U.S. Geol. Survey Library Special Collections, MS 955, 345 Middlefield Road, Menlo Park, CA 94025, (415) 329-5009.

Heartbeat of a Volcano: 1970, 20 minutes, Britannica Films, 310 South Michigan Ave., Chicago, IL 60604, (800) 621-3900. Focus on Kilauea in Hawaii.

Hot Spot: 1974, 9 minutes, Phoenix BFA Films, 468 Park Ave. South, New York, NY 10016, (800) 221-1274. Focus on Nyiragongo Volcano in Zaire.

In the Shadow of Vesuvius E: 1989, 60 minutes, Vestron Video, P.O. Box 576, Itasca, IL 60143, (800) 523-5503. Video Produced by National Geographic. Excellent footage of 1944 eruption of Vesuvius and fascinating reconstruction of the eruption events that destroyed Pompeii and Herculaneum.

Inside Hawaiian Volcanoes E: 1989, 25 minutes, Smithsonian Institution, Richard S. Fiske, Dept. of Mineral Sciences, NHB-119, Smithsonian Institution, Washington, DC 20560. Available on loan from U.S. Geol. Survey Library Special Collections, MS 955, 345 Middlefield Road, Menlo Park, CA 94025, (415) 329-5009.

Kilauea - Close-up of an Active Volcano E: 1990, 30 minutes, Káio Productions, P. O. Box 909, Volcano, HI 96785, (808) 967-7166.

Life with St. Helens: 1980, 30 minutes, PBS Video American Experience Series, 1320 Braddock Place, Alexandria, VA 22314-1698, (800) 424-7693.

Mount St. Helens - Why They Died E: 1980, 60 minutes, San Diego State University Learning Resource Center, San Diego, CA 92182, (714) 265-5726.

Mount St. Helens: Monitoring an Active Volcano E: 1985, 25 minutes, U.S. Geol. Survey, Available on loan from U.S. Geol. Survey Library Special Collections, MS 955, 345 Middlefield Road, Menlo Park, CA 94025, (415) 329-5009.

Mount St Helens—The Turmoil of Creation Continues: 1989, 90 minutes, Panorama International Productions, P.O. Box 1255, Beverly Hills, CA 90213, (818) 508-9972.

Ring of Fire - East of Krakatau: 1988, 60 minutes, Mystic Fire Video, Box 1202, Montauk, NY 11954, (800) 727-8433. Although this is primarily a documentary of culture on the island of Java, there are excellent views of volcanic phenomena, especially lahars.

Rivers of Fire: 1984, 23 minutes, The 1984 eruptions of Mauna Loa and Kilauea. Available on loan from U.S. Geol. Survey Library Special Collections, MS 955, 345 Middlefield Road, Menlo Park, CA 94025, (415) 329-5009.

Saint Helens - Growing Again: 1987, 19 minutes, Centre Productions Inc., 1800 30th St. Suite 207, Boulder, CO 80301, (800) 424-1166.

The 1902 Eruption of Mount Pelée: 1991, 45 minutes, JLM Visuals, 1208 Bridge St., Grafton, WI 53204, (414) 377-7775. A re-enactment told through footage of later disasters. Available on loan from U.S. Geol. Survey Library Special Collections, MS 955, 345 Middlefield Road, Menlo Park, CA 94025 (415) 329-5009.

The Eruptions of Mount St. Helens: 1981, 30 minutes, Video Tech., Third Ave. NW, Seattle, WA 98177, (206) 546-5401.

The Eruption of Kilauea, 1959-60: 1961, 27 minutes, U.S. Geol. Survey, **Volcano** Available on loan from U.S. Geol. Survey Library Special Collections, MS 955, 345 Middlefield Road, Menlo Park, CA 94025, (415) 329-5009.

The Living Machine: 1985, 58 minutes, Corporation for Public Broadcasting, Annenberg - CPB Project, 901 E St. Washington, DC 20004-2006, (800) 532-7637.

The Magma Chamber: 1987, 50 minutes, Osborn Court, Olney Buckinghamshire, MK 46 4AG United Kingdom, Phone 0234-711198 or 713390. Produced for BBC Horizon Series. Focuses on how studies of magma at depth aid in the prediction of eruptions.

The Volcanoes of Hawaii: 1988, 30 minutes, Norman Berger Productions, 3217 S. Arville St., Las Vegas, NV 89102-7612, (702) 876-2328 or Glenn Ege, 1313 Kaluaua Ave., Honolulu, HI 96826.

The Volcano Watchers E: 1988, 60 minutes, PBS Home Video, 1320 Braddock Place, Alexandria, VA 22314-1698, (703) 739-5380. Outstanding footage of volcanic eruptions filmed during visitations by the late Maurice and Katia Krafft, the famous French husband-wife volcanologists who perished on Japan's Unzen volcano in 1991. Possibly the best film on volcanoes ever made for the general public. Contains hard-to-find footage of dealing with volcanic hazards through diversion of flows and establishing monitoring networks for lahars.

Understanding Volcanic Hazards: Sponsored by the International Association of Volcanology and Chemistry of the Earth's Interior, this video in preparation will be available in a variety of formats and languages. It was announced at the First International Symposium on Volcanic Ash and Aviation Safety, 1991. Contact Dr. C. G. Newhall, USGS MS 905, 12201 Sunrise Valley Drive, Reston, VA 22092, (703) 648-6709 on availability.

Volcanic Eruption in Colombia: 1988, 15 minutes, Pan American Health Organization. Graphic footage of the Nevado del Ruiz disaster that claimed 20,000 lives. Some scenes are shocking and probably not suitable for young children. Available on loan from U.S. Geol. Survey Library Special Collections, MS 955, 345 Middlefield Road, Menlo Park, CA 94025, (415) 329-5009.

Volcanism E: 1990, Corporation for Public Broadcasting, Annenberg - CPB Project, 901 E St. Washington, DC 20004-2006, (800) 532-7637.

Volcano: 1953, 10 minutes, University of California at Berkeley, Extension Media Center, 2176 Shattuck Ave., Berkeley, CA 94704 (510) 642-5578.

Volcano: 1989, 23 minutes, Random House Media, Dept. 647, 4000 Hahn Road, Westminster, MD 21157, (800) 638-6460.

Volcano: The Birth of a Mountain: 1976, Britannica Films, 310 South Michigan Ave., Chicago, IL 60604, (800) 621-3900.

Volcano!: 1988, 58 minutes, Coronet Film and Video, 108 Wilmot Road, Deerfield, IL 60015, (800) 621-2131. Produced by Nova.

Volcano in Hawaii: 1990, 60 minutes, ABC Nightlines, MPI Home Video, 15825 Rob Roy Drive, Oak Forest, IL 60452, (800) 323-0442.

Volcano Special E: 1990, 22 minutes, KGO-TV San Francisco. Illustrates potential hazards from California's volcanic vents. Available on loan from U.S. Geol. Survey Library Special Collections, MS 955, 345 Middlefield Road, Menlo Park, CA 94025, (415) 329-5009.

Volcanoes: 1977, 24 minutes, Dallas County Community College District, Center for Telecommunications, 4343 N Hwy. 67, Mesquite, TX 75150-2095, (214) 324-7988.

Volcanoes of the Kenya Rift: 1988, 28 minutes, Coronet Film and Video, 108 Wilmot Road, Deerfield, IL 60015, (800) 621-2131.

Volcanoscapes E: 1988, 45 minutes, Tropical Visions Video, 62 Halaulani Place, Hilo, HI 96720, (808) 935-5557. Eruptions of Kilauea.

World Famous Volcanoes: 1988, 30 minutes total on 6 programs: Educational Video Network, 1401 19th St. Huntsville, TX 77340, (409) 295-5767. Features Vesuvius, Paricutin, Stromboli, Mauna Loa, Kilauea, and Mt. St. Helens.

LANDSLIDES and AVALANCHES

Each year landslides in the U.S. produce over 1.5 billion dollars in losses and about 25 to 50 deaths. Avoiding high-risk areas, or planning to include measures for stabilization, is a wise choice for builders and financiers. Where good geologic and slope stability maps are available, chances for successful construction and development are greatly enhanced.

Landslide Occurrences

A **landslide** consists of earth materials that move by gravitational force. The motion involves downslope movement as well as lateral spread or scatter of materials. Landslides can even involve some upslope movement, as in the case in which a massive slide runs downslope across a valley and sends debris up the opposite valley wall. The term "landslide" applies to rapid movement of earth materials, although landslide movements often begin with slow creep. An **avalanche** is a similar mass movement of snow and ice. Avalanches take about 20 lives each year in the U.S.

Downslope movement of soil and rock is a result of natural conditions on our planet's surface. The constant stress of gravity and the gradual weakening of earth materials through long-term chemical and physical weathering processes insure that, through geologic time, downslope movement is inevitable. However, when we talk about downslope movement as a hazard, we usually say that a slope is hazardous only when the downslope movement is likely to be rapid enough to threaten man-made structures. Many landslides occur in unpopulated areas and cause neither hazard nor risk. Landslides can involve volumes from as small as one falling boulder to massive movement of millions of cubic yards of material. The largest known landslide on earth occurred prehistorically in Iran, and was 14 km (9 miles) wide and 19 km (12 miles) long.

This landslide has undercut the foundation of this California home, has removed the sidewalk and threatens the road in the foreground. Landslides affect both buildings and transportation routes. Special engineering design, zoning and land use management can greatly reduce scenes such as this one. (photo by J. T. McGill, USGS)

WORLD'S MAJOR LANDSLIDES AND AVALANCHES

YEAR	LOCATION	APPROXIMATE DEATHS
218 BC	Alps (avalanches - Hannibal's army)	18,000
1248	Alps, France (avalanche)	5,000
1618	Mount Conto, Switzerland	2,430
1889	South Fork Dam, Johnstown, PA [2]	2,200
1906 - 1913	Panama Canal excavation	likely hundreds
1916 - 1917	Alps, Italy (avalanches) [1]	10,000
1920	Kansu, China[3]	200,000
1928	St. Francis Dam, Southern CA [2]	500
1934	Bihar, Nepal [4]	3,500
1941	Huaraz, Peru (avalanche and mudflow)	7,000
1945	Kure City, Japan	1,154
1949	Khait - near Garm, former USSR [4]	12,000
1958	Shizuoka, Japan	1,100
1962	Yungay, Peru	4,500
1963	Vaiont Reservoir, Italy [2]	3,000
1966	Aberfan, South Wales (tailings pile) [2]	144
1967	Rio de Janiero, Brazil	1,700
1970	Yungay, Peru (avalanche) [4]	18,000 to 25,000
1970	Alaknanda River, India [2]	600
1971	Chungar, Peru [2]	200
1971	Hindu Kush Mountains, Afghanistan [2]	1,000
1972	Buffalo Hollow, WV (tailings dam) [2]	118
1974	Mayunmarca, Peru	450
1976	Guatemala [4]	hundreds
1985	Ponce, Puerto Rico	130
1985	Stava, Italy (tailings dam) [2]	268
1985	Mamayas, Puerto Rico	129
1989	Tadzhikstan [4]	270
1991	Uttarkashi, India	2,000
1991	Ormoc, Philippines	4,081 [5]

[1] Italian and Austrian armies.

[2] Slide into river, lake or reservoir produces flood; victims drowned.

[3] Loess cliffs containing homes collapsed and flowed (dry) during earthquake accounting for about half of the cited fatalities.

[4] Landslides generated during earthquakes.

[5] Total for mudflows, mudslides and flash floods associated with typhoon

Compiled from Coates, 1985; Costa and Baker, 1981; Keller, 1985; National Research Council, 1987; Tufty, 1969 (complete citations given on pp. 8 - 11 this book) and Office of Foreign Disaster Assistance, 1992, *Disaster History.*

Dangers of Landslides

Slope failures result in an annual cost to society of about 1.5 billion dollars. Damages to highways alone from slope failure in the United States approach 1 billion dollars annually. Annual damage to buildings and building sites in the United States is about half a billion dollars. At Malibu, California, a single landslide at Big Rock Mesa recently generated costs of about 92 million dollars in damages and liabilities.

Very few landslides occur in areas where they cannot at all be anticipated. Small flows and slides that take only a few lives are common and account for an annual average estimated loss of 25 lives in the United States. Worldwide, landslides account for an average of 600 lives each year. Although steep slopes are an obvious topographic condition that should alert anyone to potential landslides, human inability to take seriously those hazards that occur infrequently can increase loss of life. Even professional engineers and regulatory officials who are aware of significant past landslide activity at a site can still be tempted to proceed with projects through unwarranted faith in the belief that "It won't happen here."

It is not possible to prevent all loss of life from small "freak accident" rockfalls, but it is possible to prevent or reduce many of the massive fatalities of the kind illustrated in the table on the preceding page. This is because rapid slope failures occur as a result of the presence of specific types of earth materials and particular conditions and processes. Areas with conditions that indicate potential for massive slides can and should be avoided for major projects and developments.

Indications of Natural Instability

Slides can be anticipated through the following criteria.

1. History of past landslides in the nearby area in the same stratigraphic units as the site in question. For instance, prehistoric wedge failures had been mapped in the Kootenai River valley of Montana, and wedge failures there plagued the site of the Libby dam after construction began in 1967. The shales of the Pierre Formation are well known by geologists in the area of Denver, Colorado, as materials in which many slope failures occur. Therefore, a geologic map that shows where this stratigraphic unit is exposed at the ground surface reveals potentially dangerous areas. Some recent landslides are easily recognized from the ground even by the untrained eye. Old landslides with the potential to move again are likely to be noticed only by experts who employ aerial photographs and remote sensing techniques. If the subtle evidence is ignored, disaster is invited.

2. Soil types that are rich in silt-to-clay-sized material, particularly soils that are rich in swelling clays. (See section on quick clays p. 15.) Usually movement occurs in these soils in spring when the soil is very saturated from thaw and snow melt. However, water is not always required to produce movement. About 200,000 lives were lost in 1920 in Kansu, China, when dry **loess** soils (fine soils developed on fine wind-blown material) went into fluid motion during an earthquake, destroyed dwellings and engulfed the inhabitants. Loose volcanic materials (see preceding section on volcanoes) often can absorb so much water that they flow quickly down even gentle slopes. A mudflow, along with gases, destroyed the Roman city of Herculaneum at the base of Mt. Vesuvius in 79 AD. Formations such as the Rissa Clay of Norway and the Leda Clay of Ontario, Canada, are particularly notorious for slope failure by flowage during liquefaction. The clays were deposited during late glacial periods in the seas that occupied these areas at that time. Where fresh ground water removed salts that were deposited with the clays in sea water, the clays became particularly unstable.

3. Downslope orientation of planes of weakness in bedrock. Translational movements occur where **bedding planes** (the planes between layers of sedimentary rocks) point in a downslope direction. Orientation of **schistosity** (alignment of platy and rod-shaped minerals in metamorphic rocks) in a downslope direction or orientation of joints parallel to the slope direction also furnishes planar weaknesses that are conducive to slides. The famous Gros Ventre landslide of Wyoming, slides in the Cretaceous rocks

Rockfall is a common hazard in mountainous regions. Motorists are sometimes injured when their vehicles strike rocks that have fallen onto highways. Even trains are sometimes derailed by rocks that fall onto railroad tracks. This boulder on Highway 6 in Colorado took the life of the driver of a gasoline tanker. (photo by R. Van Horn, USGS)

Some Kinds of Landslides Portrayed in Concept...

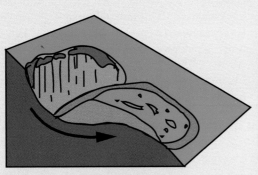

Rotational slide in soil

Planar slide in bedrock

Two basic types of landslide movements are rotational failure and planar failure. Rotational failures are common in soils; the most catastrophic slides usually involve planar block failure because huge volumes of rock and soil can move in this manner. Other forms of failure not shown here include toppling, movement of wedge-shaped blocks (wedging), buckling, and combinations of all of these.

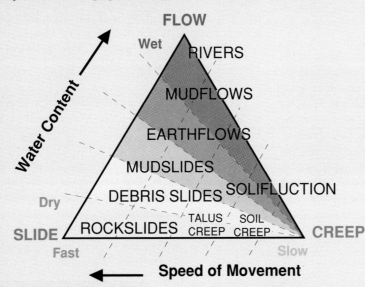

FLOW

Wet

RIVERS

MUDFLOWS

EARTHFLOWS

MUDSLIDES

DEBRIS SLIDES   SOLIFLUCTION

Dry

SLIDE   ROCKSLIDES   TALUS   SOIL   CREEP
                       CREEP   CREEP

Fast   Slow

Water Content

Speed of Movement

Types of slope failures differ from one another in speed of movement (ranging from creep to slides of over 200 miles-per-hour) and type of movement (slide *vs.* flow). The type of movement depends upon how much water is in the slide debris. With increasing water content, the movement changes from sliding motion to flowing. Amount of destruction caused by a slope failure depends on its speed and especially its size. (diagram modified from Clarkson and Kirkby, 1972, *Hillslope Form and Process*, Cambridge University Press)

Slumps often show features of sliding near their tops and flowing failure near their bases. The slide scarp (1) usually displays concave crescent-shape. Slump blocks (2) show rotational movement. Hummocks (3) are uneven mounds and ridges produced during soil flowage. Toe of slide (4) displays fluid movement. Failure plane (5) bounds the base. Fissure (6) indicates that slump is still active and that more movement is likely. Removal of toe at the base of a slope often triggers a slump failure.

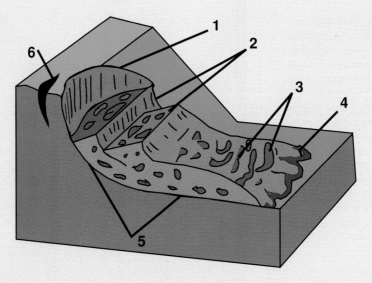

...and Portrayed as Seen in the Field

The exposed bedding plane reveals the surface along which this landslide failed. Construction of the highway (to right) removed supporting base and triggered this planar slide in Wyoming. Although this is a small slide, huge rockslides that send millions of tons of rock downslope (such as the Vaiont reservoir landslide in Italy) are well modeled by this small slide. Planar weaknesses in the rock that dip downslope produce situations that are dangerous for buildings and highways below. Dip of beds in relation to the slope is easily seen on geologic maps, so planning ahead is possible if the maps are consulted and understood. (photo by Richard Waugh)

In contrast to the sliding motion of the rockslide above, earthflows and mudflows move downslope like viscous, plastic material. Failure may be slow or fast. This earthflow in West Virginia developed on red shales and clay soils. It now advances slowly toward the home below. The utility pole engulfed in toe of flow is already tilting in response to the encroachment of the flow. (photo by Edward Nuhfer)

The entire hill side above this four-lane highway at Athens, Ohio, is involved in active slumping. The headward scarps at the top of the hill are advancing to threaten apartments sited on the hill top. Uneven hummocky ground and slump blocks are apparent on the hill side, and the toe of the slump is flowing toward the highway. Many slumps can be prevented by early planning that controls drainage, makes use of retaining structures, or pre-excavates material likely to break loose. (photo by Edward Nuhfer)

Low-altitude aerial photograph of Anchorage, Alaska, after the 1964 earthquake. Fissures at the head of landslide blocks can be seen passing through the Turnagain Heights neighborhood. The area between the major fissures dropped down as result of the consolidation and settling of porous sediments during the strong tremors. Ruins in background are remains of the Four Seasons apartment building. Landslides are a common product of earthquakes, and many slides close roads and delay rescue and repair efforts. (photo from USGS Photo Library, Denver, CO)

near Rapid City, South Dakota, and the landslide into the Vaiont Reservoir, Italy, all occurred in rocks containing weaknesses in planes that dipped steeply downslope.

Evidence for past landslides abounded in the valley used for the impoundment of the Vaiont Reservoir in Italy. Yet, engineers ignored the implications and constructed the reservoir. The catastrophe of 1963 occurred when a huge landslide shot into the reservoir and sent a wave of water over 300 feet (100 m) high across the reservoir and over the dam. The dam withstood the immense wave that overtopped it, and its strength was a credit to its designer. However, 3000 people caught in the path of the onrushing flood wave perished. Excellence in engineering design proved to be no substitute for a geological site investigation.

4. Slope undercutting. Landslides are particularly common along stream banks, reservoir shorelines, and large lake and seacoasts. The removal of supporting material by currents and waves at the base of a slope produces countless small slides each year. Particularly good examples are found in the soft glacial sediments

along the shores of the Great Lakes of the U.S. and Canada.

5. Earthquake tremors. A tremor, even a fairly mild one, can provide the *coup de grace* to a slope which has been resting for decades in a state of marginal instability. Nearly 30 campers were killed when the 1959 landslide in the Madison Canyon of Montana was triggered by an earthquake. Over 130 million tons of debris covered Canada's Highway 3 when two small earthquakes triggered the Hope Mountain slide in British Columbia in 1965. During the 1964 Alaskan earthquake huge blocks of the shoreline slid beneath the ocean at Valdez, Alaska, when rotational slumping took place in materials below sea level. Similar rotational slumping in soft materials damaged large sections of Anchorage.

6. Sensitive slopes subject to intense rainfall. When the right geological conditions exist, periods of intense rainfall can trigger the movement of unstable slopes. In one night in January, 1967, 600 people lost their lives in Brazil when a three-hour cloudburst converted green hills into mudflows and attractive stream valleys into flood torrents. In the southern and central Appalachian Mountains, periods of increased frequency of slides often coincide with severe local summer cloudbursts and thunderstorms. More widespread regional rains associated with hurricanes that move inland trigger landslides over larger areas. Studies of the Canadian Rockies also reveal a definite link between rainstorms and rockfalls. Landslides are particularly abundant during the rainy season along the West Coast of North America.

Human Causes of Rapid Slope Failures

People are very capable of causing catastrophic slope failures. Designers who are ignorant about geological materials and processes may unwittingly produce conditions at a site that are the same conditions that promote natural failures.

All loose materials such as sand or soil have a natural **angle of repose**, which is the maximum angle that can be measured on a slope when the material is stable and at rest. When any earth material is maneuvered into large piles that have side slopes that are steeper than the angle of repose of the material, the situation invites a landslide.

Mine wastes may be susceptible to absorption of water and gradual deterioration of shear strength. Sometimes these materials are stacked in huge piles with side slopes that are even steeper than the natural angle of repose (about 40°) of stable materials. When

the wastes weaken, the huge piles can fail in a landslide. This occurred in Aberfan, Wales, in 1966 when 144 people, 116 of them children, died in a flow of fine-grained mine waste. Six years later, coal mine wastes which had been used as a makeshift dam in a valley failed, and resulted in over 100 deaths and 50 million dollars damage at Buffalo Hollow, West Virginia, when the failure sent a 5-meter (15 ft.) wall of water and mud down the Buffalo Creek Valley.

Around major cities, accumulated waste is often stacked in large landfills. Some old landfills are piled high near their angle of repose. Like mine wastes, these present sources of possible danger from failure, especially in sites subject to earthquake tremors.

An unstable slope can be set into motion by removing supporting material from the toe of the slope, a situation that often results during construction on or at the base of a slope. Movement can also result from loading the slope from above. Loading from above occurs when people build a structure such as a building, a storage tank, or a highway upon materials that cannot remain stable under the additional load.

Human development of areas alters the natural drainage and increases runoff. Storm drains, roof gutters, septic tanks, or leaking water mains can focus enough water into a sensitive slope to generate movement, particularly where intensive housing development exists in several tiers on a single slope. Drainage control is very important in such areas.

Failure to appreciate the angle of repose of fill may have led to the collapse of this rock wall in northern Illinois. Soil fill was surrounded by a stone block decorative wall of insufficient strength to act as a retainer wall. Pressure accumulated as the fill settled until it suddenly broke the wall and cast blocks and fill material onto users of the parking area below. Fatalities resulted. (photo by Richard Wetzel)

Small earthquakes can trigger huge landslides. This landslide at Hope Mountain in British Columbia was triggered by a small earthquake early on a January morning. It sent millions of tons of debris hurtling into Nicolum Valley, buried the highway in over 200 feet of rubble, and killed four people. (photo by Edward Nuhfer)

Landslides and the Concept of Deep Time

Mass wasting, the downslope movement of materials, is the most prevalent of all geological processes. Through this process, materials are eventually carried into streams or onto glaciers. Thereafter, the material is transported (eroded) away by water, ice or wind. Most mass wasting takes place as creep, which is so slow that it cannot be discerned by direct observation. Instead, creep becomes evident only after some years through changes such as misaligned utility poles, out-of plumb old houses, and bulges in stone retainer walls. As a hazard, creep is so slow that it is harmless and probably represents the more gradual of geological processes. However, not all downslope movement is gradual. Occasionally sections of rock and soil move quickly. A melting snowman is a good analogy of change. Most of the snowman disappears at nearly imperceptible rates by slow, gradual melting, but occasionally a piece breaks and falls away. The piece is rarely seen falling because a fall occurs in only a tiny fraction of the time taken for melting. The falling events are analogous to the type of mass wasting characterized by rock falls or toppling blocks. The frequent "Falling Rock" sign seen on our highways is a reminder of the perpetual problem of falls, but we rarely see a rock actually in motion toppling onto a highway.

Some slope failures occur seasonally. In many areas in the early spring, one sees small slumps that have occurred along the banks of streams, in pastures, or along slopes adjacent to the highway. While it cannot be predicted exactly when a slump will occur in spring, we can anticipate that more slumps will occur in seasons when the soils are wet with water from recently melted snow.

Some landslides occur on the irregular timetables of events such as earthquakes and storms which trigger movement. (See also chapters on occurrences of earthquakes and floods through deep time.) These triggering events cannot be predicted, but the particular

Unlike natural lakes, flood-control reservoirs in steep valleys are often subject to seasonal water level variations that can exceed 100 feet. When the reservoirs are lowered quickly after a high water period (usually spring), the water level in the reservoir drops faster than water can exit from the pores and capillaries of the saturated rocks and soils. This leaves waterlogged soils resting tenuously on steep banks, and these soils easily slump into the reservoir. As this material is removed, the soils that lie on slopes above have no toe support downslope. Sliding then develops further up-slope and contributes to abnormal sediment filling rates in the reservoir.

geological conditions in an area which will make it prone to movement can be mapped, thus clearly showing where the higher landslide risks will be for homes and other structures during a future storm or earthquake. Such maps can help planners, lenders, homeowners and insurers.

Massive sliding or flowing failures that involve thousands of tons of material and that move at speeds well in excess of 100 miles-per-hour are the most infrequent of mass wasting events. Such massive movements usually leave scars and other tell-tale signs on the landscape that enable these areas to be recognized as slide-prone many centuries after the event occurs. These events cannot be predicted, but many can be anticipated from evidence of older prehistoric slides, and the area can be avoided for dense development or construction of sensitive facilities such as dams or power plants. The landslide which destroyed the Vaiont Reservoir in Italy should have been anticipated because landslide scars abounded in the valley, and the geological conditions were obviously ideal for massive failures.

Through deep time, there have been a few huge landslides (called *sturzstroms*) involving billions of cubic yards of material. Movement of one of these has never been witnessed by humans, but they are evident from the rock record in places like the Shasta terrain of California, and they are clearly evident from high-altitude space-probe photographs of the surface of planet Mars.

In summary, mass wasting through deep time is characterized by (1) gradual movement as creep, (2) fairly regular seasonal times of increased landslide activity, and (3) irregular punctuations when massive slide events are triggered by major regional rainstorms or earthquakes. Times of major slide events cannot be predicted. Generally, the larger the landslide, the more infrequently it occurs over time.

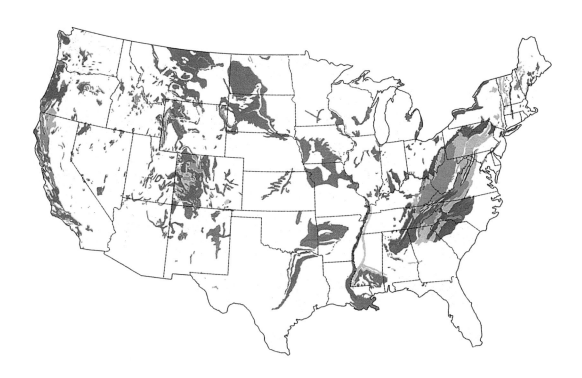

Map showing primary areas of landslide problems within the conterminous United States. Hazards decrease in severity in the order red, yellow, green, blue and violet. (map reproduced from Hays, 1981, USGS Professional Paper 1240-B. Readers may wish to consult the larger, more detailed *Map Showing Landslide Areas in the Conterminous United States* by D.H. Radbruch-Hall and others that accompanies USGS Professional Paper 1183.)

Roles of the Geologist in Minimizing Slope Stability Hazards

In field evaluation. The more an area is susceptible to landsliding, and the more humans encroach into it, the greater the necessity for a complete geologic investigation.

The involvement of professional geologists should be absolutely mandatory in the site characterization for any structure whose failure may endanger human lives or significant amounts of property. No structure is safer than its geological setting.

Geologic examinations of slopes require evaluation of at least the following categories:

1. The evaluation of topography—relief, steepness and shape of slope
2. The types and conditions of the bedrocks that underlie the slope
3. The type and thickness of soils present
4. The angle and direction of bedding planes or rock fabric
5. The frequency and the direction of any discontinuities (such as joints), the extent of the discontinuities, and the kind of infilling material present in them
6. The amount and type of vegetation on the slope
7. The sources of moisture and the moisture-retaining properties of the materials
8. The nature of surface and subsurface drainage, and any human-made drainage
9. A determination of the earthquake history of the area
10. Evidence of past slides, flows or rockfalls
11. An evaluation of possible volume of earth materials susceptible to failure, the possible styles in which they may fail, and the area that may be affected by failure.

In public service. At the regional level, geologists serve as data gatherers, compilers and organizers of basic information that will become available for future use in development of the areas. Geologists employed by state geological surveys and the U.S. Geological Survey provide a tremendous service by constructing geological and slope stability maps. Mapping is based on field study of the soils and rock formations and is aided by remote sensing methods that include satellite and high-altitude photography and computer technology. Geologists' published maps are used by engineers, contractors, developers and homeowners.

In research. The quantitative estimation of slope safety is a common task performed by engineering geologists and geotechnical engineers. Calculating a **"factor of safety"** by estimating the ratio of those forces that tend to hold material in place to those forces that tend to drive it downslope is a requisite of most engineering design projects that involve any construction on a sloping terrain. The more that is known about the nature of the geological materials and processes present at a site, the more likely a site will be developed without later regret. Research provides better ways to investigate sites and evaluate data. The mining and civil engineering professions benefit particularly from slope stability research.

A vigorous research program on the topic of massive earth movements has been ongoing in Russia for several years. Study of the way landslides move aids in the design of methods of blasting that move materials efficiently during mining and major construction projects. Benefits of such research serve the public whenever applied by engineers.

Computers provide continued research opportunities to model slope failures and rockfalls, and new programs remove the tedium from calculations that formerly were a necessary evil in conventional factor of safety calculations.

In this age of electronic and biological technology, it might seem to the lay reader that most answers to problems that involve something as apparently primitive as falling rock would have been answered, but such is not the case. In particular, the mechanisms that cause rocks to move surprisingly great lateral distances during rock avalanches are still not well understood. Slope stability and rock movement remain very suitable areas for research in our age of high technology.

In education. Geology is the most essential of all sciences for understanding what constitutes good land use. It is important that citizens understand slope hazards because so many home sites and developments are on slopes. Slope hazards should be covered in introductory geology and earth science courses, and such courses should be taught only by teachers with extensive formal education in geology.

Geologists in some universities are involved in teaching engineering geology and environmental

Portion of the slope-stability map produced for Clarksburg, West Virginia, by Peter Lessing and others of the West Virginia Geological and Economic Survey. Recent landslides are shown in dark red, older slides in solid pink, slide-prone areas in red stipples and stable ground in white. Red X's show rockfall areas. A citizen can purchase the full-sized map for only $5.00. What a bargain for the thousands of homeowners and citizens in the vicinity of Clarksburg! Every city should have such fine maps.

geology to future designers. Geology should be part of the education of any civil or environmental engineer, environmental scientist or architect. Development and construction projects that are designed using the contributions of professional geologists have proven to be more successful in reducing damages from landslide hazards than those in which the geology is omitted or is performed by someone without credentials in geology. Yet only a few graduating civil engineers actually take a course in engineering geology, and only half take any geology courses.

Geologists are also involved in public education through establishing scientific areas where the public can investigate landslides, often by guided tour. One of the most expensive slides in history occurred near Thistle, Utah, in 1983, and over 200 million dollars was required for the relocation of a major highway and railroad. The site is now used as an educational resource and a classic area for scientific study. So also are the sites of the Madison Canyon landslide, Montana, and the Gros Ventre landslide, Wyoming.

References on Landslides & Avalanches

"E" Denotes references particularly suitable for educators.

Abrahams, A. D., (ed.), 1986, *Hillslope Processes*: London, Allen & Unwin.

Anderson, M. G., and Richards, K. S., (eds.), 1987, **Slope Stability**: New York, John Wiley.

Armstrong, B., and Williams, K., 1992, *The Avalanche Book* (2nd ed.) E: Golden, CO, Fulcrum.

Brabb, E. E., 1985, **On the line, losing by a landslide**: Natural Hazards Observer (November, 1985), Institute of Behavioral Science, University of Colorado, Boulder, CO.

Bromhead, E. N., 1985, *The Stability of Slopes*: New York, Methuen.

Brundsden, D., and Prior, D. B., 1984, *Slope Instability*: New York, John Wiley.

Christopherson, E., 1960, *The Night the Mountain Fell - The Story of the Montana - Yellowstone Earthquake* E: Yellowstone Publications, P.O. Box 411, West Yellowstone, MT 59758. A narrative on the 1959 Madison Canyon landslide.

Chowdhury, R. N., 1978, *Slope Analysis*: Amsterdam, Elsevier.

Close, U., and McCormick, E., 1922, **Where the mountains walked** E: National Geographic, v. 41, pp. 445 - 520. (Kansu, China, - 1920 earthquakes and landslides).

Coates, D. R., (ed.), 1977, **Landslides**: Geol. Soc. Amer. Reviews in Engineering Geology, v. 3, 278 p.

Committee on Ground Failure Hazards, Commission on Engineering and Technical Systems, National Research Council, 1985, **Reducing losses from landsliding within the United States**: Washington, DC, National Academy Press.

Committee on Ground Failure Hazards Mitigation Research, National Research Council, 1990, *Snow Avalanche Hazards and Mitigation in the United States*: Washington, DC, National Academy Press.

Costa, J. E., and Wieczorek, G. F., (eds.), 1987, **Debris flows, avalanches: process, recognition and mitigation**: Geol. Soc. Amer. Reviews in Engineering Geology, v. 7, 248 p.

Crawford, C. B., 1961, **Engineering studies of Leda Clay**: in *Soils in Canada*, R. F. Legget, ed., Royal Soc. Canada Spec. Pub. n. 3, pp. 200 - 217.

Crozier, M. J., 1986, *Landslides: Causes, Consequences and Environment*: New York, Chapman & Hall.

Cummans, J., 1981, **Mudflows resulting from the May 18, 1980, eruption of Mount St. Helens** E: U.S. Geol. Survey, Circular 850 B.

Cupp, D., 1982, **Avalanche!** E: National Geographic, v. 162, pp. 280 - 305.

Ehlig, P., 1986, **Landslide and landslide mitigation in southern California**: Geol. Soc. Amer. Guidebook and Volume Field Trip nos. 3, 13, and 16.

Evans, D., and Lownes, R., 1992, **Big Rock Mesa landslide and litigation**: in *Engineering Geology Practice in Southern California*, Assoc. Engrg. Geologists, Spec. Pub., Belmont, CA, Star Pub. Co., pp. 555 - 574.

Fleming, R. W., and Taylor, F. A., 1980, **Estimating the cost of landslide damage in the United States** E: U.S. Geol. Survey Circular 832.

Fleming, R. W., and Varnes, D. J., 1991, **Slope movements**: in *The Heritage of Engineering Geology; The First Hundred Years*, G. A., Kiersch (ed.), Geol. Soc. Amer. Centennial Special Volume 3, pp. 201 - 218.

Hoek, E., and Bray, J., 1981, *Rock Slope Engineering* (2nd. ed.): London, Inst. Mining & Metallurgy.

Hollingsworth, R. A., and Kovacs, G. S., 1981, **Soil slumps and debris flows: prediction and protection**: Bull. Assoc. of Engrg. Geologists, v. 18, pp. 17 - 28.

International Snow Science Workshop Committee, 1990, **Proceedings of the International Snow Science Workshop: October 9-13, 1990, Bigfork, Montana**: International Snow Science Workshop Committee, P. O. Box 372, Big Fork, MT 59911, 337 p. Focus on avalanche control.

Keefer, D. K., 1984, **Landslides caused by earthquakes**: Geol. Soc. Amer. Bull. 95, pp. 406-421.

Keefer, D. K., and others, 1987, **Real-time landslide warning during heavy rainfall**: Science, v. 238, pp. 921 - 925.

Kenney, N. T., 1969, **Southern California's trial by mud and water** E: National Geographic, v. 136, pp. 552 - 573.

Kiersch, G. A., 1964, **Vaiont Reservoir disaster** E: Civil. Engrg., v. 34, pp. 32 - 39.

Kockelman, W. J., 1986, **Some techniques for reducing landslide hazards**: Bull. Assoc. Engrg. Geologists, v. 23, pp. 29 - 49.

Krohn, J. P., and Slosson, J. E., 1976, **Landslide potential in the United States** E: California Geology, Vol. 29, No. 10, pp. 224 - 231.

Leighton, F. B., 1976, **Urban landslides: targets for land use planning in California** E: Geol. Soc. Amer. Spec. Paper n. 174, pp. 37 - 60.

McDowell, B., 1962, **Avalanche!** E: National Geographic, v. 121, pp. 855-880. (Avalanche in Peru)

Mears, A. I., 1992, **Colorado snow-avalanche area studies and guidelines for avalanche-hazard planning**: Colorado Geol. Survey (an update of 1979 Special Publication 7).

Melosh, H. J., 1990, **Giant rock avalanches**: Nature, v. 348, pp. 482 - 483.

Nilsen, T., Wright, R., Vlassic, T., and Spangle, W., 1979, **Relative slope stability and land use planning in the San Francisco Bay region, California** E: U.S. Geol. Survey Prof. Paper 944.

Peck, R. B., 1967, **Stability of natural slopes**: Amer. Soc. Civil. Engrs. Jour. Soil Mech. and Foundations, v. 93, pp. 403 - 417.

Perla, R. I., and Martinelli, M., 1975, *Avalanche Handbook*: U.S. Forest Service Agriculture Handbook.

Plant, N., and Griggs, G. B., 1990, **Coastal landslides and the Loma Prieta earthquake**: Earth Science, v. 43, pp. 12 - 18.

Radbruch-Hall, D., and others, 1982, **Landslide overview map of the conterminous United States** E: U.S. Geol. Survey Prof. Paper 1183, 25 p.

Schaefer, S. J., and Williams, S. N., 1991, **Landslide hazards - an example from Zunil, Guatemala** E: Geotimes, v. 36, n. 5 (May), pp. 20 - 22.

Schuirman, G., and Slosson, J. E., 1992, *Forensic Geology*: New York, Academic Press. (Contains three excellent case studies on landslides with an emphasis on litigation caused by these.).

Schultz, A. P., and Jibson, R. W., (eds.), 1989, **Landslide processes of the eastern United States and Puerto Rico**: Geol. Soc. Amer. Spec. Paper 236, 102 p.

Schultz, A. P., and Southworth, C. S., (eds.), 1987, **Landslides of eastern North America** E: U.S. Geol. Survey Circular 1008, 43 p.

Schuster, R. L., 1989, **Long-term landslide hazard mitigation programs: structure and experience from other countries**: Bull. Assoc. Engrg. Geologists, v. 26, pp. 109 - 133.

Schuster, R. L., (ed.), 1986, **Landslide dams: processes, risk, and mitigation**: Amer. Soc. Civil Engrs., Geotech. Spec. Pub. n. 3, ASCE, 345 East 47th St., N.Y., N.Y., 10017-2398, 162 p.

Schuster, R. L., and Fleming, R. W., 1986, **Economic losses and fatalities due to landslides** E: Bull. Assoc. Engrg. Geologists, v. 23, pp. 11 - 28.

Schuster, R. L., and Krizek, R. L., (eds.), 1978, **Landslides, analysis, and control**: Natl. Research Council, Transportation Research Board, Special Report 176, 234 p.

Selby, M. J., 1982, *Hillslope Materials and Processes*: New York, Oxford Univ. Press.

Selby, M. J., 1987, **Slopes and Weathering** E: in *Human Activity and Environmental Processes*, K. J. Gregory and D. E. Walling, (eds.), New York, Wiley, pp. 87 - 116.

Sidle, R. C., Pierce, A. J., and O'Loughlin, C. L., 1985, **Hillslope stability and land use**: Am. Geophys. Union Water Res. Monograph, n. 11, 140 p.

Siebert, L., 1984, **Large volcanic debris avalanches**: Jour. Volcanology & Geothermal Res., v. 22, pp. 163 - 197.

Soule, J. M., 1980, **Engineering geologic mapping and potential geologic hazards in Colorado**: Intnl. Assoc. Engineering Geology Bull. 21, Krefeld, Germany (distributed by U.S. National Committee on Geology, Washington, DC, 2101 Constitution Ave. NW, Washington, DC 20418).

Terzaghi, K., 1950, **Mechanism of landslides**: Geol. Soc. Amer. Berkey Volume, pp. 83 - 123.

Transportation Research Board, Natl. Research Council, 1992, **Rockfall prediction and control and landslide case histories**: Transportation Research Record n. 1343., Washington, DC, Natl. Research Council, Transportation Research Board.

Varnes, D. J., and others, 1984, **Landslide hazard zonation: a review of principles and practices**: UNESCO, 7 Place de Fontenay, 75700 Paris, 63 p.

Voight, B., (ed.), 1978, *Rockslides and Avalanches*: Amsterdam, Elsevier.

Wieczorek, G. F., 1984, **Preparing a detailed landslide-inventory map for hazard evaluation and reduction**: Bull. Assoc. Engrg. Geologists, v. 24, pp. 337 - 342.

Wold, R. L., Jr., and Jochim, C., 1989, **Landslide loss reduction: A guide for state and local government planning** E: Federal Emergency Management Agency, P. O. Box 70274, Washington, DC 20024.

Zaruba, Q., and Mencl, V., 1982, *Landslides and Their Control*: Amsterdam, Elsevier.

Videotapes on Landslides and Avalanches

Buffalo Creek Flood: An Act of Man: 1975, 40 minutes, Appalshop Films, 306 Madison St., Box 743 A, Whitesburg, KY 41858, (213) 666-6500. Focus on Buffalo Creek disaster from burst tailings dam.

Debris Flow Dynamics: 1987, 23 minutes, U.S. Geol. Survey. Compiled by John Costa and G. P. Williams. Contains footage of Japanese and Chinese debris flows. Available on loan from U.S. Geol. Survey Library Special Collections, MS 955, 345 Middlefield Road, Menlo Park, CA 94025, (415) 329-4009.

Debris Flows of the Tibetan Plateau: 1978, 35 minutes, People's Republic of China. Available on loan from U.S. Geol. Survey Library Special Collections, MS 955, 345 Middlefield Road, Menlo Park, CA 94025, (415) 329-4009.

Landslide, the 1979 Abbotsford Disaster: 1984, 40 minutes, University of Otago, New Zealand. Available on loan from U.S. Geol. Survey Library Special Collections, MS 955, 345 Middlefield Road, Menlo Park, CA 94025, (415) 329-4009.

The Rissa Landslide: 1985, 25 minutes, Norwegian Geotechnical Institute, Order from Leif Carserud, Sveriges Geologiska Undersökning: Killiangatan 10, 223 50 Lund Sweden, Telephone 009 46 46 13 14 56. One of the most spectacular landslide films ever made. Shows massive block of marine quick clays in actual movement.

Soil Mechanics in Permafrost Regions: 1975, 30 minutes, Genesys Systems Inc., 1057 E. Meadow Circle, Palo Alto, CA 94303, (415) 494-3701.

Slope Stability of Waste Dams and Embankments: 1979, 28 minutes, U.S. Dept. of Labor, National Mine Health and Safety Academy, P. O. Box 1166, Beckley, WV 25802-1166, (304) 256-3257.

USGS Landslide Prediction Efforts: 1987, 120 minutes. An educational tape by geologists of the USGS on methods of landslide prediction. Available on loan from U.S. Geol. Survey Library Special Collections, MS 955, 345 Middlefield Road, Menlo Park, CA 94025, (415) 329-4009.

Zunil, Guatemala, Landslide: 1991, 22 minutes, Harry Reid Center for Environmental Studies, Suite 201, 100 Washington St., Division of Earth Sciences, Reno, NV 85903, (702) 784-6151.

Slide Sets of Landslides and Avalanches

Philippines II: Faulting, Structural Damage, Liquefaction and Landslides from the Luzon, Philippines, Earthquake of July 16, 1990: 1992, 64 slides, Earthquake Engineering Research Institute (EERI), 499 14th St., Suite 320, Oakland, CA 94612-1902, (510) 451-0905.

Laguna Landslide and **Thistle Landslide**: undated, 36 and 37 slides respectively, Geophoto Publishing Company, P.O. Box 1960, Orem, UT 85049, (801) 226-4009.

SUBSIDENCE

Subsidence seldom causes fatalities, but it brings heartbreaking financial losses to property owners. Readers who live in areas where underground mining has occurred or where limestones or other rocks with natural, large voids underlie their property should be aware of the potential for subsidence. Obtaining property insurance that includes coverage against subsidence hazards can be worthwhile in many areas.

Occurrences of Subsidence

Subsidence is local sinking of the land surface with little or no horizontal motion. Special natural or man-made geologic conditions produce subsidence.

Tectonic processes (large-scale geologic processes) are one means of producing subsidence. One tectonic process that brings about natural subsidence occurs when regional areas of strong, competent rock are lowered by settling along major faults. When settling is abrupt, the subsidence is associated with major earthquakes. During the Alaskan earthquake of 1964, an area of 100,000 km² (over 42,000 square miles) subsided in a single block that extended from Kodiak Island eastwards past Anchorage, Alaska. Tectonic subsidence that is more gradual and not associated with major earthquakes still has important implications for residents. For instance, geologists now know that the Nile delta is subsiding at a rate that has important implications for the well-being of the city of Cairo and the nation of Egypt. Subsidence along coastal areas means loss of important land and greater susceptibility to effects of floods, wave erosion and storm surge. Gradual subsidence of the Mississippi delta has similarly important (although less immediate) implications for residents of that Gulf Coast area too.

The town of Portage, along the coast of Alaska, was built on a block of land which subsided over 6 feet during the 1964 Alaskan earthquake. The town then flooded at every high tide. (photo from USGS Photo Library, Denver, CO)

Collapse of soluble rocks or compression of weak rock and soil are major causes of natural subsidence. Other than tectonic subsidence, the ultimate cause of subsidence is usually insufficient support of the overlying soils and rocks. Areas prone to natural subsidence occur over soluble rocks where dissolved voids produce lack of support of overlying material. Soluble rocks include rock salt and gypsum beds, but by far the most common soluble rock is limestone, a rock composed of calcium carbonate. Over time, water seeps through cracks in the rock and percolates downward while dissolving the rock and creating ever-enlarging voids.

When viewed from the air, many limestone terrains are seen as pock-marked with sinkholes (depressions caused by collapse of large voids), thus reflecting the caverns and galleries developed beneath the ground surface. Such terrain is termed karst topography. In many areas of the country sinkholes have been used for dumps and garbage pits, and the users have been unaware that sinkholes are open conduits to the ground water supply. As a result valuable water supplies have been ruined through sheer ignorance of geology. Most drainage in karst terrain is underground through open fractures and caverns rather than through surface streams. The sinkhole areas that occur within the limestones of the southeastern United States, especially Florida, Kentucky and Alabama, are examples of subsidence into natural voids. In karst terrain the additional weight of new construction at a site above a hidden cavern may cause the surface to collapse immediately. If there is no immediate failure, then slight subsidence

Sign warns motorists in the Dry Creek area of Selby County, Alabama, about sinkholes that may appear suddenly in the highway built upon cavernous limestone. (photo by Paul Moser, Alabama Geological Survey)

A new sinkhole develops in Selby County, Alabama. (photo by Paul Moser, Alabama Geological Survey)

Sinkhole at Winter Park, Florida, engulfed homes, cars, recreational vehicles and part of a municipal swimming pool as the affected area expanded in early May of 1981. Damage developed over a period of a few hours, and within months the hole filled with water to form a new lake. A lowered water table caused by a dry season was thought to be the reason for failure during 1981. (photo by Florida Geological Survey)

associated with the structure may allow precipitation to collect and percolate into the ground toward the structure. The process has been called "induced recharge," which once started, tends to increase water inflows that ultimately weaken the roof of the cavity, causing it to fail. Even removal of trees from a forested area can induce recharge and initiate subsidence. Sometimes, sinkholes in soluble rocks become filled with mud and clay and clay-filled cavities do not support heavy structures well. The structure may settle unevenly into the soft clay-filled cavity even though it is supported elsewhere by strong bedrock. The University of Wisconsin campus at Platteville, Wisconsin, has several buildings that have suffered damage from settling into clay-filled cavities.

Mine subsidence occurs where large underground voids have been created by humans. Even the deepest mines can eventually have an effect on local lowering of the ground surface. Most metallic mines will result in subsidence within a small local area because the ore deposit is generally vertical or at least restricted

Clay-filled cavities in limestone and dolostone, like that below in southwestern Wisconsin, will result in damage if heavy structures are built upon them. Structures then rest partly on sound bedrock and partly on soft clay. The latter eventually deforms and allows structures to subside unevenly and crack. (photo by Edward Nuhfer)

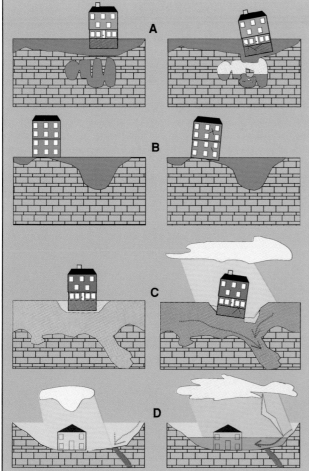

Limestone terrain provides subsidence hazards that usually can be overcome by prior planning and site evaluation. "A" shows construction above an open cavern which later collapses. This is one of the most difficult situations to detect, and the possibility of this situation beneath a structure warrants insurance protection for homes built on karst terrain. "B" is a situation where a heavy structure presumed to lie above solid bedrock actually is partially supported on soft, residual clay soils that produce very gradual subsidence and damage to the structure. This occurs where inadequate site evaluation can be traced to lack of geophysical studies and inadequate core sampling. "C" and "D" show the close relationship between hydrology and subsidence hazards in limestone terrain. In "C," the house is situated on porous fill (light shading) at a site where surface and groundwater drainage move supporting soil (darker shading) into voids in limestone (blocks) below. The natural process is then accelerated by infiltration through fill around the home. "D" shows a karst site where normal rainfall is absorbed by subsurface conduits, but water from an infrequent heavy storm cannot be carried away quickly enough to prevent flooding of low-lying areas. (Hazard models in part from L. D. Harris, 1973, Sinkholes in Knox County, Tennessee, USGS Map I-767-F)

beneath a small surface area. On the other hand, economic deposits that occur in extensive, continuous strata result in a type of mining that extends beneath a large area. Underground mining of coal, limestone, salt and some iron and chromium ores are examples of the latter. Such mines usually remove from 50 to 90 percent of the rock within the stratum being mined. This loss of support causes the overlying rock to collapse into the void, and the collapse eventually manifests at the ground surface. About one quarter of all United States land over areas mined for coal has subsided. Subsidence beneath the Appalachian coal

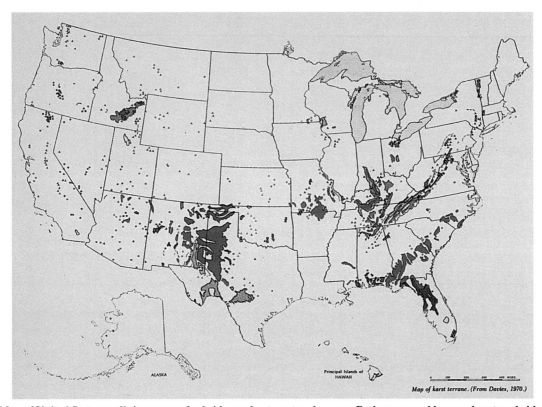

Map of karst terrane. (From Davies, 1970.)

Map of United States outlining areas of subsidence due to natural causes. Red, green and brown denote subsidence in limestone terrain; dark yellow denotes sinking above evaporite beds consisting of salt and gypsum. Blue denotes subsidence in areas underlain by lava tubes (natural cavities that formed when the lava was molten) which may collapse and cause structures above them to subside. Purple shows where sinkholes develop due to settling of gravel. (from Hays, USGS Professional Paper 1240-B, 1981) The reader may wish to procure W. E. Davies' and others' 1986 map, *Engineering Aspects of Karst* (1:7,500,000), which is a larger map with detailed text that is available from the USGS.

Grocery store in residential area south of Pittsburgh, Pennsylvania, subsides into an abandoned coal mine. (photo by Edward Nuhfer)

fields of Pennsylvania, West Virginia, Ohio and Kentucky or the western coal fields near Sheridan and Rock Springs, Wyoming, are just two examples of many areas prone to mine subsidence.

Fluid withdrawal causes subsidence. Rock is not the only supporting medium of the ground surface. Fluids entrapped in the small pores of the rock also provide support. If this support is removed by pumping

Aerial photograph near Sheridan, Wyoming, shows characteristic rectangular pattern of sinkholes above abandoned coal mines. The mine operated from the early 1900s through the 1940s. (photo by C. R. Dunrud, USGS)

Underground fires in coal seams have been a major cause of subsidence. Workers at the Percy site in southern Pennsylvania encounter choking gases as they attempt to isolate the fire that otherwise would soon spread beneath homes in the background. (photos by Edward Nuhfer)

The red, lava-like glow reveals the high temperatures developed in underground coal fires. This fire follows abandoned mine workings around Sheridan, Wyoming, and leaves behind voids certain to cause subsidence. Vapors released from such fires are a health hazard. Fires are often started by careless burning of trash near a coal seam; others start by natural processes. Extinguishing such fires is never easy. (photo by C. R. Dunrud, USGS)

of wells, then subsidence can result at the ground surface. Most damage from subsidence of this type occurs in areas where the underlying sediments have not yet been compacted and cemented into strong rock, and extensive withdrawal of water or petroleum occurs in them near urban developments. Water withdrawn between 1960 and 1967 from wells near the southern end of San Francisco Bay produced land subsidence of up to 4 m (12 ft.) in the area of San Jose, California. Construction of levees to prevent flooding and repair of wells alone cost more than 13 million dollars. Fluids can also be withdrawn from the subsurface due to construction of geothermal power plants (power plants which use high-pressure steam found in hot areas of the earth to drive turbines). Subsidence displacements above 4.5 m (above 11 ft.) due to fluid withdrawal at geothermal power plants in New Zealand have been measured. Notable

Schematic below shows how fluid withdrawal causes subsidence by removing supporting fluids and allowing mineral grains to draw together. This process can work at scales from small domestic water wells up to commercial oil wells.

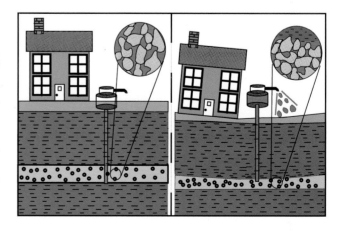

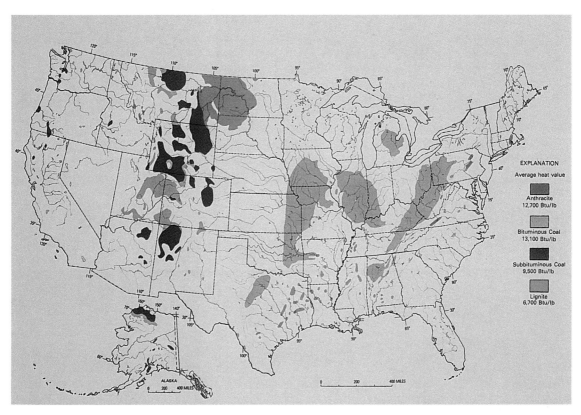

Locations of coal-mining areas in the United States. Most underground mining produces later opportunities for subsidence. Land-use planning above mined areas should always take possible subsidence into account and make use of whatever mine maps are available. (map from Hays, 1981, USGS Professional Paper 1240-B)

subsidences due to fluid withdrawal have been described in the San Joaquin Valley of California; Houston and vicinity, Texas; New Orleans, Louisiana; south-central Arizona; and in the Wilmington-Long Beach area of southern California. At the city of Long Beach, California, oil withdrawal caused part of the city to subside 31 feet! In arid regions such as near Deming, New Mexico; Riverside, California; and in south-central Arizona, large **earth fissures** appear at the ground surface over large areas as a result of subsidence due to water withdrawal.

Water also provides support even in the large openings that include abandoned mines and in karst terrain. When the water table is lowered below these openings, collapse often follows, along with resulting surface subsidence.

Drainage of surface waters can have a pronounced subsidence effect on soils, particularly when water is drained from highly organic soils and peats that lie in wetlands and coastal areas. Subsidence rates can vary from less than 1 to over 10 cm/yr (up to 4 in/yr), and amounts of subsidence up to 3.5 m (over 11 ft.) have been recorded. States with notable

subsidence due to drainage of organic-rich soils include California, Florida, Louisiana, Michigan and New York.

Hydrocompaction is a type of subsidence produced by the addition of water. When water enters some soils, several processes can result in compaction. One is that the surface tension of thin films of water actually pulls the grains more tightly together. Any home gardener who has freshly tilled fluffy soil has witnessed this kind of hydrocompaction after a heavy rainstorm. Other processes include the softening or removal of material such as clays and calcite that act like cements to strengthen and support the soil when it is dry. Soils susceptible to hydrocompaction are usually fine-grained and porous. Loess (wind-deposited silts) and soils derived from old lake sediments are notorious for being susceptible to hydrocompaction. The Colorado Geological Survey noted that soils subject to hydrocompaction along the Interstate 70 route in western Colorado between Rifle and Debecque subsided almost a meter within one month. The California Aqueduct canals crossed an area with severe hydrocompaction problems; the area was pre-saturated by ponding, and the ground sank

91

Fractures in this structure were produced by subsidence when unconsolidated sediments beneath the Pacific Garden Mall in Santa Cruz, California, settled during the 1989 Loma Prieta earthquake. (photo by C. Stover, USGS)

more than 10 feet prior to canal construction. In one extreme domestic case, a home subsided when a garden hose was accidentally left on for an extended period near the foundation of a house.

Earthquake tremors can trigger subsidence. The fluids from uncompacted natural sediments can escape through newly created fractures, and the mineral grains then rearrange themselves, collapsing closer together as the fluids depart. Such compaction in the Bootlegger Cove Formation caused extensive damage to portions of Anchorage, Alaska, during the 1964 earthquake. The Pacific Garden shopping mall in Santa Cruz, California, was severely damaged when the river deposits underlying the mall shifted and compacted during the 1989 Loma Prieta earthquake.

Human-placed **fill** consisting of soil, rock and waste debris is also prone to subsidence during tremors and earthquakes. The fill is almost impossible to compact to the point where developments can be safely built on it in earthquake country. The Marina district of San Francisco was built upon the site of a former lagoon which was filled in 1915 with sand, soil and debris from the famous 1906 San Francisco earthquake. Parts of this heavily developed area were totally destroyed by subsidence of this fill during the

1989 Loma Prieta earthquake. Artificial fill is notorious for local subsidence even in areas which are not affected by earthquakes. Sometimes the subsidence results when the fill is poorly compacted. Other times, the fill may include degradable materials such as refuse, which eventually breaks down and leaves void space that eventually invites subsidence.

Permafrost soils are those soils near polar regions that, except for shallow layers, remain permanently frozen. These are sometimes discussed under the topic of slope stability because of their propensity to flow laterally. They are also particularly prone to local subsidence. The melting that takes place during the brief polar summer season permits shallow layers to liquefy, to flow, and to subside under the weight of structures. Homes that are not adequately constructed so as to keep their heat from melting the soils at the foundation can produce local subsidence. Permafrost soils also shift, expand and heave when they refreeze during cooler seasons. About 20 percent of the earth's surface is underlain by permafrost. More than 32,000 square miles of the high mountain area in the western United States has alpine permafrost. Alaska is underlain by 500,000 square miles of permafrost, and off its northern coastline, permafrost creates special problems for construction of docks and offshore drilling rigs.

The delicate thermal equilibrium of permafrost can be disrupted by altering the snow or vegetation cover. The upper active layer of frozen ground will thaw in summer, will release water if any ice has been present, and will be susceptible to erosion. Construction of all types—roads, bridges, factories, homes, railroad tracks, storage tanks, pipelines and utility lines—must be preceded by plans to reduce or eliminate damage that will otherwise certainly occur as a result of heaving, subsidence and slippage. The geology within permafrost is unique because ground water movement is controlled by various thawed zones rather than by consistent **aquifers** (rocks permeable to water) and **aquicludes** (rocks impermeable to water), thus complicating water supply and waste disposal problems. Water may issue from the ground and in the winter form sheet-like masses of ice that can complicate any construction project.

Subsidence and the Concept of Deep Time

Subsidence is easy to anticipate based on knowledge of the geology and mining history of an area. However, a natural subsidence event is the most difficult of all geologic hazards to predict. Openings in soluble rocks that will some day collapse to become sinkholes are usually roofed with solid rock and hence are not easily detected. Collapse is sporadic and unpredictable. The karst terrain pock-marked with sinkhole depressions provides ample evidence that collapses are frequent through geologic time, but these collapses are not perceived as common over a single human lifetime.

Tectonic subsidence that results from earthquakes occurs only from some of the major earthquakes that affect a wide area. Quake-induced subsidence of uncompacted materials is even harder to predict than an earthquake itself, because not every area with subsidence potential will actually collapse during a single earthquake. However, the locations of materials that are likely to subside severely during an earthquake can be mapped, and development can then be avoided in the highest-risk areas.

Sensitive instruments can monitor slow regional subsidence that is ongoing in some areas, and this allows scientists to estimate rates, within certain limits, and to predict long-term consequences for the future.

Extreme shifting and tilting of these power lines occur because of shifting of the permafrost soils in which they are set. (photo by T. L. Pewe, USGS)

93

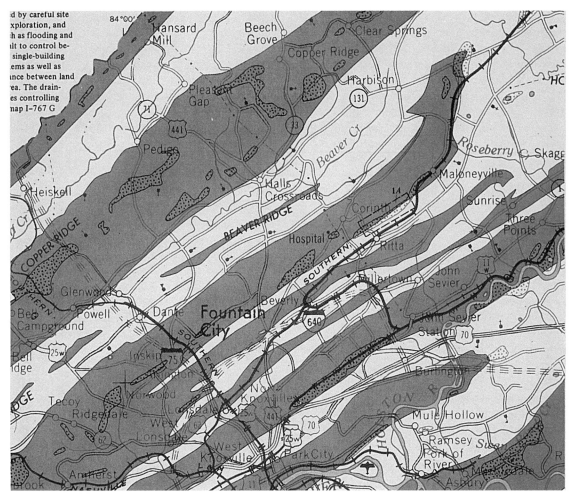

Geologic maps are the best tools to use to anticipate subsidence. This map (a part of USGS Map I-767-F, *Sinkholes in Knox County, Tennessee)* **focuses on karst hazards and outlines limestone areas in blue and particularly high-risk areas in red stipples.**

Subsidence that results from human activities is much more frequent over time, and numerous occurrences in local regions are easily perceived within a single human lifetime. Artificial openings such as mines and tunnels are far more unstable than are natural caverns. Hence construction over an undermined area offers a much higher risk than construction within an area underlain by karst geology.

Subsidence due to fluid withdrawal is measurable, predictable and controllable. This is because the changes that occur are gradual and closely related to generally known volumes of fluid withdrawal. This kind of subsidence through time can be described with mathematical equations and modeled on computers. Future consequences then can be anticipated much more clearly.

Dangers from Subsidence

Other than rapid tectonic subsidence events, losses due to subsidence are very localized and pose far more danger to property and the economy than to life. Potential hazards to life occur primarily if a subsidence failure occurs beneath a major transportation route such as beneath a highway or railroad, or in the rarer instance when the subsidence occurs above a burning underground coal mine. While the potential is there for loss of life, actual occurrences of loss of life have been almost non-existent. Some examples of common damages follow.

1. **Physical destruction and damage (to homes, buildings, highways, bridges, dams, etc.) by uneven (differential) settling and earth fissures that often develop in a subsiding area**
2. **Encroachment of water onto lowlands adjacent to the sea, lakes or rivers**
3. **Changes in gradient that affect drainage in stream channels, man-made drainage, pipelines and sewer lines**
4. **Collapse of oil and water well casings**
5. **Leaking and seepage from landfills, canals and reservoirs**
6. **Pollution of ground water supplies by surface pollutants traveling through conduits and fissures produced by subsidence**

There is no practical way to reverse, to halt or to retard natural tectonic sinking. Once human-induced land subsidence has been detected, corrective measures can only retard or halt the sinking; only fractional amounts of lost surface elevation may be regained. Enormous monetary losses are possible. In 1984 the Geological Society of America estimated an annual cost of human-induced subsidence of 100 million dollars. In 1985 the Ground Failure Hazard Committee of the National Research Council estimated $500 million as total annual subsidence losses in the U.S.

Roles of the Geologist in Mitigating Subsidence Damage

In public service. Despite the fact that subsidence events are often difficult to predict, the areas in which subsidence can be anticipated are based on mappable geological characteristics. Geologists in public service (such as those employed by geological surveys, bureaus of mines, departments of transportation and municipalities) and private consultants who work with engineering and environmental firms are all actively engaged in mitigating subsidence damage. These geologists prevent costly mishaps that might otherwise occur from building important structures over areas that may be particularly prone to subsidence. Geologists are specialists in dealing with subsurface resources that include minerals, petroleum and groundwater, and they are able to use their knowledge of these fields as an aid to anticipating subsidence.

At this time, however, mapping of hazardous areas is far from complete. Drilling and mining occurred in the United States for almost two centuries before permits were required and records were kept. Therefore, the locations of many old mines may never be known. The most economical safeguard lies in a general geological investigation from public records

This brick home was declared a total loss to mine subsidence damage. Note that cracking occurs throughout the house, along the red brick side from cellar to roof (toward far left chinked with pink fiberglass insulation) to the concrete block foundation. Such homes are condemned and must be vacated. (photo by Edward Nuhfer)

and published maps and literature (available through state surveys) to see if the hazard might exist locally. If concern is warranted, subsidence insurance, where available, is a prudent investment. Subsidence insurance should be obtained by all homeowners located in seriously endangered areas. Once subsidence begins, there is no reversing it, and damage to structures such as homes is often total. While the risks of

subsidence loss are numerically small, the actual loss can be a lifetime investment.

In research. Geologists involved in subsidence research study features that range from regional tectonics to individual sites of homes. Modeling of subsidence on computers helps to understand the mechanisms, rates and risks of subsidence.

References for Additional Reading on Subsidence

"E" indicates references suitable for educators.

Allen, A. S., 1969, **Geologic settings of subsidence** [E]: in D. J. Varnes and G. E. Kiersch, (eds.), Geol. Soc. Amer., Reviews in Engineering Geology II, pp. 305 - 342.

Allen, D. R., 1973, **Subsidence, rebound and surface strain associated with oil producing operations, Long Beach, CA**: in *Geology, Seismicity, and Environmental Impact*, Assoc. of Engrg. Geologists Special Pub., Los Angeles, CA, pp. 101 - 111.

American Society of Civil Engineers, 1988, **Geotechnical aspects of karst terrains**: Amer. Soc. Civil Engrs. Conf. Proceedings, Nashville, TN., New York, A.S.C.E.

Beck, B. F. (ed.), 1984, *Sinkholes: Their Geology, Engineering and Environmental Impact* [E]: Boston, A. A. Balkema. (A book produced based on the first multidisciplinary conference on sinkholes held in Orlando, Florida, in October, 1984).

Beck, B. F., and Wilson, W. L. (eds.), 1987, *Karst Hydrogeology: Engineering and Environmental Applications*: Boston, A. A. Balkema.

Bradley, M. D., and Carpenter, M. C., 1986, **Subsiding land and falling ground water tables: public policy, private liability and legal remedy** [E]: Economic Geography, v. 62, pp. 241 - 253.

Bushnell, K. O., 1977, **Mine subsidence** [E]: in *"Lots" of Danger - Property Buyers Guide to Land Hazards of Southwestern Pennsylvania*, J. L. Freedman (ed.), Pittsburgh Geol. Soc., pp. 9 - 16.

Coates, D. R., 1987, **Subsurface impacts**: in *Human Activity and Environmental Processes*, K. J. Gregory and D. E. Walling (eds.), New York, John Wiley, pp. 271 - 304.

Cory, F. E., 1973, **Settlement associated with subsidence in the thawing of permafrost**: 2nd. Intnl. Conf. on Permafrost, Natl. Acad. Sci., pp. 599 - 607.

Davies, W. E., and others., 1984, **Engineering Aspects of Karst** [E]: 1:7,500,000-scale map from U.S. Geol. Survey National Atlas. Sold as a separate wall map with informative text on back.

Davis, G. H., Small, J. B., and Counts, H. B., 1963, **Land subsidence related to decline in artesian pressure in the Ocala Limestone at Savannah, GA**: Geol. Soc. Amer., Engineering Geology Case Histories n. 4, pp. 1 - 8.

DuMontelle, P., Bradford, S. C., Bauer, R. A., and Killey, M. M., 1981, **Mine subsidence in Illinois: facts for the homeowner considering insurance** [E]: Illinois State Geol. Survey Division of Illinois Institute of Natural Resources, Envtl. Geol. Notes 99, 24 p.

Ege, J. K., 1984, **Formation of solution-subsidence sinkholes above salt beds**: U.S. Geol. Survey Circular 897.

Ferrians, O. J., Kachadorian, R., and Green, G. W., 1969, **Permafrost and related engineering problems in Alaska**: U.S. Geol. Survey Prof. Paper 678.

Foose, R. M., (ed.), 1979, **Selected papers, engineering geology of karst terrain**: Bull. Assoc. Engrg. Geologists, v. 16, n. 3.

French, H. M., (ed.), 1986, **Focus: permafrost geomorphology** [E]: The Canadian Geographer, v. 30, n. 4. (Issue contains many articles on permafrost.).

French, H. M., 1987, **Permafrost and ground ice** [E]: in *Human Activity and Environmental Processes*, K. J. Gregory and D. E. Walling (eds.), John New York, John Wiley & Sons, pp. 237 - 269.

Gass, T., **Sinkholes**: Water Well Jour., v. 35, pp. 36-37.

Gray, R. E., and Meyers, J. F., 1970, **Mine subsidence and support methods in Pittsburgh area**: Amer. Soc. Civil Engrs. Jour. Soil Mechanics Division, v. 96, SM4.

Higgins, C. G., and Coates, D. R., 1990, **Groundwater geomorphology; the role of subsurface water in earth-surface processes and landforms**: Boulder, CO, Geol. Soc. Amer. Spec. Paper 252.

Holzer, T. L., (ed.), 1984, **Man-induced land subsidence** [E]: Geol. Soc. Amer., Reviews in Engineering Geology VI, 232 p.

International Association of Engineering Geologists, 1981-82, **Bull. Issues n. 24 and n. 25 (37 papers) devoted to Construction problems on soluble rocks (including karst)**: IAEG, Krefeld, Germany (distributed by U.S. Natl. Comm. on Geology, 2101 Constitution Ave., Washington, DC 20418).

International Association of Hydrologic Science, 1991, **Land subsidence**: IAHS Pub. 200, 2000 Florida NW, Washington, DC 20009.

Isphording, W. C., and Flowers, G. C., 1988, **Karst development in coastal plain sands**: Bull. Assoc. Engrg. Geologists, v. 25, pp. 95 - 100.

Ivey, J. B., 1978, **Guidelines for engineering geologic investigations in areas of coal mine subsidence— a response to land use planing needs**: Bull. Assoc. Engrg. Geologists, v. 15, pp. 163 - 174.

Jennings, A. N., 1985, *Karst Geomorphology*: Blackwell, available from NWWA, P. O. Box 182039, Dept. 017, Columbus, OH 43218.

Johnson, A. I., (ed.) 1991, **Proc. fourth international symposium on land subsidence**: International Association of Hydrologic Science, IAHS Pub. 200, 2000 Florida NW, Washington, DC 20009.

Kenny, R., 1992, **Fissures—legacy of a drought** [E]: Earth, May, pp. 34 - 41.

Knight, F. J., 1971, **Geologic problems of urban growth in limestone terrains of Pennsylvania** [E]: Bull. Assoc. Engrg. Geologists, v. 8, pp. 94 - 95.

Kroll-Smith, J. S., and Couch, S. R., 1990, *The Real Disaster Is Above Ground: A Mine Fire and Social Conflict*: Univ. of KY Press, Ithaca, NY. Details problems with underground coal mine fires in Centralia, PA.

Larson, M. K., and Pewe, T. L., 1986, **Origin of land subsidence and earth fissuring, northeast Phoenix, Arizona** [E]: Bull. Assoc. Engrg. Geologists, v. 23, pp. 139 - 166.

Legrand, H. E., and Stringfield, V. T., 1973, **Karst hydrology, a review**: Jour. of Hydrology, v. 20, pp. 97- 120.

Marsden, S. S., and Davis, S. N., 1967, **Geological subsidence** [E]: Sci. Amer., v. 216, n. 6, pp. 93 - 100.

National Academy of Sciences and others, 1991, **Mitigating losses from land subsidence in the United States** [E]: National Research Council, Washington, DC 20418.

Newton, J. G., 1987, **Development of sinkholes from man's activities in eastern United States** [E]: U.S. Geol. Survey Circular 968.

Pewe, T. L., 1984, **Fissures in Arizona** [E]: Earth Science, v. 37, n. 2, pp. 19 - 21.

Poland, J. F., 1969, **Subsidence in United States due to groundwater withdrawal**: Am. Soc. Civil Engrs. Jour. Irrigation and Drainage Div., v. 107.

Poland, J. F., and Davis, G. H., 1984, **Guidebook to studies of land subsidence due to groundwater withdrawal**: UNESCO, 7 Place de Fontenay, 75700 Paris, France.

Prokopovich, N. P., 1976, **Some geological factors determining land subsidence** [E]: International Assoc. of Engrg. Geologists Bull., n. 14, p. 75 - 81, Krefeld, Germany.

Saxena, S. K., (ed.), 1979, **Evaluation and prediction of subsidence**: Amer. Soc. Civil Engrs. Conf. Proc., NY, 600 p.

Schlemon, R., and Davis, P., 1992, **Ground fissures in the Temecula area, Riverside County, CA**: in *Engineering Geology Practice in Southern California*, Assoc. Engrg. Geologists Spec. Pub., Belmont, CA, Star Pub. Co., pp. 461 - 483.

Schuirman, G., and Slosson, J. E., 1992, *Forensic Engineering*: New York, Academic Press. Chapter 9, "Land Subsidence on a Large Scale: Dire Consequences," pp. 210 - 241 details case study of a Hispanic residential section of San Diego.

Singh, M. M., (ed.), 1986, *Mine Subsidence*: Society of Mining Engineers, Littleton, CO, 143 p.

Wagner, F. W., and Durabb, E. J., 1977, **New Orleans, the sinking city**: Environ. Comment, June, pp. 15- 17.

White, W. B., 1988, *Geomorphology and Hydrology of Karst Terrains*: New York, Oxford Univ. Press.

Windham, S. R., and Campbell, K. M., 1981, **Sinkholes follow the pattern** [E]: Geotimes, v. 26, n. 8, pp. 20- 21.

FLOODS

Floods are the most destructive of all geologic hazards and take immense tolls on lives and property. Yet flooding streams serve an important, increasingly recognized function in both local and regional environmental balance. Human development of drainage basins has a profound effect on drainage, flooding and erosion as well as on water quality and aquatic life. Flood control has become intimately entangled with water use rights, and this has made flood control the most fiercely politicized issue of land use planning and environmental management.

Occurrence of Floods

A **flood** is any high flow of surface waters that overtops the normal confinements and/or covers land that is normally dry. Natural floods occur at some time along most of the major river systems of the world.

Riverine floods occur primarily when water from rainfalls or melting snow is directed to a major stream from its drainage basin. The larger floods involve either unusually rapid regional melting of snow in the early spring or major weather events such

as hurricanes that bring heavy rainfalls over a large region. In northern latitudes, ice jams brought about by moving cakes and sheets of ice released during spring thaw often cause floods. Initially, broken ice jams the channel, and this causes water to back up to flood the area above the ice jam. When the jam breaks, the result is like a burst dam, and a rushing wall of water floods the areas downstream.

Flash floods occur naturally when occasional cloudbursts pour large amounts of rainfall into small drainage basins. Although flash floods are of short duration, they are devastating to local residents. The

Main Street of downtown Northport, Alabama, during flood. (photo by Alabama Geological Survey)

The power of flash floods to move materials is shown in the aftermath of the 1976 Big Thompson Canyon flood in Colorado. A battered truck is buried to the windows in flood-transported soil and rock debris. (photo from USGS Photo Library, Denver, CO)

The flood roaring through Big Thompson Canyon denuded soil and trees from the valley sides and scoured the foundation from beneath the red cabin. This flood destroyed a number of homes and killed over one hundred victims who could not scale the steep canyon walls quickly enough. (photo from USGS Photo Library, Denver, CO)

flash flood in 1976 on the Big Thompson River in Colorado took about 140 lives and created over 30 million dollars in damage. In 1942, 8.5 inches of rain fell at Bayfield, Wisconsin, within 12 hours. Boulders were washed through city buildings and the harbor was filled with sand and mud. Coffins were even washed out of graves. Sometimes flash-floods destroy man-made dams and release large volumes of water catastrophically downstream.

In rare instances rapid melt of local snowpack or glacial ice due to volcanic action causes flash floods. Snowpack meltwaters produced during the May 18, 1980, eruptions of Mount Saint Helens sped downslope to create flash floods and mudflows. A huge prehistoric flood (Wright Valley flood) occurred in Antarctica near the Ross Sea when a volcanic eruption occurred beneath thick glacial ice. Smaller historic meltwater floods caused by volcanic heating have occurred in Iceland and Ecuador.

Storm surge floods begin near a low coastal area when onshore winds and low barometric pressures in storms such as hurricanes cause the sea level to rise locally above the coastal lowlands. Seawater then rushes into the mouths of river channels and covers the lower floodplains and deltas. If the time of the storm coincides with the time of high tide, the devastation will be catastrophic. Sometimes riverine and storm-surge processes occur simultaneously in a single river basin. Floodwaters rushing down-valley then combine with the invading ocean waters entering upstream. Because storm-surges affect coastal areas, we detail these in the final chapter on coastal hazards.

Human interference in the fluvial (stream) environment is a major factor causing floods and increasing their consequences. The most easily pictured flood of this type is the result of a burst dam, fortunately an infrequent event. The bursting of one such dam on the Little Conemaugh River caused the 1889 flood in Johnstown, Pennsylvania, which took 3,000 lives. A second bursting dam occurred there in July, 1977, and caused 77 fatalities.

Loose garbage, logs and debris can briefly form unintended dams that temporarily back up water and cause local floods. The Buffalo-Creek disaster of 1972 that killed 125 people in West Virginia can scarcely be called a failure of a designed dam. The "dam" was merely a pile of old mining waste that was dumped into a hollow. The disastrous event led to prompt action in removing similar waste dams. It also resulted in regulations limiting the size of water-retention ponds that can be built on active mines and added the requirement that dams for these temporary ponds must be removed upon completion of mine reclamation.

Constructing soil and wood levees and dikes along rivers as an attempt to control floods dates back many centuries before Christ. Bursts of these artificial dikes (see discussion on Yellow River below) are frequent and cause some of the most deadly floods of all. Early flood control management along the Mississippi River also relied on construction of higher levees, even though major floods occurred again and again through the late 1800s and early 1900s. Until early 1927 the Corps of Engineers remained steadfastly dedicated to the premise that levees alone could control flooding, despite all evidence to the contrary. In 1927, a levee breach 18 miles north of Greenville, Mississippi, sent a wall of water across more than 2.3 million acres of land even as over 5,000 laborers tried to save the levee. The number that perished in that breach alone has never been clearly known. When the flood ended, over half a million people were homeless as the result of over 100 breaches in the levees. The 1927 disaster brought an end to the near-fanatical reliance on levees and led to a much broader approach to flood control management.

Floods are heavily influenced by human activities in the drainage basin. Farming, overgrazing, deforestation or construction may increase the size and frequency of floods by modifying the ability of the land to absorb water. Several other human activities

This flood occurred in Estes Park, Colorado, when a cloudburst destroyed two dams at Lawn Lake and Cascade Lake. (photo by R. D. Jarrett)

WORLD'S MOST SEVERE FLOODS
(exclusive of floods produced by storm surge)

YEAR	FLOOD LOCATION	LIVES LOST
1887	Yellow River, China	900,000 to 6,000,000
1911	Yangtze River, China	100,000
1931	Yangtze River, China	3,700,000
1939	Yellow River, China	200,000

Estimates of lives lost in such major floods conflict depending upon the source and methods of estimation. Maximum numbers in 1887 and 1931 include deaths from flood-induced famine. Sources for these figures are Clark and others (1982), Tufty (1969) and Office of Foreign Disaster Assistance, 1992, *Disaster History.*

can promote flooding. These include choking of natural channels with sediment from some mining or construction projects (as occurred in California placer mining in the late 1800s), poor planning in the development and paving of large areas (the 1972 flood in Rapid City, South Dakota, is an example) or construction of dams that later fail catastrophically (such as the Teton dam in Idaho in 1976).

Runoff refers to the process by which quantities of rainwater travel overland. **Infiltration** occurs when water seeps into the ground and is released slowly, if at all, to streams. Runoff increases when forests are cleared, grassy vegetation is removed (as during mining and excavation), areas are paved, and homes are built. Rainfall that enters a developed basin rushes across any cleared slopes, pavements and roofs, enters artificial drains and sewers, and passes immediately onward to streams. In a well-vegetated drainage basin, the vegetation and the natural, thick, porous, spongy, organic soils decrease runoff. Much more water seeps into the ground than runs across its surface. Because infiltrated water is released to streams slowly over many months, a stream fed by a drainage basin that has high infiltration and low runoff characteristics will be much more resistant to flooding.

Floods are the most devastating of all geological agents. Only global plagues, world wars and the Holocaust have exceeded floods in causing catastrophic loss of life. The sites of the worst natural disasters in history are uncontested as being the floods along China's rivers. Texts conflict only on whether the loss of life was greatest in the 1887 Yellow River flood or the 1931 Yangtze River flood.

The Yellow River is often called "China's Sorrow" and has taken more lives than any other single natural feature. The Yellow River carries 1.6 billion tons of silt each year, more than enough to build a wall around the world 6 meters (20 feet) high and 5 meters (16 feet) thick. As the silt is deposited in the river channel over the last 500 miles of its course across the flat North China Plain, the channel becomes filled with sediment and, as the river bottom rises, so does the water level. To prevent frequent flooding, residents along the river had to increase the height of the levees and dikes by the amount the river bottom rose due to siltation. The river thus gradually became perched high above the alluvial plain between two parallel dikes that extended for hundreds of miles. Deaths along this river resulted primarily when levees and dikes were breached through natural failure during seasons of high rainfall or through intentional breaching during wartime. When breaches occurred at the start of the greatest floods, they widened in minutes into huge openings more than a half-mile wide. Walls of water poured across the low alluvial plains and eventually covered an area of about 10,000 square miles (25,000 square kilometers). This is an area comparable to that of Lake Erie. When this occurred, it took years to repair the dikes and dry the flooded areas. Thus the loss of life from the floods extended over years, including not only the drowned, but also those who died from exposure, starvation and flood-associated diseases such as cholera.

Most of the deaths in the 1931 flood of the Yangtze River are attributed to starvation. The Yangtze was home to nearly one-quarter of a billion people who produced nearly half of the nation's grains. When

101

SEVERE RIVERINE and FLASH FLOODS in the UNITED STATES (1937-1993)

YEAR	FLOOD LOCATION	LIVES LOST	LOSS (millions of dollars*)
1937	Ohio and lower Mississippi river basins	137	417.7
1938	Southern California	79	24.5
1947	Lower Missouri and Middle Mississippi basins	29	235.0
1951	Kansas and Missouri	28	923.2
1955	West Coast	61	154.5
1955	Northeastern U.S. (Hurricane Diane)	187	714.0
1963	Ohio River	26	97.6
1964	California and Oregon	40	415.8
1969	California	60	399.2
1969	James River Basin, Virginia	154	116.0
1977	Big Thompson River, Colorado	139	30.0
1977	Kansas City, Missouri and Kansas	25	80.0
1983	Arizona	13	416.0
1986	California	17	270.0
1989	Hurricane Hugo	49	10,000
1990	May floods in South - Central U.S.	7	600
1990	June flash flood near Shadyside, Ohio	26	8
1990	Texas, Louisiana, Arkansas, Oklahoma	14	1,000
1991-92	Texas, December 1991 - March 1992	15	150
1992	Southern California, February	4	>40
1993	Southwestern U.S. and southern CA (data current only to mid-January)	9	> 160

*Loss figures are approximations. Accurate losses from floods are difficult to acquire. Totals should include private and federal insurance payments, disaster relief, damages to public works, uncompensated private damages and lost revenues, but that data is not always included in compilations. Figures here are not corrected for currency inflation. (data from U.S. Army Corps of Engineers *Annual Flood Damage* reports; *World Almanac*, 1993; and W. W. Hays, 1981, USGS Prof. Paper 1240-B, p. B40) The U.S. Army Corps of Engineers noted in the period 1980-1989 that flood damages averaged 2.2 billion dollars a year, but flood control structures saved an average of 10.7 billion dollars annually during that period.

the flood crested at nearly 100 feet above its normal stage, productivity of that important area was destroyed. A later flood in 1954 took 30,000 lives despite heroic efforts to contain the rising waters.

In the United States, the annual average is 100 lives lost and property damage of between 1 billion and 3 billion dollars. With 3 million miles of streams existing in the United States, and 6 percent of the land containing a large percentage of the nation's population and property, repeated threats from flooding are to be expected. Over 20,000 communities are affected by flooding, and evacuation of more than 300,000 people occurs annually. Major cities of the United States have significant portions of their development located within floodplains.

Flood Occurrence and the Concept of Deep Time

Floods are so frequent that most individuals will observe several in their lifetimes. While many people should anticipate floods at least every few years and take regular precautions in dealing with them, most action taken to mitigate flood risk actually comes during the immediate aftermath of a flood. The frequent basis on which floods occur does not give the full story about floods in the context of deep time. The longest historical record of floods comes from the Nile River. **Nilometers** were probably the first stream gauging stations and have been in use since about 3500 B.C. The long record of Nile floods typifies change through time in most streams—pronounced irregularity characterized by frequent small floods, occasional large floods, and rare enormous floods. The larger floods occur at no regular intervals. The mathematical pattern of these events charted through time is called a **fractal**. It is similar to the pattern of the rainfall at a site through time. Large flood events are not predictable any more than are large rainstorms or hurricanes. However, flood effects can be anticipated from climatic records, historical records and geological studies. The geologic record left within the sediments along a stream can often tell how frequently prehistoric floods have occurred in the area and how large they were.

Computer programs that take into account local surface topography, geology and land use can be used to deduce flood effects by **modeling** them. These programs allow input of a hypothetical rainfall (amount, intensity and affected area) and give as output the likely water levels in streams during and after the rainfall event.

Floods can occur at any month of the year, but the most frequent floods result from seasonal events that occur regularly through time. Floods that occur in accord with annual rhythms of spring rains and snow

Flood plains of major rivers experience frequent flooding. This aerial view shows spring flooding of the Missouri River downstream from the mouth of the Osage River junction in April of 1973. Floodplains that are inundated frequently merit either flood control structures or limits on development. Reconstruction of flood-damaged homes on flood-prone sites using federal insurance claims payments results in a repeated drain on the flood insurance fund by a relatively small number of insured structures. (photo by Richard Waugh)

Torrential rains spread inland by Hurricane Camille in summer of 1969 caused floods in many rural areas that were not normally considered as endangered, including this cabin in southern West Virginia used by West Virginia University's geology field camp. This is an example of the infrequent flood that surprises many citizens who believe they live where floods do not occur. (photo by Edward Nuhfer)

thaw or monsoons (seasonal winds that blow shoreward from seas and oceans and bring heavy rains) are anticipated to occur frequently and within given seasons. Significant floods can be expected from regular seasonal processes at least every two or three years on many rivers.

Most readers recognize that hurricanes cause coastal storms, but hurricanes also cause large inland riverine floods by bringing moisture far inland from the coast. Hurricane-induced floods are also seasonal, but they are not as predictable as smaller, more frequent seasonal events. Numbers of hurricanes vary from year to year, and movements of hurricanes are generally unpredictable. A hurricane produces significant flooding somewhere in the eastern United States at least once or twice in a decade and more frequently in the Gulf Coast. Regarding specific areas within the eastern United States, a major storm like a hurricane will produce a very large flood every century or two. This is normally the kind of flood that engineers and planners try to anticipate in the "100-year flood" used in flood control design and zoning.

It is important to realize that the 100-year flood is not the maximum flood that occurs along rivers. Catastrophic floods occur every few thousand years. Their infrequency makes them difficult to anticipate and unreasonable to use as the basis for engineering design of control structures. In fact, a thousand-year flood represents a time span which is about ten times

the useful life of many dams. Nevertheless, important historical floods fall into this category. The Big Thompson Canyon flood of 1976 was an event that probably is expected only about once every 5,000 years; the 1936 floods in the Connecticut Valley of Massachusetts also represent an event that occurs perhaps only every few thousand years. These huge floods are usually local and result from rainstorm events that are just as infrequent as the floods they produce. An astonishing 31.5 inches of rain fell in about six hours, when Hurricane Camille brought devastating flash floods to Nelson County, Virginia, in 1969.

Infrequent enormous floods of sizes beyond anything recorded in history are seen in deep time. The channeled scablands of eastern Washington resulted about 15,000 years ago when an immense ice dam that retained glacial Lake Missoula failed. The lake was in what is today the western part of Montana. Several hundred cubic miles of water rushed across 2,000 square miles and carved channels hundreds of feet deep in solid rock. The dam failed repeatedly during the wane of the Pleistocene, sending waters again and again across Idaho and eastern Washington. Closer examination of the sedimentary deposits in other areas also reveals periods of enormous floods. Such areas include the glaciated regions of the north-central United States, the present-day Mediterranean Sea (which has not always been a sea through deep time) and the Wright Valley flood in Antarctica.

A nilometer on Roda Island near Cairo, Egypt. Several varieties existed; the earliest ones simply recorded the levels of the high water marks. These early stream gauging stations provide the longest hydrologic record in history. (photo by P. E. LaMoreaux)

A levee along the Mississippi River begins to experience leakage that may lead to piping of water through the levee and an eventual catastrophic failure. Sandbags have been applied on snow fence in an effort to brace the levee. (photo by U.S. Army Corps Engineers)

Dangers from Floods

Primary losses caused by rampaging flood waters are the deaths or serious injuries of people and animals, structural damage to buildings, roadbeds and utilities, and destruction of equipment and property. In developed countries, good communication and monitoring systems give citizens early warnings, and good transportation systems permit rapid evacuation and prevent massive loss of life over large areas. Ideally loss of life should not occur at all after adequate warning is given, but the ideal response doesn't always occur. Lack of focused education leaves many citizens without the critical ability to distinguish between **flash-flood watch**, which means that weather conditions have developed that may lead to a flood, and a **flash-flood warning**, which means that flooding has already begun in certain areas and that real responses are required such as investigating the local situation immediately and possibly moving to higher ground. Because the urgency of the term "flash flood warning" is sometimes not understood, listeners may not take the announcement seriously until it is too late. Even in the most developed countries major loss of life can occur from quick events such as burst dams or flash flooding.

If flood waters force a path through a weakness along a levee, a "boil" or upwelling of water may be established at the base of the levee, through it, or on the floodplain just outside it. Piling sandbags around the boil raises the water head to build pressure that helps to slow the seepage and prevent erosion that may cause major failure. Levees must be monitored for damage and maintained to keep them strong. Even an animal burrow can provide the weakness that allows a boil to develop during flooding. (photo by U.S. Army Corps Engineers)

Longer term secondary damage from floods includes backing up of sewers, flooding of septic tanks, landfills, waste disposal areas and farms, which leaves the resulting flood waters polluted with animal, human and industrial wastes. These can contaminate wells and other water supply sources and even marine fisheries near the areas of river discharge. Disruption of normal utility services and water supplies results, and dealing with massive incidence of disease is a possibility. Additional long-term damages include equipment malfunctions, hunger, homelessness, and losses to commerce, education, and employment.

Mitigating the Effects of Floods

Effective reduction of losses from floods comes from three primary actions by citizens.

1. Investment in flood control structures such as dams and flood walls. Large expenditures have been made by the American public to mitigate flood damages, and the structures have successfully protected many areas. Yet these expenditures have not produced anything like a complete solution. Flood damage losses have not decreased significantly since 1937, despite significant investments in flood control structures. This is because flood plains become more heavily developed as they become better protected. Urban damage from flooding continues to account for a major share of the increase in damage.

2. Zoning of flood plains to prevent developments that will likely lead to loss. Actions include preventing high populations from settling in flood-prone areas by restricting flood-prone <u>land</u> to uses such as recreation, parking areas and agriculture. Other zoning restrictions include required siting of structures so that they are built on elevations higher than the maximum anticipated flood, and limiting flood plain development by other legal measures.

3. Purchase of appropriate flood insurance. Many homeowners who live in areas susceptible to flooding do not have appropriate insurance. Today in many communities, a person cannot obtain federally secured financing to buy, build or improve structures in flood hazard areas. New structures built in compliance with National Flood Insurance Program (NFIP) standards are far less likely to experience a loss than older, noncompliance structures. Today about half the structures in floodplains are new and in compliance, and zoning and building code regulations are reducing losses significantly. Older, noncompliance structures enjoy subsidized insurance rates because they are exempted in the NFIP by a grandfather clause. The grandfathered structures are a major source of flood insurance claims, and thus a small portion of all properties insured for flood damage accounts for a large portion of NFIP payments. Since October 1, 1991, lower flood insurance premiums became available to residents of participating communities that have demonstrated success in managing reduction of flood losses.

This channelized stretch of Mill Creek, Wisconsin, is shown by the linear channel and lack of irregularities. Straightening streams in this manner increases water flow and helps prevent local flooding, but does so at great cost to the aquatic life in the stream. The devastation that channelizing wreaks on streams greatly reduces its attraction as a flood control measure. (photo by Richard Waugh)

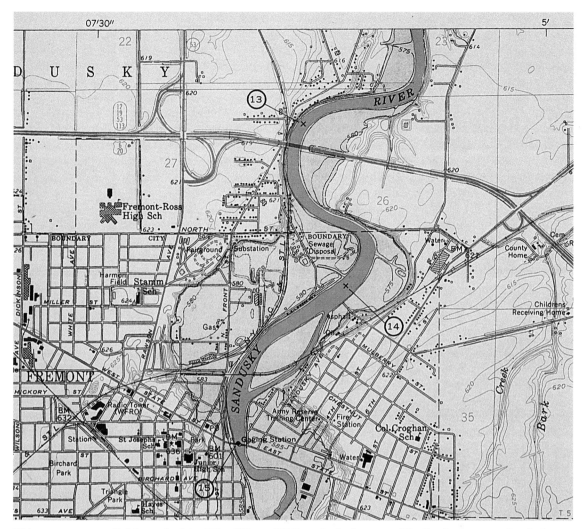

This map was compiled by geologists of the Ohio and U.S. geological surveys. The flood-prone area bordering the Sandusky River appears in light blue. The sewage plant lies in the area of potential flood. Wastes that enter a river during flood can spread pollution and even disease in undeveloped countries with few purification plants. (map from USGS Hydrologic Atlas 47)

Controversies over Flood Control

Few interactions between man and nature have sparked more controversy than flood control. The earliest human controls were dikes and levees used by the Egyptians to enhance agriculture. By about 3000 B.C. the Egyptians under King Menes had dammed the Nile and diverted its course. Since before 2000 B.C., the Chinese had utilized dikes and levees in attempts to suppress floods Chinese emperors were or were not remembered fondly in accord with their success in managing water resources and flood hazards. Dikes and levees were still the primary means of control espoused by the United States government until after 1927.

Channelization, or straightening a stream to increase its capacity to send large flows of water quickly downstream, has also been used as a flood control measure. Channelization is controversial because, while it improves flow, it also permanently devastates the straightened stream segment and converts it into a stretch that is incapable of supporting diverse aquatic life.

Dams were not built in Europe until about 200 years ago, and the first major flood control dams were built in the United States in 1913. After 1927, dams and locks were constructed across nearly all of the major rivers of the United States.

Today there are over 50,000 dams in the United States, and where dams should or should not be built has been a source of major political controversy. Agricultural and natural resource interests have favored construction of many small dams in the upstream tributaries to control floods. Large industrialists and developers favor construction of large dams downstream. Each interest group has supported its own government agency whose philosophy is in accord with its interest, and this has led to bitter political contests where interest in winning sometimes overrides interest in providing good management.

In the eastern United States, dams, in conjunction with flood walls, have provided increased stability and control. The controls have enabled eastern rivers to become important commercial boat and barge routes. Dams in the west have permitted irrigation of arid regions that are now our nation's major sources of agricultural produce. Hydroelectric power generation at many dams provides clean energy, and reservoirs located behind dams are used for everything from critical water supplies for cities and farms to recreational boating and fishing. The highest per capita boat ownership occurs today in states that formerly had no significant natural lakes or navigable rivers.

Dams also bring costs and consequences. Agricultural land gained from irrigation is offset by loss of land as deltas and flood plains downstream of dams erode because they are no longer replenished by silt. Reservoirs behind dams spread water over large areas and may cover useful forest, recreational waterways, scenic valleys, historical areas and fertile agricultural land. Water impounded in a large area is susceptible to evaporation, and in arid regions this may be so great as to result in significant loss of useful water and increased salinity of the water remaining. Impoundments may also leak water into the subsurface, especially into geological formations that lie within the reservoir above the former stream level, and that water may then be lost to both human use and the river environment.

As more dams are built, quality and quantity of usable water downstream of dams deteriorate. The Colorado River has been practically eradicated by the time it enters the Gulf of California, and the quality of the Rio Grande has been so reduced by dams and irrigation projects that it has become a source of political conflict between Mexico and the United States. Large dams bring abrupt changes to riverine environments that have been established over

thousands of years, and irreparable ecological damage can occur. Commercial marine fisheries may suffer after construction of a major dam when fish populations decrease because of upstream impoundment of nutrients and disruption of coastal wetlands spawning habitat. The sardine industry of the Mediterranean was reduced after construction of the Aswan dam on the Nile River. Upstream, the mud-flat areas of the reservoir can increase populations of undesirable disease-bearing organisms such as certain species of snails.

Dams do not prevent all floods. No dam can be designed for the catastrophic flood that occurs every few thousand years. When such floods occur, some dams burst and cause enormous loss of life. In 1981, a study by the Corps of Engineers listed 2,884 dams as unsafe out of 8,639 surveyed. Most were deemed unsafe because of inadequate spillway design. Worldwide about three dams fail annually.

Construction of a dam does not provide a one-time permanent solution against flood damage. Siltation behind dams insures that they have only a limited useful life. When full, they retain an immense amount of mud within a river valley and are then often termed "sediment dams." Many dams in this country are approaching the end of their useful life, and financial decisions will need to be made regarding their maintenance and replacement in comparison to adopting alternative flood control methods.

Many scientists and engineers are advocating zoning and flood plain management as an alternative to major engineering works such as dams, channelization and channel paving projects. Good zoning and management policy is often at odds with pressures from urban growth, from land development, and from agencies and private organizations that compete for funding and influence. There are no simple answers that satisfy all interests and situations.

Roles of the Geologist in Flood Prediction and Control

The training of geologists offers two good reasons for their involvement in mitigating the effects of floods. The first is an educational curriculum that focuses on an understanding of natural processes. This begins in freshman physical geology courses with the study of the effects of running water and continues in many advanced courses that focus on river processes. The second is an educational focus on deep time which provides geologists with the knowledge about how rivers develop and how floods occur over deep time. Hydrology of both ground water and surface waters is one of the major areas in which geologists are employed. Their duties are diverse and include monitoring of water quality, producing of maps, and performing research on fluvial processes that include erosion and sedimentation. A few specific examples follow but these are by no means all-inclusive.

In anticipating floods. Applied geology in flood control begins with reconstructing the history of past flooding of an area, especially the important geologic history that precedes recorded history. Based upon landforms and types of soils and sediments present, it is possible to deduce the extent and magnitude of some record floods that occurred in the past. It is not a simple matter to piece together the detailed history of a river or to estimate what the "100 - year flood" will actually be in terms of water levels and extent. Geologists examine the sediments of the stream valley and look for subtle signs of scour and erosion that may reveal immense past floods larger than those recorded. Without study of the geology these would never otherwise be anticipated. Geologists also make records from flood scars recorded in tree rings or in other growths that reveal flood damage. Since 1969, geologists (many with the USGS as part of the Federal Emergency Management Agency (FEMA) National Flood Insurance Program) have been involved in mapping flood-prone areas throughout the nation on more than 13,000 topographic maps. Current (1992) efforts are directed toward mapping areas (1) downstream from larger reservoirs that have high potential for overtopping their spillways, and (2) channels susceptible to flash floods in areas of potential future urban development.

By investigating the size of the drainage channels and the runoff potential associated with particular land use in the drainage basin, it is also possible to use a computer to quantitatively model hypothetical floods for an area based on various scenarios of rainfall amount and intensity. Engineers, geologists and applied mathematicians are all involved in modeling. Predicting the magnitude of future floods can be aided by use of historical data where good records are available. Once a major rainfall occurs on streams which contain monitoring devices, the data yielded allows the magnitude and timing of water flow and associated flood stages throughout the length of the channel to be more accurately predicted.

In geology for engineered control structures. The success of any flood-control structure, particularly dams, depends on accurate geologic assessment of the nature of the foundation materials, the slope stability around the impoundment, and the sedimentation likely to occur within an impoundment. Some of the greatest flood disasters in history resulted where flood control structures were built without adequate characterization of geology. The Saint Francis Dam in California in 1928 (450 killed), the Malpasset dam in France in 1962 (421 killed), the Vaiont Reservoir in Italy in 1963 (3,000 killed), and the Teton Dam in 1976 (11 killed) are a few examples where inadequate evaluation of the geology led to significant fatalities and economic losses. A study in Spain in 1962 examined the cause of failure in over 300 dams and designated foundation failure as the greatest single factor.

The role of the geologist is not limited to flood control structures but includes all types of construction that take place in flood plains. By delineating the areas of potential flooding, the geologist defines zoning boundaries that should exclude the location of certain projects such as waste storage dumps, certain types of industry, and housing projects. Bridge failures, such as the 1987 failure on the New York State Freeway and the 1972 bridge failure on Interstate 90 near Rapid City, South Dakota, both occurred because the scouring of alluvium, a normal geological process during floods, was not anticipated during bridge design. The bridge supports were undercut and failure occurred because design did not take into account the geological conditions. Design of structures such as dams and flood walls lies within the province of the engineer, but the investigation of the geologic conditions of the site should always be undertaken and supervised by a qualified geologist.

Geology is also useful as an aid to investigate cost effectiveness of some structures. Warm Springs Dam in California cost over 440 million dollars to build as a water supply. Ground water could probably have supplied the same users for a cost of only about 10 million dollars, but geologists were never consulted. The dam at Fishtrap Reservoir on the Levisa Fork in Kentucky was built without making an adequate study to determine how much sediment would fill the reservoir behind the dam. After the dam was built, it was discovered that the useful life might be less than half of what was expected. Only then were geologists called in to investigate—more to explain the mechanisms for an ongoing economic disaster rather than to prevent it.

In education. There are a number of earth science teachers in our schools systems today who are either geologists or who have significant education (36 or more credits in geology). Unfortunately there are not enough such teachers. Despite the frequency of floods and the immense expenditures spent on remediation and on flood control, few American citizens receive education about fluvial processes.

A populace familiar with streams and stream processes is more likely to support sound management policy that protects property and minimizes losses. An educated public is less likely to be swayed by unwise arguments that spring simply from vested political or economic interests. Citizens should demand that all students take an earth science course taught by a teacher with solid qualifications in geology.

References for Additional Readings on Floods

"E" denotes references especially suitable for educators

Arnold, J. L., 1988, **The evolution of the 1936 Flood Control Act**: GPO n. 008-022-00245-6, Government Printing Office, Washington, DC 20402, 126 p.

Association of State Floodplain Managers, 1987, **Reducing losses in high-risk flood hazard areas**: FEMA Pub. n. 116, 500 C St. SW, Rm. 324, Wash., DC 20492.

Association of State Floodplain Managers, 1987, **Realistic approaches to better floodplain management**: Inst. of Behavioral Sci., Univ. Colorado at Boulder, CO 80309, 53 papers.

Association of State Floodplain Managers, and Kusler, J. A., 1989, **Avoiding public liability in floodplain management: recent cases and trends in the courts**: Assoc. of State Floodplain Managers, P.O. Box 2051, Madison, WI 53701.

Baker, V. R., (ed.), 1988, *Flood Geomorphology*: New York, John Wiley.

Belt, C. B., Jr., 1975, **The 1973 flood and man's constriction of the Mississippi River** E: Science, v. 189, pp. 681 - 684.

Biswas, A. K., 1972, *History of Hydrology*: Amsterdam, North Holland Pub. Co.

Brown, W. R., and Cutcheon, B. W., 1975, *Historical Catastrophes: Floods* E: New York, Addison Wesley.

Bue, C. D., 1967, **Flood information for flood plain planning** E: U.S. Geol. Survey, Circular 539.

Buffey, P. M., 1977, **Teton dam verdict: A foul-up by the engineers** E: Science, v. 195, pp. 270 - 272.

Burby, R. J., and others, 1988, **Cities under water: ten cities' efforts to manage floodplain land use** E: Monograph 47, Institute of Behavioral Sci., Univ. Colorado, Boulder, CO 80309.

Chadwick, W. L., and others, 1976, **Report to U.S. Dept. of the Interior and State of Idaho on Failure of Teton Dam**: U.S. Govt. Printing Office, Washington, DC 20402.

Clark, C., and others, 1982, *Flood* E: Alexandria, VA, Time-Life Books Planet Earth Series 176 p. An outstanding book for students and lay readers, it contains detailed, well-illustrated accounts of catastrophic floods and dam failures.

Committee on Natural Disasters, National Research Council, 1991, *The New Year's Eve Flood on Oahu, Hawaii, December 31, 1987 - January 1, 1988*: Washington, DC, National Academy Press.

Committee on Natural Disasters, National Research Council, 1991, *Hurricane Elena, Gulf Coast, August 29 - September 2, 1985* E: Washington, DC, National Academy Press.

Costa, J. E., 1978, **The dilemma of flood control in the United States**: Environmental Management, v. 2, pp. 313 - 322.

Costa, J. E., 1978, **Holocene stratigraphy in flood-frequency analysis**: Water Resources Research, v. 14, pp. 626 - 632.

Costa, J. E., 1985, **Floods from dam failures**: U.S. Geol. Survey Open-File Report OF 85-0560.

Crippen, J. R., and Bue, C. D., **Maximum floodflows in the conterminous United States**: U.S. Geol. Survey Water Supply Paper 1887, 52 p.

Degen, P., 1984, *Johnstown Flood of 1889 - Tragedy on the Conemaugh* E: Philadelphia, PA, Eastern Acorn Press, Division of Eastern Natl. Park & Monument Assoc.

Drieger, C., and Kennard, P., 1984, **Ice volumes on Cascade volcanoes**: U.S. Geol. Survey Open File Report 84-581.

Ellen, S. D., and others, 1988, **Landslides, floods and marine effects of the storm January 3-5, 1982, San Francisco Bay region, California**: U.S. Geol. Survey Prof. Paper 1434.

Emerson, J. W., 1971, **Channelization: A case study**: Science, v. 173, pp. 325 - 326.

Federal Emergency Management Agency, 1992, **An assessment report on floodplain management in the United States** E: FEMA, 500 C Street, Washington, D.C. 20472.

Howard, A. D., and Remson, I. (eds.), 1978, *Geology in Environmental Planning* E: McGraw-Hill, chapters 3 and 4.

Illinois Dept. of Transportation Division of Water Resources, 1991, **Floodplain compliance: Enforcing your community's floodplain management ordinance**: IL Dept. Trans. Div. Water Resources, 201 West Center Court, Schaumburg, IL 60196-1096.

James, L. D., Laurent, E. A., and Hill, D. W., 1971, **The floodplain as a residential choice**: Atlanta, GA, Georgia Inst. Technol. Environmental Resources Ctr.

Jansen, R. B., 1980, **Dams and public safety: a water resources technical publication**: Water and Power Resources Service, Denver Federal Center, P. O. Box 25007, Denver, CO 80225.

Judkins, G., (ed.), 1976, *The Big Thompson Disaster* E: Denver, CO, Lithographic Press.

Lee, L. T., Chrostowski, J., and Eguchi, R. T., 1978, **Natural hazards: riverine floods, storm surge, tsunami loss models**: Natl. Tech. Inf. Serv. n. PB-294682/AS-PCA-10.

Leopold, L. B., 1968, **Hydrology for urban land planning: A guidebook on the hydrologic effects of urban land use** E: U.S. Geol. Survey Circular 554.

McCain and others, 1979, **Storm and flood of July 31 - August 1, 1976, in the Big Thompson River and Cache la Poudre River basins, Larimer and Weld counties, Colorado**: U.S. Geol. Survey Prof. Paper 1115 B.

McCullough, D. G., 1968, *The Johnstown Flood* E: New York, Simon and Shuster.

Mathewson, C. C., and Keaton, J. R., 1988, **Flood hazard recognition and mitigation on alluvial fans**: ASCE Proc. of Hydraulic Engineering Symp., Colorado Springs, CO.

National Park Service, Association of State Wetland Managers, and Association of State Floodplain Managers, 1991, **A casebook in managing rivers for multiple uses** E: Assoc. State Floodplain Managers, Madison, WI, 53701-2051, 86 p. The organization at this address also provides many other useful publications.

National Science Foundation, 1980, **A report on flood hazard investigation**: NSF, 2101 Constitution Ave., Washington, DC. 20418.

National Weather Service, 1991, **Shadyside, Ohio, flash floods June 14, 1990** E: Warning and Forecast Branch, Natl. Weather Service, 1325 East West Highway, Silver Spring, MD 20910.

Natural Hazards Research and Applications Information Center (NHRAIC), 1991, **Floodproof retrofitting: homeowner self-protective behavior** E: Publications Clerk, NHRAIC, P. O. Box 482, University of Colorado, Boulder, CO 80309-0482.

Outland, C. F., 1977, *Man-made Disaster - the Story of St. Francis Dam* E (revised ed.): Glendale, CA. Arthur. H. Clarke Co.

Parker, D. J., 1991, **Flood disasters in Britain: lessons from flood hazard research**: Flood Hazards Research Ctr., Middlesex Polytechnic, Queensway, Enfield, EN3 4SF, U.K.

Paulson, R. W., and others, 1991, **National water summary 1988-89**: U.S. Geol. Surv. Water Supply Paper 2375, 591 p.

Rahn, P. H., 1975, **Lessons learned from the June 9, 1972, flood in Rapid City, South Dakota** E: Bull. Assoc. Engineering Geologists v. 12, pp. 83 - 97.

Rahn, P. H., 1986, **Fluvial Processes** E: Chapter 8 in *Engineering Geology, An Environmental Approach*, P. H. Rahn, New York, Elsevier, pp. 241 - 302.

Rantz, S. E., 1970, **Urban sprawl and flooding in southern California** E: U.S. Geol. Survey Circular 601 B.

Rogers, J. D., 1992, **Reassessment of the St. Francis Dam failure**: in *Engineering Geology Practice in Southern California*, Assoc. Engrg. Geologists Spec. Pub., Belmont, CA, Star Pub. Co., pp. 639 - 666.

Schaeffer, J. R., Ellis, D. W., and Spieker, A. M., 1970, **Flood hazard mapping in metropolitan Chicago**: U.S. Geol. Survey, Circular 601-C.

Schneider, W. J., and Goddard, J. E., 1974, **Extent and development of urban flood plains** E: U.S. Geol. Survey Circular 601 J.

Smith, N., 1972, *A History of Dams*: Secaucus, NJ, Citadel Press.

Starosolsky, O., and others, 1989, *Hydrology of disasters; proceedings of the technical conference*: London, James and James.

Tennessee Valley Authority, 1991, **Conserving your valuable floodplain resources**: TVA Flood Protection Section, Evans Bldg. Room 1A, Knoxville, TN 37902.

U.S. Army Corps. Of Engineers, 1991, **Flood proofing techniques, programs and references** E: U.S. Army Corps. of Engineers, Natl. Flood Proofing Committee, Attn. CECW-PF, 20 Massachusetts Ave., Washington, DC 20314-1000.

Vance, M., 1990, **Flood insurance: A bibliography**: P. O. Box 229 Monticello, IL 61856, Vance Bibliographies, 13 p.

Ward, R., 1978, *Floods*: New York, NY, John Wiley.

White, G. F., and others, 1975, **Flood hazards in the United States: a research assessment**: Monograph NSF-RA-E-75-006, Institute of Behavioral Sci., Univ. Colorado, Boulder, CO 80309.

Wilson, W. A., 1990, **Issues to floodproof retrofitting** E: Assoc. of State Floodplain Managers, P. O. Box 2051, Madison, WI 53701.

Videotapes on Floods

Best Build II: Construction in a Riverine Floodplain E: 1988, 20 minutes, Natl. Flood Ins. Program, Best Build Series, P. O. Box 710, Lanham, MD 20706, (800) 638-6620 - 7.

Best Build III: Protecting a Flood-Prone Home E: 1990, 30 minutes, Natl. Flood Ins. Program, Best Build Series, P. O. Box 710, Lanham, MD 20706, (800) 638-6620 - 7.

Buffalo Creek Flood: An Act of Man: 1975, 40 minutes, Appalshop Films, 306 Madison St., Box 743 A, Whitesburg, KY 41858, (213) 666-6500. Focus on Buffalo Creek disaster from burst tailings dam in West Virginia.

Buffalo Creek Revisited: 1984, 31 minutes, Appalshop Films, 306 Madison St., Box 743 A, Whitesburg, KY 41858, (213) 666-6500.

Community Rating System: 1992, 13 minutes, National Flood Insurance Program Community Rating System (NFIP - CRS) Publications, P. O. Box 501016, Indianapolis, IN 42650-1016, (317) 845 - 1750.

Flood Control: 1992, 20 minutes, Films for the Humanities and Social Sciences, P.O. Box 2053, Princeton, NJ 08543-2053, (800) 257-5126.

Floods in South E: 1990, 60 minutes, ABC Nightlines, MPI Home Video, 15825 Rob Roy Drive, Oak Forest, IL 60452, (800) 323-0442.

Flood Forecasting: 1987, 20 minutes, Britannica Films, 310 South Michigan Ave., Chicago, IL 60604, (800) 621-3900. Call for current prices. Occasional special sale prices on videos are given.

Managing the Floods of '86 - California's Ordeal E: 1986, 9 minutes, U.S. Dept. Interior Bureau of Reclamation, P.O. Box 25007, Mail D-1500, Denver Federal Center, Denver, CO 80225-0007, (303) 236-6972. Focus on California floods in late winter through early spring of 1986.

River Town E: 1984, 28 minutes, Bullfrog Films, Inc., Oley, PA 19547, (800) 543-3764. Focuses on Soldiers Grove, Wisconsin, a frequently flooded town that not only relocated out of the floodplain area, but became a model solar energy community.

Teton - Decisions and Disaster E: 1976, 60 minutes, Copyrighted and produced by KAID-TV, Boise, ID and KUID-TV Moscow, Idaho. Available for loan from U.S. Dept. Interior Bureau of Reclamation, P.O. Box 25007, Mail D-1500, Denver Federal Center, Denver, CO 80225-0007, (303) 236-6972. Focus on the background of the Teton Dam and the disaster which followed from the dam break. Particularly interesting for mature social science students because of the extreme viewpoints between conservation and exploitation expressed regarding water rights.

The Awesome Power: 1989, 15 minutes, National Oceanic and Atmospheric Administration. Focuses on flash floods. Available on loan from U.S. Geol. Survey Library Special Collections, MS 955, 345 Middlefield Road, Menlo Park, CA 94025, (415) 329-5009.

The Johnstown Flood E: 1989, 30 minutes, Johnstown Area Heritage Association, 319 Washington St., Johnstown, PA 15901, (814) 539-1889.

The Living Desert E: 1954, 45 minutes, Walt Disney. Available at many rental outlets, this old film focuses primarily on desert wildlife but has excellent footage of a flash flood from its beginning through its wane.

Walls of Water: 1978, 29 minutes, Pennsylvania State University Audiovisual Services, Special Services Building, University Park, PA 16802, (800) 826-0132. Focus on the Johnstown Flood.

Water E: 1989, 59 minutes, Bullfrog Films, Inc., Oley, PA 19547, (800) 543-3764. This film designed for educators is also available on videodisc. Includes section on purpose and construction of dams.

COASTAL HAZARDS - STORM SURGE, TSUNAMIS and COASTAL EROSION

Losses from coastal hazards are extremely severe and will continue to increase even more as shorelines become more densely developed. Loss of life has been greatly decreased in developed countries as a result of satellite weather warning systems and good evacuation routes. Economic losses can be decreased by developing only on favorable geological materials and by managing developments in accord with natural shoreline processes.

Occurrences of Coastal Hazards

Coastal areas along large lakes and oceans are some of the most charming and desired areas for human residence and recreation. Already, over half of our population in the United States lives on or very near to the coasts. These areas are also sensitive ecological areas where wetlands are important for wildlife and for fisheries. Yet these areas provide their own special hazards. On a day-to-day basis, wave erosion gradually undercuts bluffs and periodically causes areas of the shoreline to recede and collapse. Common waves result primarily from winds blowing over the surface of the water. These waves, in turn, are the primary generators of nearshore currents. Accelerated events of erosion caused by fluctuations in water levels (particularly along the Great Lakes) and by occasional storms have cost many property owners their homes and the land itself on which their homes were built. Today, severe erosion occurs along about 25% of the nation's coastline and produces an annual loss of about 900 million in 1990 dollars.

Storm surge is the term used to describe the abnormal sudden rise in sea level that accompanies wind and other atmospheric conditions that cause water to pile up over a low coast and spill into low

Destroyed area of Romain Retreat, on Bulls Bay, southern coast of South Carolina. Storm surge here during Hurricane Hugo was almost 20 feet. Forty-three homes were present before the storm. (photo from National Weather Service NOAA National Hurricane Center)

coastal river valleys. Loss of life occurs by drowning and structural collapse. Property damage from a single event can reach billions of dollars. In natural catastrophes within the United States, storm surge accounts for both the event with the greatest loss of life (Galveston, Texas, in 1900, with 6,000 lives lost) and the two costliest natural disasters (Hurricane Hugo, in 1989, at over 10 billion dollars, 7 billion on the U.S. mainland, and Hurricane Andrew in 1992 at about 30 billion dollars).

Undeveloped countries with large populations in low-lying coastal valleys are prone to terrible losses from storm surge coastal flooding. The most severe storm surge in recent history occurred in Bangladesh in 1970, where a tropical cyclone (typhoon) with winds over 100 miles per hour combined with high tides to create a 20-foot tidal surge into the Bay of Bengal that inundated lowlands. Here, more than 300,000 lives were lost.

Tsunamis are produced by purely geologic agents such as earthquakes, avalanches and volcanic eruptions. "Tsunami," the Japanese term for "harbor wave," is the proper name for huge waves generated by geologic agents. These same agents sometimes also cause large waves to occur on inland lakes. The common term "tidal wave" is a misnomer. Tides are the regular, rhythmic and predictable rise and fall of local sea levels that result from gravitational forces that change according to relative positions of the earth, moon and sun. While the highest spring tidal ranges in some areas may exceed 40 feet (such as at the Bay of Fundy), tides do not produce "tidal waves" or any other sporadically large waves. However, the time of high tide that coincides with either a storm surge or tsunami can greatly accent its destructive force. Tsunamis are typically larger than storm surge. Tsunamis are not common, but when they occur, waves more than 80 feet high might be expected.

WORLD'S MAJOR STORM SURGES

YEAR	LOCATION	DEATHS
1099	Netherlands & England	100,000
1737	Bay of Bengal	300,000
1881	Southeast China	300,000
1906	Hong Kong	10,000
1932	Cuba	2,500
1942	Bengal, India	40,000
1953	Netherlands	1,800
1963	Bangladesh	22,000
1965	Bangladesh	57,000 in 3 storms
1970	Bangladesh	300,000
1971	Orissa State, India	9,600
1977	India	14,000
1985	Bangladesh	10,000
1991	Bangladesh	139,000

(early data from Tufty, 1969; post-1900 data from *World Almanac* (1993) and Office of Foreign Disaster Assistance, *Disaster History*, 1991.)

Aerial view of Valdez, Alaska, after tsunami damage. The wave was generated locally during the Alaska quake of 1964 when a huge block of land slid into the sea, carrying portions of the town with it. The landslide generated a huge wave that slammed into the waterfront within minutes and penetrated into two blocks of the town, producing 30 fatalities. (photo by U.S. Dept. of Interior, distributed by NOAA, Boulder, CO)

WORLD'S MAJOR TSUNAMIS

YEAR	ORIGIN	DAMAGE LOCALE	DROWNINGS (COMMENTS)
1628 B.C	Santorini (Thera) eruption	Crete, Greece, Egypt	(Minoan civilization devastated)
1640	Komagatake Volcano	Hokkaido, Japan	1,470
1707	West Pacific earthquake	Osaka Bay, Japan	4,900
1755	Offshore Lisbon earthquake	Western Europe, North Africa	20,000 - 30,000
1792	Unzen Volcano avalanche into sea	Kyushu, Japan	10,000 (landslide killed 5000 more)
1812	Offshore Santa Barbara, CA earthquake	Santa Barbara, CA	(reported waves 30 ft. high)
1815	Tambora eruption	Indonesia	10,000
1868	Peru/Chile earthquake	Hilo, Hawaii	(waves 30 ft. high - carried boats 2 mi. inland)
1883	Krakatau eruption	Indonesia	36,000 (waves more than 100 ft. high)
1896	Honshu earthquake	Sanriku, Japan	27,000
1905	Norway, landslide into fjord	Loen Lake, Norway	61
1918	Landslide, Philippines	Philippines	100
1933	Honshu earthquake	Sanriku, Japan	3,000 (waves 75 ft. high)
1936	Norway, landslide into fjord	Loen Lake, Norway	73
1946	Aleutian Islands earthquake	Wainaku, Hawaii	173 (waves 55 ft. high)
1960	Chilean earthquake	Chile, Hawaii, Japan	1,900
1964	Alaska earthquake	Crescent City, CA; Valdez area, AK	122
1971	Peru avalanche into lake in Andes	Chungar, Peru	600
1976	West Pacific earthquake	Philippines	3,000
1979	Werung Volcano with avalanche into sea	Lomblem Island, Indonesia	539
1992	Southwest Nicaragua earthquake	Masachapa & 200 miles of coast & nearby islands	116 (waves 30 ft high)

(data from Office of Foreign Disaster Assistance, *Disaster History*, 1991; *World Almanac*, 1993; D. R. Coates, *Geology and Society*, 1985; and United Nation's, *UNDRO NEWS*, 1992. As of early 1993, 63 people remained unaccounted for in addition to the 116 killed in the 1992 tsunami in Nicaragua.)

Fortunately, tsunamis are brief and their effects are restricted to the immediate coastline. Because tsunamis have their origins in local geologic events that occur within minutes, they provide far less warning than is provided by a tropical storm, which can be seen developing and moving. Satellite images now provide many days of warning time to prepare for major storm-related hazards. Only a few hours at most elapse between the time when the triggering landslide, earthquake or eruption takes place and the resulting tsunami strikes the coast.

Along the East Coast and Gulf Coast, the primary coastal hazard is storm surge rather than tsunamis.

The Pacific Ocean is ringed by plate boundaries, and the potential for *tsunamis* produced by accompanying earthquakes and volcanoes is greater for the nations that border that ocean.

The orientation and bathymetry of the West Coast of the United States tend to protect it from the full effects of many tsunamis. However, the 1964 earthquake in Alaska produced a 20-foot tsunami and severe damage in Crescent City, California. Nearly 30 blocks of the business district were destroyed and 11 deaths resulted. Many residents along the West Coast live within areas that are endangered by tsunamis.

The Importance of Geological Materials in Shoreline Erosion

One of the wisest actions a prospective property owner along a lake or ocean shore can take is to learn about the nature of the geological materials under the property. The stability of shorelines depends upon the inherent strength of the geological materials, their degree of exposure to waves and their vegetative cover. Natural shorelines are composed of materials that range from soft clays to hard bedrock. Even common storms can cause disastrous recession of shorelines underlain by soft, unconsolidated deposits. Some shores recede at over 20 meters (60 feet) per year. The number of homes and structures now currently hanging over water on U.S. coasts shows profoundly just how many contractors, developers, engineers and homeowners incorrectly estimated the rate of shoreline recession. The attractive appearance of sites underlain only by unconsolidated materials can inspire unwarranted confidence for building. In a

Soft, unconsolidated deposits are particularly susceptible to wave erosion, even when capped with resistant blacktop or concrete. A moderate winter storm damaged structures, including a parking area, while causing recession of the shoreline at a recreational beach at Isla Verde, Puerto Rico, in 1988. (photo by David M. Bush, Duke University)

Desperation to protect this hotel near Fort Lauderdale, Florida, is evident. The building is sited on soft sand, and neither the sandbags nor the attached breakwater will save it if a major storm occurs. This is an example of ignoring the nature of both beach processes and geological foundation materials. Heavier structures like seawalls will simply destroy the recreational use of the local beach that initially provided the incentive to locate a hotel here. (photo by Paul Moser)

Sand movement affects homeowners in major coastal storms. LEFT - Scour produced in late stages of storm surge eroded the pilings of these homes almost to their bases on Folly Island, South Carolina.

RIGHT - Sand removal became a problem for these residents of Garden City, South Carolina, after it was moved into this development by overwash. Both events occurred during Hurricane Hugo. (both photos by Rodney Priddy and E. Robert Thieler, Duke University)

truly major storm, these materials, even where well vegetated, can be stripped away and the shoreline can recede a significant distance in only a few hours.

Coastal **sand dunes** are the least durable of unconsolidated deposits. They are composed of materials easily moved by wind or water and are particularly inhospitable areas for plant growth. These dunes are normally stabilized only where a very delicate community of vegetation becomes established over long periods of time. The vegetation can be destroyed even by occasional foot traffic, and barren dunes are especially susceptible to wind and wave erosion. If natural offshore barriers such as reefs or sandbars are destroyed, then increased exposure of these delicate dunes to waves results. Unless barriers strong enough to withstand currents and waves are maintained or are artificially restored, roads and structures are at immediate risk.

Other unconsolidated deposits established along coastlines include old glacial till, soft terraces built of marine or lacustrine mud and sand, and thick residual soils. In unconsolidated deposits, suitable vegetation serves as important barriers to waves and currents and greatly reduces rates of land erosion. In marine coastlines, only a few salt-tolerant plants, such as mangrove trees in Florida and the Bahamas or *Spartina* (salt marsh cordgrass) in England and the east coast of the U.S., are suited to grow all the way to the water line. In some places, thick growths of mangroves are so effective in trapping sediment that they produce a net gain in land area. In freshwater coastlines, a diverse vegetation may grow all the way to the shoreline and reduce erosion during normal rains and winds. When natural vegetation has been destroyed or replaced by less suitable flora, effects of shoreline erosion will be much greater.

Bedrock includes diverse indurated geological substances, but aside from weak rocks such as shale and chalk, bedrock cliffs are by far the most stable sites for shoreline foundations. Most resist wave erosion, even from wave surges, to a remarkable degree. A homeowner who wisely selects a bedrock site at a reasonable elevation is not likely to experience the sea or lake entering the back door or the disappearance of 100 feet of shore front property in a single storm. Many who ignore the local geology and build or buy cabins, houses, condos or other structures on bluffs consisting of sand, glacial till or other unconsolidated materials can expect just such an experience. No engineered structure is more stable than the geological material on which it rests.

Coastal Hazards and the Concept of Deep Time

Shorelines are probably the most dynamic of all geological environments. The eye-catching presence of wind and water energy over vast expanses of land, sky and sea is the major aesthetic attraction of shorelines. This energy seems always at work producing changes, whether it be in the constant movement of sand by longshore currents or in the cataclysmic power of the tsunami.

It is easy to see short-term changes that occur in minutes as sand gets carried in zigzag patterns down the beach in the back-and-forth rhythm of waves. Tidal rise and fall in response to the gravitational forces of sun and moon are obvious. The regular shifts in tide on a daily basis are perhaps the most repetitive and predictable agents affecting the geologic environment.

Seasons produce extreme changes along many shorelines. Beaches that are sandy and inviting in gentle warm summer can be stripped to cobble and bedrock in winter as more powerful storms crash onto the shore and drag the sand to deeper water offshore. In fresh water lakes in temperate zones or along oceans in polar climates, ice pack grinds against the shore, rearranging even boulders and gouging out

MAJOR HURRICANES and STORM SURGES AFFECTING COASTAL UNITED STATES and HAWAII

DATE	LOCATION	DEATHS
July, 1715	Florida (Ten Spanish galleons sank)	1,000
August, 1856	Isle Derniere, LA	400
August, 1881	Georgia and South Carolina	700
August, 1893	South Carolina & Georgia	1,000
August - September, 1900	Galveston, TX - hurricane	6,000
September, 1909	Louisiana and Mississippi	350
August - September, 1915	Gulf Coast	525
September, 1919	Texas and Florida	300
September, 1926	Florida and Alabama	243
September, 1928	Lake Okeechobee, Florida	1,836
August - September, 1935	Florida Keys	408
September, 1938	New York and New England	600
August, 1955	Hurricane Diane, NE. U. S.	184
June, 1957	Hurricane Audrey, TX & LA	390
September, 1965	Hurricane Betsy, SE. U. S.	75
August, 1969	Hurricane Camille, MS, LA & E. U. S.	256
August, 1972	Hurricane Agnes, Florida to New York	118
August, 1979	Hurricane Frederic, Gulf Coast	13
August - September, 1979	Hurricane David, Caribbean and SE. U. S.	1,100
August, 1980	Hurricane Allen, Caribbean and SE. U. S.	273
September, 1989	Hurricane Hugo, S. Carolina and Caribbean	54
August, 1991	Hurricane Bob, NE. Atlantic coast	18
August, 1992	Hurricane Andrew, Florida & Louisiana	38
September, 1992	Hurricane Iniki at Kauai, Hawaii	4

(data from National Oceanic and Atmospheric Administration's Technical Memorandum NWS NHC 31, 1990; *The World Almanac*, 1993; and D. R. Coates, *Geology and Society*, 1985) For brevity, only those storms affecting the mainland U.S. are shown here. This table omits many Caribbean hurricanes, such as Gilbert in 1988, that did great damage in the Caribbean but only minor damage in the continental U.S. Sizes of hurricanes should not be inferred on basis of casualties.

loose chunks of bedrock. Spring rains and snow melt cause sea cliff springs to flow and even wash away parts of rock cliff. Swollen rivers then bring mud and sand, the raw material that nature uses to build beaches, sand bars and spits to parts of the coast. As summer returns, sand is again washed onto the beaches and remains there until autumn squalls begin to carry it away again. These seasonal process are regular and anticipated.

Storms and hurricanes, like floods, can be anticipated but their timing cannot be predicted. The same long-term patterns that produce floods also produce shoreline changes, and some of these changes are permanently destructive to residents. Describing shoreline recession in terms of a certain length-per-year may mislead a listener into picturing a gradual,

uniform process. Shoreline recession is anything but gradual and uniform. There may be no recession for over a decade; then suddenly more than a hundred feet of waterfront property vanishes within a few hours during a single violent storm. The 100-year storms and those great storms whose effects are separated by intermissions of deep time are coastal counterparts of the 100-year floods and enormous deep-time floods noted in the previous chapter.

In deep time, we have to consider yet another factor—"sea level" is not constant over deep time! At the shoreline, effects are profound as relationship of land level and sea level changes. In the Great Lakes and smaller lakes as well, a few dry seasons can depress the water level by more than a foot, and wet seasons can raise it by the same magnitude. In fact, the

The Dynamic Beach

Longshore current direction ⟶

BEACH

Path of sand movement

A

Deposition / Erosion

Groin

B

Deposition

Erosion

C

Breakwater

A. Beaches are in motion, and sand doesn't simply rest on a beach. A beach is like a river of sand, and the sand flows in a zig-zag path along the shoreline in response to wave-driven longshore currents.

B. Protective structures affect the beach well beyond the site of the structure. A groin may capture sand and add waterfront land to some property, but it always does so at the expense of taking away land down-current through erosion. Dotted line shows the original shoreline configuration prior to groin installation.

C. Even though the detached sea wall does not physically touch the beach, it weakens the waves and thus the longshore currents between the wall and the beach. This causes sand to build up in this quiet area, but starves the beach of sand down-current and results in erosion. Any manipulation of a natural beach has adverse consequences as well as benefits.

119

SAFFIR-SIMPSON HURRICANE SCALE

RATING	CONDITIONS	EFFECTS
1	Winds 74-95 mph; storm surge 5 ft. above normal	Damage to unanchored mobile homes and trees; some coastal road flooding
2	Winds 96-110 mph; storm surge 6-8 ft. above normal	Roofing and window damage to homes; heavy damage to trees, mobile homes and docks. Flooding occurs 2 to 4 hours ahead of arrival of storm center.
3	Winds 111-130 mph; storm surge of 9-12 ft. above normal	Mobile homes destroyed, structural damage to small homes. Flooding near coast damages larger structures. Land less than 5 ft. above sea level may be flooded for miles inland.
4	Winds 131-155 mph; storm surge 13-18 ft. above normal	Major erosion of beach areas, failure of shore protection devices. Major damage to all nearshore structures; land lower than 10 ft. above sea level may flood inland for up to 6 miles. Major evacuation warranted.
5	Winds greater than 155 mph; storm surge greater than 18 ft. above normal	Complete roof failure on residences and public buildings. Major damage from flooding to lower floors of buildings on land less than 15 ft. above sea level. Devastation within 500 yards of coastline. Massive evacuation warranted from low areas up to 10 miles from the coast.

On the Saffir - Simpson Scale, hurricanes Hugo (1989) and Andrew (1992), were rated at 4. Chart condensed from NOAA, 1978, *Tropical Cyclones of the North Atlantic Ocean, 1871 - 1987*, p. 25.

RIGHT - Enhanced infrared satellite imagery of Hurricane Hugo as it spirals with its eye near Charleston, South Carolina.

BELOW LEFT - Folly Beach south of Charleston before Hurricane Hugo. Large buildings are the newly remodeled Atlantic House Restaurant and tourist shops.

BELOW RIGHT - The same site after Hugo. This developed area had a history of chronic problems with beach erosion. It was a certain site for disaster when the infrequent, but inevitable, major storm passed through. (photos by National Weather Service, NOAA, National Hurricane Center)

Folly Beach homes before Hurricane Hugo. Evidence of efforts to control beach erosion by engineering is revealed in the hard barrier of riprap rock facing the beach. The barrier was designed to protect homes by preventing wave erosion of the soft sand on which the houses are built.

BELOW is the same housing area after Hurricane Hugo. The riprap rock barrier has been breached and nearly leveled by waves and storm surge.

In an act with the flavor of a defiant parting gesture, Hugo deposited the riprap blocks from the barrier wall into the very living rooms of the homes the wall was intended to protect. (photos from National Weather Service, NOAA, National Hurricane Center)

water levels in the Great Lakes have varied above and below their present levels by hundreds of feet through deep time. Presently, the crust is rising in the area around northern Lake Superior at one or two inches (several centimeters) per century, thus slowly tilting the lake basin, like a giant teacup, to the south. The levels of the oceans have also changed, primarily in response to a good portion of the planet's water being bound up in glaciers that were spread across the northern continents during the ice ages. About 20,000 years ago, the waterfront of the present United States extended about 200 miles further into the Atlantic Ocean. As the glacial ice melted, the water ran back to the oceans, which have continued to rise accordingly over the past 200 centuries.

When water levels rise, the erosion along coasts increases. Even a small rise makes a difference, as homeowners along the Great Lakes shorelines can truly attest.

Changes in climate determine both the frequency and severity of coastal hazards, because hazards associated with storms are products of weather and climate. Increasing of ocean surface temperatures through global warming should lead to more frequent and larger hurricanes, especially along the Gulf and Atlantic Coasts. Any rising sea level that resulted from melting the ice caps over the next few decades would seriously increase the effects of storm surge on these coastal communities. An abrupt global warming period, whether resulting from human effects or from natural variations, would likely increase damages caused by coastal hazards.

In summary, geologic hazards along shorelines are a product of many short-term rhythms and longer term events acting together to make coastlines the most changeable of all Earth's environments.

Dangers from Coastal Hazards

Storms bring wind and rain and occasional storm surge that involves catastrophic flooding. The low barometric pressures near the centers of major regional storms (hurricanes) cause the ocean to bulge upwards. This raises the local elevation of sea water over an area of many square miles. Winds associated with the storm push across the surface of the sea, and the traction generated by this push gets transmitted to underlying water. This traction is relentless and eventually gets water moving even to depths of several hundred feet. As the storm moves close to land, the

moving water begins to drag against the bottom, and more and more energy is directed into shallower and lesser volumes of water. Large waves are the result. The composite result of the low barometric pressure and the pile-up of water forces immense amounts of water over low-lying areas in a storm surge. The worst case for loss of life occurs when hurricane winds encroach toward the coast at the times coincident with high tide. Then every mechanism is in place to raise the local sea level and drive the ocean waters, with accompanying violent winds and rain, over coastal lowlands.

Hurricanes are rated in severity according to the speed of their winds and the height of the storm surge they produce. The **Saffir-Simpson Hurricane Scale** ranks severity on a scale between 1 and 5. The ratings are based on sustained wind speed and height of storm surge at affected areas.

Flooding produces great losses, and tornado winds that accompany hurricanes can cause comparable degrees of damage. Property damage occurs when natural barriers such as sand dunes and man-made barriers such as stone walls are destroyed. Thereafter thousands of square feet of land and all structures on it can be swept away in hours, and the shoreline can be completely reconfigured—all during a single storm. Thereafter, the storm may move inland, bringing wind damage and immense rainfalls that will produce large floods along streams and landslides in sloping terrain.

Pressures to develop coasts are similar to the pressures to develop floodplains. People want to live there and many are willing to take the risks. For those who choose to live along coastlines, an informed risk greatly increases chances of avoiding catastrophe. In developed countries, early warning systems for both tsunamis and major storms exist, and transportation facilities are usually adequate to allow evacuation, but even there risks exist to property and perhaps to the overall global quality of life.

Local risks involve personal safety and economics. Risks to property can be reduced by construction of protective barriers such as seawalls, groins and jetties, and the cost of maintenance of these structures increases the costs to society, especially to the residential areas that require them. Risks to property may also be mitigated by obtaining appropriate insurance against the events that occur over longer time spans, such as storm surges and tsunamis. Those who fail to insure themselves against such hazards are at least as negligent as citizens who risk living on a floodplain without flood insurance. Some citizens who live with flood dangers often are unaware that they live at a locality which occasionally is flooded; residents of a shoreline see water daily and should have no doubt about their position.

Possible Global Consequences of Coastal Development

One long-term risk of overdevelopment of coasts may be global catastrophe. Development brings pragmatic problems of pollution and waste disposal. The ocean, unlike a river basin, is a global source of life. Plankton in the ocean yield life-giving oxygen to the atmosphere. All oxygen in our atmosphere is produced by photosynthetic organisms. Marine plankton produced an oxygenated atmosphere over our planet hundreds of millions of years before terrestrial plants became important contributors. Plankton continue to remain important oxygen producers, and they support the entire food chain of the oceans.

Wetlands, marshes and living coral reefs are essential for marine life, particularly for fish and other marine life. Wetlands also serve as sinks that remove harmful pollutants from both the water and atmosphere. (Recall that in the section on acid drainage in this book we noted that wetlands were found to be so effective at removing some pollutants that artificial wetlands are constructed to serve as actual biological water treatment plants.) Coral reefs remove carbon dioxide from sea water (most of this carbon dioxide comes ultimately from the atmosphere) and convert it into limestone. Human development involves excavating, and excavations increase sediment yield during runoff. Sediment is deadly to coral reefs, and some reefs in the Caribbean have been nearly destroyed by sediment. Unlike restoring a river, there will be no restoring an ocean if humans succeed in seriously damaging it. It is a sobering fact that our developing of coastlines has already been responsible for loss of about 50% of our nation's wetlands, and pollution has forced the closing of one-third of the nation's shellfish beds.

Roles of the Geologist in Reducing Coastal Hazards

Coastal areas are complex systems, and dealing with coastal hazards is a responsibility of many professionals, including biologists, chemists, meteorologists, engineers, physical geographers,

oceanographers and environmental scientists. Yet, there are some areas of reducing coastal hazards that require geologists as the dominant scientists.

In tsunami warnings. Unlike storm surge, where the development of the storm can be monitored in a timely manner on weather instruments and satellites, tsunamis result from instantaneous and unpredictable geological events. The waves generated spread from the source of disturbance like ripples on a pond and can cross the entire Pacific Ocean in less than a day. Nearby areas may have less than an hour's notice. Immediate recognition of the location and magnitude of the triggering geologic event is imperative to provide time for evacuation of high-risk areas. Tsunamis rippling across the open ocean are no larger than any normal wave and pass ships unnoticed. These waves become visible and build to great heights only where they approach coastal areas with appropriate shoreline and bottom configurations. By this time it is too late to warn coastal inhabitants. In the Pacific Ocean, an international tsunami warning system headquartered in Hawaii utilizes a system of tidal gauges and seismic stations to provide warning. When a significant earthquake or volcanic disturbance occurs within the ocean, geologists who specialize in geophysics and seismology are the first to note the location and magnitude of the event. If tidal gauging stations near the site begin to show significant response, then a **tsunami warning** can be issued to all endangered locations.

In mapping and public service. Ordinary wave erosion is a chronic problem in shoreline areas, and the most cost-effective method of dealing with economic losses is allowing construction only on suitable geological materials. The geologist is the sole professional who is trained to map the distributions and thicknesses of these materials. From field studies, geologists can select the most stable sites for development and sometimes can deduce the extent of previous fluctuations in water level that have occurred at the site over deep time. The extent of loss of property and life that ensues along coastlines during wave surge of any origin greatly depends upon the degree to which the knowledge of geology has been incorporated into structural design and land use zoning. Geologists in government, academia and the private sector produce coastal maps that often enable the public to investigate development of property with some knowledge of the geologic materials. The series *Living with the Shore*, produced by Duke University, is an outstanding example of this service.

123

In engineering structures. Geology plays an important role in the stabilization of both shore protection devices and offshore structures. Man-made islands, walls, breakwaters and groins, piers, offshore oil drilling platforms, and deep-water ports are all exposed to waves and wave-generated currents that may erode unsuitable foundations. Geological foundations beneath prospective structures require prior evaluation by qualified geologists.

Assessment of suitability of particular structures cannot be made by simply concentrating on the design of the structure itself. Overall knowledge of shoreline processes is essential. Shoreline processes are studied by geologists during their educations, and many geologists specialize in the study of shoreline, shallow marine and reef processes. When the natural geological, meteorological and climatological conditions of an area are understood, it is possible to evaluate benefits *versus* ultimate costs of such structures.

In research. Because shorelines represent an immense global system, the study of human effects on this system must come through research that involves global perspectives of space, and deep time perspectives of change. These perspectives require learning about past shoreline positions and elevations, and climatic conditions that persisted in the past. This involves extensive monitoring and gathering of data. Geologists in many universities and government agencies are involved with this important research, as well as research on local areas that helps to assess shoreline processes and their rates.

SUMMARY of PART III

The earth is a dynamic planet with a number of wondrous, constantly ongoing processes. Process-based hazards result from the dynamics of our planet's deep interior (earthquakes and volcanoes), its shallow interior (subsidence) and its surface environment (landslides, floods and coastal hazards). The surface processes account for the largest losses of life and property and are heavily influenced by weather and climate. A human lifetime is short in comparison to the recurrence of many hazards at a single place on the earth's surface. Thus long time intervals that occur between major catastrophic events contribute to complacency and lack of preparation that would minimize losses. Between fall, 1989, and early 1993, process-based hazards cost the U.S. over 50 billion dollars in losses, making this the most costly period of economic losses from natural hazards in the nation's history

The appendices which follow this section provide access to self-help for any reader who may be confronting a geologic hazard.

References for Additional Reading on Coastal Hazards
"E" Denotes references particularly suitable for educators.

Adams, W. M., 1970, **Tsunami effects and risk at Kahuku Point, Oahu, Hawaii**: in *Engineering Geology Case Histories* n. 8, Geol. Soc. Amer., pp. 63 - 70.

Adams, W. M., (ed.), 1970, *Tsunamis in the Pacific Ocean* E: Honolulu, HI, East-West Center Press.

All-Industry Research Advisory Council and National Committee on Property Insurance, 1989, **Surviving the storm: building codes compliance and mitigation of hurricane damage**: 1200 Harge Road, Suite 310, Oak Brook, IL 60521.

Bascom, W., 1980, *Waves and Beaches: The Dynamics of the Ocean Surface* (revised ed.): Garden City, NY, Anchor Press.

Bernard, E. N., (ed.) 1991, *Tsunami Hazard*: Hingham, MA, Kluwer Academic Publishers.

Bird, E. C. F., 1987, **Coastal Processes**: in *Human Activity and Environmental Processes*, K. J. Gregory and D. E. Walling, (eds.), New York, John Wiley & Sons, pp. 183 - 205.

Coastal Hazards Advisory and Mitigation Project, 1989, **Recommendations for Rebuilding after Hurricane Hugo** E: Coastal Hazards Advisory and Mitigation Project, 110 Lowry Hall, Clemson University Dept. Civil Engineering, Clemson, SC 29634-0911.

Committee on Coastal Erosion Zone Management, 1990, *Managing Coastal Erosion* E: Washington, DC, National Academy Press.

Committee on Engineering Implications of Changes in Relative Mean Sea Level, 1987, **Responding to changes in sea level—Engineering implications**: Washington, DC, National Academy Press.

Dolan, R., Godfrey, P. J., and Odum, W. E., 1973, **Man's impact on the barrier islands of North Carolina** [E]: Amer. Scientist, v. 61, pp. 152 - 162.

Dolan, R., and others., 1985, **Coastal erosion and accretion** [E]: 1: 7,500,000-scale map from U.S. Geol. Survey National Atlas. Sold as a separate wall map with informative text on back.

Dolan, R., and Lins, H., 1986, **The Outer Banks of North Carolina** [E]: U.S. Geol. Survey Prof. Paper 1177-B.

Dudley, W. C., and Lee, M., 1988, *Tsunami* [E]: Honolulu, HI, Univ. Hawaii Press.

Dunn, G. E., and Miller, B. I., 1964: *Atlantic Hurricanes* [E]: Louisiana State Univ. Press, Baton Rouge, 377 p.

Emmer, R. E., and others, 1992, **Planning for sea level rise along the Louisiana Coast: A workbook:** Envtl. Social Sci. Research Inst., Dept. Sociology, University of New Orleans, New Orleans, LA, 80 p.

Friedman, D. G., 1990, *U.S. Hurricanes and Windstorms*: DYP Insurance and Reinsurance Research Group Ltd., Bridge House, 181 Victoria St., London, EC4V 4DD, England.

Great Lakes Basin Commission, 1975, **Shore use and erosion** [E]: P. O. Box 999, Ann Arbor, MI 48106, Great Lakes Basin Framework Study Appendix 12.

Hayes, M. O., 1967, **Hurricanes as geological agents: case studies of hurricanes Carla, 1961, and Cindy, 1963** [E]: Bur. Econ. Geol., Univ. TX, Rept. Inv. n. 61, 56 p.

Inman, D. L., and Brush, J. D., 1973, **The coastal challenge** [E]: Science, v. 181, pp. 20 - 32.

Insurance Information Institute, 1990, **Hurricane awareness** [E]: Available through National Insurance Consumer Helpline, (800) 942-4242. Free brochure.

Jeleniansky, C. P., 1978, **Storm surges**: in *Geophysical Predictions*, Natl. Acad. Sci., Washington, DC, pp. 185-192.

Kaufman, W., and Pilkey, O. H., 1983, *The Beaches are Moving; the Drowning of America's Shoreline* [E]: Durham, NC, Duke University Press.

Kimball, S., Anders, F., and Dolan, R., 1989, **Coastal Hazards** [E]: 1: 7,500,000-scale map from U.S. Geol. Survey National Atlas with informative text .

Komar, P. D., 1983, *CRC Handbook of Coastal Processes and Erosion*: Englewood Cliffs, NJ, CRC Press.

Lander, J. F., and Lockridge, P. A., 1989, **United States tsunamis (including United States Possessions) 1690 - 1988**: Natl. Geophysical Data Center, 325 Broadway, Boulder, CO 80303.

Laska, S., and Emmer, R., 1992, **A bibliography of coastal erosion and sea level rise:** Envtl. Social Sci. Research Inst., Dept. Sociology, University of New Orleans, New Orleans, LA, 45 p.

Leatherman, S. P., 1988, *Barrier Island Handbook* (3rd ed.) [E]: College Park, MD, University of Maryland.

Lopez, S. H., 1985, **Coastal design with natural processes** [E]: Amer. Soc. Landscape Architects Tech. Inf. Series n. 9, 32 p., Washington, DC 20009. An excellent issue that focuses on coastal restoration and good land use.

Lyskowski, R., and Rice, S. (eds.), 1992, **The Big One: Hurricane Andrew** [E]: Miami Herald, P.O. Box 02140, Miami, FL 33101-2140 (305) 376-2788.

McGowen, J. H., Garner, L. E., and Wilkinson, B. H., 1977, **The Gulf Shoreline of Texas: processes, characteristics, and factors in use** [E]: Bur. Econ. Geol., Univ. Texas, Circular 73 - 7, 27 p.

Miller, D. J., 1960, **Giant waves in Lituya Bay, Alaska**: U.S. Geol. Survey Prof. Paper 354 - C, pp. 51 - 86.

Monday, J. L., 1992, **Learning from Hurricane Hugo: implications for public policy**: FEMA/FIA, 500 C St., S.W., Washington, DC 20472.

Morrison, H. R., and Lee, C. E., 1981, *Americas Atlantic Isles* [E]: Washington, DC National Geographic Society.

National Research Council, 1989, **Great Lakes water levels: shoreline dilemmas**: Natl. Research Council, Water Science and Technology Board, 2101 Constitution Avenue, HA-278, Washington, DC 20418.

NOAA/NWS, 1992, **The Halloween Nor'easter of 1991:** NOAA/NWS, Room 14124, 1325 East-West Highway, Silver Spring, MD 20910.

Pilkey, O. H., and Neal, W. J., 1988, **Coastal geologic hazards** [E]: in Geol. Society America, *The Atlantic Continental Margin: U.S.*, Decade of North American Geology (DNAG), v. I-2, pp. 549 - 556.

Pilkey, O. H., and Neal, W. J., (eds.) various years, **Living with the Shore** E: Durham, NC, Duke University Press. A very useful series for homeowners, real estate workers and insurers. The volumes in this series are separated by state, with detailed analyses of the shorelines of each.

Pipkin, B. W., Robertson, H., and Mills, R., 1992, **Coastal erosion in Southern California**: in *Engineering Geology Practice in Southern California*, Assoc. Engrg. Geologists Spec. Pub., Belmont, CA, Star Pub. Co., pp. 461 - 483.

Platt, R. H., Beatley, T., and Miller, H. C., 1991, **The folly at Folly Beach and other failings of U.S. coastal erosion policy** E: Environment, v. 33, n. 9, pp. 7 - 33.

Platt, R. H., and others, 1992, **Coastal erosion—has retreat sounded?**: Univ. of CO Institute Behavioral Sciences, Monograph n. 53, 195 p.

Pugh, 1987, *Tides, Surges and Mean Sea Level*: New York, John Wiley.

Shepard, F. P., and Wanless, H. R., 1971, *Our Changing Coastlines* E: New York, McGraw - Hill.

Silvester, R., 1974, *Coastal Engineering*: (v. I, 457 p., v. II, 338 p.) New York, Elsevier.

Soloviev, S. C., 1978, **Tsunamis**: in *The Assessment and Mitigation of Earthquake Risk - Natural Hazards*, UNESCO, Paris, pp. 118 - 139.

Sorensen, J. H., and Mitchell, J. K., 1975, **Coastal erosion hazard in the United States** E: Monograph NSF-RA-E-75-014, Inst. Behavioral Sci., Univ. CO, Boulder, 65 p.

Stauble, D. K., (ed.), 1989, **Barrier islands: process and management**: New York, NY, Amer. Soc. Civil Engineers.

Thieler, E. R., and Bush, D. M., 1991, **Hurricanes Gilbert and Hugo send powerful messages for coastal development** E: Jour. Geol. Ed., v. 39, pp. 291 - 299.

U.S. Army Corps of Engineers, 1981, **Low cost shore protection** E: U.S.A.C.E. Section 54 Program, Washington, DC. A series of pamphlets for property owners, community planners and contractors. Provides directory of U.S.A.C.E. regional offices for help.

U.S. Army Coastal Engineering Research Center, 1984, *Shore Protection Manual*: U.S. Govt. Printing Office, Washington, DC, 2 volumes.

Williams, G. P., and Gray, H. P., 1973, **Erosional and depositional aspects of Hurricane Camille in Virginia, 1969** E: U.S. Geol. Survey Prof. Paper 804.

Williams, J. W., (ed), 1987, **Engineering geology in the marine coastal zones of the United States**: Bull. Assoc. of Engrg. Geol., v. 24, n. 2 & 3.

Williams, S. J., Dodd, K., and Gohn, K. K., 1990, **Coasts in Crisis** E: U.S. Geol. Survey Circular 1075. Beautiful color photos with imaginative layout, annotated reference list and list of federal agencies responsible for coastal management and protection.

Videotapes on Storm Surge and Beach Erosion

Best Build I: Constructing a Sound Coastal Home: 1987, 20 minutes, Natl. Flood Ins. Program, Best Build Series, P. O. Box 710, Lanham, MD 20706, (800) 638-6620 - 7.

Hurricane: It's Not Just Another Storm! E: 1991, 20 minutes, FEMA Region IV, Suite 700, 1371 Peachtree Street, N.E., Atlanta, GA 30309.

In the Path of a Hurricane: Pan American Health Organization, The World Health Organization Emergency Preparedness/Relief Coordination Office, 525 23rd Street, N. W., Washington, DC 20037.

Superstorms: 1990, 30 minutes, Crocus Entertainment Inc., 630 Twelve Oaks Center, Wayzata, MN 55391, (800) 942-2992. Emphasis on human disregard for natural processes in floodplains and coastal regions.

The Beach - A River of Sand E: 1966, 21 minutes: Britannica Films, 310 South Michigan Ave., Chicago, IL 60604, (800-621-3900). Call for current prices. Occasional special sale prices on videos are given. Made originally by Shell Oil Company. Excellent illustrations of beach processes and sand movement. Despite its age this remains one of the best movies to show classes of students how beaches are created and maintained by nature.

The Beaches Are Moving E: 1990, 60 minutes: Contact Dr. Orrin Pilkey, Dept. of Geology, Duke University, P. O. Box 6729 CS, Durham, NC 27708, (919) 684-4238.

An excellent set of 35 mm slides on the effects of Hurricane Hugo, is available from National Audiovisual Center, Customer Services Section, 8700 Edgeworth Drive, Capitol Heights, MD 20743-3701, (301) 763-1896. At the time of this writing (Sept., 1992) no set for Hurricane Andrew was available.

Appendix A:
Sources of Help from Professional Geologists

These appendices are designed to help users of this book evaluate presence of a hazard on their property and to take action to minimize danger or losses. Preventing losses may involve procuring appropriate insurance (Appendix B, p. 131).

If your intention is to obtain personal help, a good first step is to access educational or general information sources by making a telephone call or writing a letter to your local state geological survey (see pp. 128 - 130). Ask for a list of publications and their procedures for answering public service requests.

The United States Geological Survey (USGS) produces a wealth of outstanding resources. Every citizen should know about this agency and its services. **A Guide to Obtaining USGS Information**, U. S. Geol. Survey Circular 900, tells how to access the vast storehouse of information of the USGS. Circulars are free. Write *Books and Open-File Reports Section, USGS, Federal Center, Box 25425, Denver, CO 80225*, and request your own copy of Circular 900. You may also contact the Public Inquiries Office closest to your area.

Geologists employed with the USGS are highly qualified specialists (many hold doctorates in geology). They are forbidden by law to do private consulting, but serve the public through production of maps and publications and through pure research.

Public Inquiries Offices of the United States Geological Survey (USGS)

ANCHORAGE, AK: Room 101, 4230 University Drive, Anchorage, AK 99508-4664, (907) 271-4320
DENVER, CO: 169 Federal Building, 1961 Stout Street, Denver, CO 80294, (303) 894-2850
MENLO PARK, CA: Building 3, Room 3128, Mail Stop 533, 345 Middlefield Road, Menlo Park, CA 94025, (415) 329-4390
RESTON, VA: 503 National Center, Room 1-C-402, 12201 Sunrise Valley Drive, Reston, VA 22092, (703) 648-6892
SALT LAKE CITY, UT: 8105 Federal Building, 125 South State Street, Salt Lake City, UT 84138 (801) 524-5652

If you are a property owner or buyer who wants to assess the geologic hazards under a particular site, begin by examining the checklist below. Cross out any risks that you know do not apply to your property. In most cases, only a single hazard will likely apply to a given site. If you have categories to which you have answered "yes" or "unknown," proceed on in these appendices for sources of help in your area.

PROPERTY OWNERS' and HOME BUYERS' CHECKLIST for POSSIBLE GEOLOGIC HAZARDS

HAZARD	POSSIBLE RISK?	DEGREE OF RISK ASSESSED?	INSURANCE COVERAGE?
SWELLING SOILS			
ACID DRAINAGE			
ASBESTOS			
RADON GAS			
OTHER GASES			
EARTHQUAKES			
VOLCANOES			
LANDSLIDES and AVALANCHES			
SUBSIDENCE			
FLOODS			
STORM SURGE			
TSUNAMIS			
COASTAL EROSION			

Your first action after completing the previous table should be to fill in the gaps regarding the unknown geological situation of home or property in question. Contact with the state geological survey should be made to fill in as many of these gaps as possible. The best way to contact the survey is to furnish them with the marked location of your property on a good map, ideally the 7 1/2 minute topographic quadrangle of your town or city. If you have no such map available, one can be purchased from the state survey. Simply phone them, give your address, and ask for the name of the appropriate quadrangle. The service of providing the information is usually free of charge; maps and publications must be purchased but costs are very reasonable.

The state survey should be able to provide you with the pertinent information which they have. Remember that geologists are still in the process of mapping and compiling data, and not everything you want may be actually available. If important gaps are missing, you may wish to use the services of a professional geologist who may make an on-site assessment.

If a geological consultant is required, you can obtain reference to a certified professional geologist in your area from **The American Institute of Professional Geologists** (AIPG), 7828 Vance Drive, Suite 103, Arvada, CO 80301, (303) 431-0831. This is the organization who commissioned this book. It also represents a source for consultants in virtually every specialty area of geology. The Institute maintains a listing of geologists and their specialties by geographic location. All geologists listed with AIPG are certified by the Institute on the basis of education and work experience. Most can consult and act as expert witnesses. There are many very capable geologists who are not listed with AIPG but, unfortunately, there exists a much smaller number of individuals without degrees or qualifications in geology who nevertheless call themselves geologists. In some states, registration boards of geologists keep such persons from offering bogus geological services to the public; other states have no provisions to protect the public from charlatans. We advise readers to ask their state survey, their state's registration board (for those which have them) or AIPG if they are uncertain about who may be qualified locally to perform consulting.

State (and Territory) Geological Surveys

State geological surveys provide some of the most useful services of all to private citizens, to domestic state industries and to other government agencies. Their geologists are usually highly qualified people with educations comparable to employees of the USGS. However, most are more heavily engaged in direct public service rather than in research and publication. State employees are generally forbidden by law to do private consulting, at least within the state in which they are employed. However, they are able to answer service requests of private citizens, to make information available by mail and by phone, to provide maps and publications and, in a few urgent cases, to provide on-site visits. State surveys may also provide lists of geologists from the private sector who are available to consult. Readers of this book will be pleasantly surprised if they write to their state survey requesting a list of publications and an explanation of services provided. Most will be amazed at the services provided for little cost and often for free. The contacts for the state geological surveys follow.

ALABAMA
Geological Survey of Alabama
P.O. Drawer O
Tuscaloosa, AL 35486
(205) 349-2852

ALASKA
Alaska Division of Geological and
Geophysical Surveys
794 University Avenue Suite 200
Fairbanks, AK 99709
(907) 479-7625

ARIZONA
Arizona Geological Survey
845 North Park Avenue, Suite 100
Tucson, AZ 85719
(602) 621-7906

ARKANSAS
Arkansas Geological Commission
Vardelole Parham Geology Center,
3815 West Roosevelt Road
Little Rock, AR 72204
(501) 371-1488

CALIFORNIA
California Dept. Conservation,
Mines & Geology Division
801 K Street Mail Stop 12-30
Sacramento, CA 95814 - 3531
(916) 445-1923

COLORADO
Colorado Geological Survey
1313 Sherman Street, Room 715
Denver, CO 80203
(303) 866-2611

CONNECTICUT
CT Dept. of Envtl. Protection
Natural Resources Center, 165
Capitol Avenue, Room 553
Hartford, CT 06106
(203) 566-3540

DELAWARE
Delaware Geological Survey
University of Delaware
Newark, DE 19716
(302) 451-2833

FLORIDA
Florida Bureau of Geology
903 West Tennessee Street
Tallahassee, FL 32304
(904) 488-4191

GEORGIA
Georgia Geological Survey
Dept. Natural Resources, Room 400
19 Martin Luther King Jr Drive S.W.
Atlanta, GA 30334
(404) 656-3214

HAWAII
Hawaii Division of Water and Land
Development
P.O. Box 373
Honolulu, HI 96809
(808) 548-7533

IDAHO
Idaho Geological Survey
Univ. of ID., Morrill Hall, Rm. 332
Moscow, ID 83843
(208) 885-7991

ILLINOIS
Illinois State Geological Survey
Room 121, 615 E. Peabody
Champaign, IL 61820
(217) 333-5111

INDIANA
Indiana Geological Survey
611 North Walnut Grove
Bloomington, IN 47405
(812) 335-2862

IOWA
Iowa Geological Survey Bureau
123 North Capitol Street
Iowa City IA 52242
(319) 335-1575

KANSAS
Kansas Geological Survey
Univ of KS 1930 Constant Ave.
West Campus
Lawrence, KS 66045
(913) 864-3965

KENTUCKY
Kentucky Geological Survey
228 Mining & Mineral Rescs. Bldg.
Lexington, KY 40506
(606) 257-5500

LOUISIANA
Louisiana Geological Survey
P.O. Box G
Baton Rouge, LA 70893
(504) 388-5320

MAINE
Maine Geological Survey
State House Station 22
Augusta, ME 04333
(207) 289-2801

MARYLAND
Maryland Geological Survey
2300 St. Paul Street
Baltimore, MD 21218
(301) 554-5503

MASSACHUSETTS
Massachusetts Executive Office of
Environmental Affairs
100 Cambridge St., 20th Floor
Boston, MA 02202
(617) 727-9800

MICHIGAN
Michigan Geological Survey
Division
MI Dept. Natural Resources
Box 30028
Lansing, MI 48909
(517) 334-6923

MINNESOTA
Minnesota Geological Surv.
Univ. of MN 2642 University
Avenue
St. Paul, MN 55114
(612) 627-4780

MISSISSIPPI
Mississippi Bureau of Geology
Dept. of Natural Resources
P.O. Box 5348
Jackson, MS 39216
(601) 354-6228

MISSOURI
Missouri Division of Geology and
Land Survey
Missouri Dept. Natural Resources,
P.O. Box 250,111 Fairgrounds Road
Rolla, MO 65401
(314) 364-1752

MONTANA
MT Bureau of Mines & Geology
Montana College of Mineral Science
and Technology
Butte, MT 59701
(406) 496-4180

NEBRASKA
NB Conservation and Survey Div.
Inst. of Agricultural and Natural Res.
Univ. NE, 113 Nebraska Hall
Lincoln, NE 68588
(402) 472-3471

NEVADA
NV Bureau of Mines and Geology
University of Nevada at Reno
Reno, NV 89557
(702) 784-6991

NEW HAMPSHIRE
New Hampshire Dept. of
Environmental Services
117 James Hall, University of New
Hampshire
Durham, NH 03263
(603) 862-3160

NEW JERSEY
New Jersey Geological Survey
Division of Water Resources
CN-029
Trenton, NJ 08625
(609) 292-1185

NEW MEXICO
New Mexico Bureau of Mines and
Mineral Resources
Campus Station
Socorro, NM 87801
(505) 835-5420

NEW YORK
State Geological Survey
3136 Cultural Education Center
Albany, NY 12230
(518) 474-5816

NORTH CAROLINA
North Carolina Dept. of Natl.
Resources and Community
Development
P.O. Box 27687
Raleigh, NC 27611
(919) 733-3833

NORTH DAKOTA
North Dakota Geological Survey
University Station
Grand Forks, ND 58202
(701) 777-2231

OHIO
Ohio Dept. of Natl. Resources
Division of Geological Survey
4383 Fountain Square, Bldg. 8
Columbus, OH 43224
(614) 265-6605

OKLAHOMA
Oklahoma Geological Survey
830 Van Fleet Oval Room 163
Norman, OK 73019
(405) 325-3031

OREGON
OR Dept. Geol. & Minl. Industries
1400 SW Fifth Ave., Room 910
Portland, OR 97201
(503) 229-5580

PENNSYLVANIA
PA Bureau of Topographic and
Geologic Survey
P.O. Box 2357, Dept. of
Environmental Resources
Harrisburg, PA 17105
(717) 787-2169

PUERTO RICO
Sevicicio Geologico de Puerto Rico
Apartado 5887 Puerta de Tierra
San Juan, PR 00906
(809) 724-8774

RHODE ISLAND
University of RI Dept. of Geology
315 Green Hall
Kingston, RI 02881
(401) 792-2265

SOUTH CAROLINA
South Carolina Geological Survey
5 Geology Road
Columbia, SC 29210
(803) 737-9440

SOUTH DAKOTA
South Dakota Geological Survey
Science Center, USD
Vermillion, SD 57069
(605) 677-5227

TENNESSEE
Tennessee Division of Geology
Dept. of Conservation
Customs House 701 Broadway
Room B-30
Nashville, TN 37219
(615) 742-6991

TEXAS
Texas Bureau of Economic Geology
University Station, Box X
Austin, TX 78713
(512) 471-1534

U. S. VIRGIN ISLANDS
Caribbean Research Institute
College of the Virgin Islands
St. Thomas, U.S. Virgin Islands
00801
(809) 774-9200

UTAH
Utah Geological & Mineral Survey
606 Black Hawk Way
Salt Lake City, UT 84108
(801) 581-6831

VERMONT
Vermont Office of the State
Geologist
103 S. Main St., Center Building
Waterbury, VT 05676
(802) 244-5164

VIRGINIA
Virginia Division of Mineral
Resources
P.O. Box 3667, McCormick Road
Charlottesville, VA 22903
(804) 293-5121

WASHINGTON
Washington Geology and Earth
Resources Division
WA Dept. of Natural Resources
Mail Stop PY-12
Olympia, WA 98504
(206) 459-6372

WEST VIRGINIA
West Virginia Geological and
Economic Survey
P.O. Box 879, Mt. Chateau Res. Ctr.
Morgantown, WV 26507
(304) 594-2331

WISCONSIN
Wisconsin Geological and Natural
History Survey
3817 Mineral Point Road
Madison, WI 53705
(608)-263-7384

WYOMING
Geological Survey of Wyoming
P.O. Box 3008, Univ. Station
Laramie, WY 82071
(307) 742-2054

Access to Professional Organizations

For working professionals, particularly those in land use planning and government, there are professional organizations concerned with research and abatement of natural hazards that are useful to join or contact. The list is too long to provide here in a book intended primarily for lay readers, but it has been published in the January, 1991, edition of *Natural Hazards Observer* (v. 15, n. 3, pp. 9-12) Their list is available for $0.50 from Univ. of Colorado, Campus Box 482, Boulder, CO 80309-0482, (303) 492-6818.

Geotimes, the monthly magazine of the American Geological Institute (AGI) carries a periodic issue that contains an updated directory of geological organizations. Their list also contains many societies that have little to do with geologic hazards, but most of the societies whose publications we have cited in this book can be found there. Contact AGI, 4220 King Street, Alexandria, VA 22302-1507, (703) 379 - 2480.

Appendix B:
Sources of Help from Insurance Professionals

The general lack of education in geology brings problems to the public consumer, especially if local insurance agents are unfamiliar with local geologic hazards. The authors have experienced first-hand the difficulty in obtaining appropriate information on available insurance from local agents with respect to geologic hazards. Agents who have read this book will probably be much better able to assist property owners.

However, should you not feel that you are able to obtain sufficient information locally to meet your needs, you should contact your state's insurance commissioner. At the state level, offices of state insurance commissioners are the insurance profession's equivalents of the geological profession's state geological surveys in regard to providing public assistance. A call to the state commissioner's office may give you the answers about what types of insurance are available in your state. The list below comes courtesy of **The Insurance Information Institute.**

State (and Territory) Insurance Commissioners

ALABAMA
Commissioner of Insurance
1665 Hot Springs Rd.
Carson City, NV 89710
(702) 687-4270 or (800) 992-0900

ALABAMA
Commissioner of Insurance
135 South Union Street
Montgomery, AL 36104
(205) 269-3550

ALASKA
Director of Insurance
P.O. Box D
Juneau, AK 99811
(907) 465-2515

AMERICAN SAMOA
Insurance Commissioner
Office of the Governor
Pago Pago, AS 96797
(684) 633-4116

ARIZONA
Director of Insurance
3030 North 3rd Street Suite 1100
Phoenix, AZ 85012
(602) 255-5400

ARKANSAS
Insurance Commissioner
400 University Tower Building
Little Rock, AR 72204
(501) 371-1325

CALIFORNIA
Commissioner of Insurance
100 Van Ness Avenue
San Francisco, CA 94102
(415) 557-1126 or (800) 233-9045

COLORADO
Commissioner of Insurance
303 W. Colfax Ave. Suite 500
Denver, CO 80204
(303) 866-6274

CONNECTICUT
Insurance Commissioner
165 Capitol Avenue
Hartford, CT 06106
(203) 297-3801

DELAWARE
Insurance Commissioner
Rodney Bldg., 841 Silver Lake Blvd.
Dover, DE 19901
(302) 739-4251 or (800) 282-8611

FLORIDA
Insurance Commissioner
State Capitol Plaza Level 11
Tallahassee, FL 32399-0300
(904) 488-3440 or (800) 342-2762

GEORGIA
Insurance Commissioner
2 Martin L. King, Jr., Drive
Floyd Memorial Bldg.
704 W. Tower
Atlanta, GA 30334
(404) 656-2056

GUAM
Insurance Commissioner
P.O. Box 2796
Agana, GU 96910
011 - (371) 477-5106

HAWAII
Insurance Commissioner
P.O. Box 3614
Honolulu, HI 96813
(808) 548-5450 or (800) 548-5450

IDAHO
Director of Insurance
500 S. 10th Street
Boise ID 83720
(208) 334-2250

ILLINOIS
Director of Insurance
320 W. Washington St. 4th Fl.
Springfield, IL 62767
(217) 782-4515

INDIANA
Commissioner of Insurance
311 W. Washington St #300
Indianapolis, IN 46204-2787
(317) 232-2385 or (800) 622-4461

IOWA
Commissioner of Insurance
Lucas State Office Bldg. 6th Floor
Des Moines, IA 50319
(515) 281-5705

KANSAS
Commissioner of Insurance
420 South W. Ninth Street
Topeka, KS 66612
(913) 296-7801 or (800) 432-2484

KENTUCKY
Insurance Commissioner
229 West Maine Street P.O. Box 517
Frankfort, KY 40602
(502) 564-3630

LOUISIANA
Commissioner of Insurance
P.O. Box 94214 Capitol Station
Baton Rouge, LA 70801
(504) 342-5900

MAINE
Superintendent of Insurance
State House Station 34
Augusta, ME 04333
(207) 582-8707

MARYLAND
Insurance Commissioner
501 St. Paul Pl., 7th Floor S.
Baltimore, MD 21202
(301) 333-2520 or (800) 492-6116

MASSACHUSETTS
Commissioner of Insurance
280 Friend Street
Boston, MA 02114
(617) 727-7189

MICHIGAN
Insurance Commissioner
P.O. Box 30220
Lansing, MI 48933
(517) 373-9273

MINNESOTA
Commissioner of Commerce
133 E. 7th Street
St. Paul, MN 55101
(612) 296-6848 or (800) 652-9747

MISSISSIPPI
Commissioner of Insurance
1804 Walter Sillers Building
Jackson, MS 39205
(601) 359-3569

MISSOURI
Director of Insurance
301 W. High St. 6 N., P.O. Box 690
Jefferson City, MO 65102-0690
(314) 751-4126

MONTANA
Commissioner of Insurance
126 North Sanders Mitchell Building
Rm. 270
Helena, MT 59601
(406) 444-2040 or (800) 332-6148

NEBRASKA
Director of Insurance
Terminal Bldg., 941 O St., Suite 400
Lincoln, NE 68508
(402) 471-2201

NEW HAMPSHIRE
Insurance Commissioner
169 Manchester Street
Concord, NH 03301
(603) 271-2261 or (800) 852-3416

NEW JERSEY
Commissioner of Insurance
CN 325-20 West State Street
Trenton, NJ 08625
(609) 292-5363

NEW MEXICO
Superintendent of Insurance
Department of Insurance
P.O. Drawer 1269
Santa Fe NM 87504
(505) 827-4500

NEW YORK
Superintendent of Insurance
160 West Broadway
New York, NY 10013
(212) 602-0429 or (800) 522-4370

NORTH CAROLINA
Commissioner of Insurance
P.O. Box 26387
Raleigh, NC 27611
(919) 733-7349 or (800) 662-7777

NORTH DAKOTA
Commissioner of Insurance
Capitol Building Fifth Floor
600 East Blvd.
Bismarck, ND 58505-0320
(701) 224-2440 or (800) 247-0560

OHIO
Director of Insurance
2100 Stella Court
Columbus, OH 43266-0566
(614) 644-2658 or (800) 282-4658

OKLAHOMA
Insurance Commissioner
P.O. Box 53408
Oklahoma City, OK 73105-3408
(405) 521-2828

OREGON
Insurance Commissioner
21 Labor and Industries Bldg.
Salem OR 97310
(503) 378-4271

PENNSYLVANIA
Commissioner
1326 Strawberry Sq. 13th Fl.
Harrisburg, PA 17120
(717) 787-5173

PUERTO RICO
Commissioner of Insurance
Fernandez Jucos Station
P.O. Box 8330
Santurce, PR 00910
(809) 722-8686

RHODE ISLAND
Insurance Commissioner
233 Richmond Street
Providence, RI 02903
(401) 277-2223

SOUTH CAROLINA
Chief Insurance Commissioner
1612 Marion Street
P.O. Box 100105
Columbia, SC 29201-3105
(803) 737-6117

SOUTH DAKOTA
Director of Insurance
Insurance Building
910 E. Sioux Avenue
Pierre, SD 57501
(605) 773-3563

TENNESSEE
Commissioner of Insurance
500 James Robertson Pkwy.
Nashville, TN 37243-0566
(615) 741-2241 or (800) 342-4029

TEXAS
Commissioner of Insurance
1110 San Jacinto Blvd.
Austin, TX 78701-1998
(512) 463-6464

UTAH
Commissioner of Insurance
3110 State Office Bldg.
Salt Lake City, UT 84114
(801) 538-3800

VERMONT
Commissioner of Insurance
State Office Building 120 State
Street
Montpelier, VT 05602
(802) 825-3301

VIRGIN ISLANDS
Commissioner of Insurance
18 Kongen's Garden
St. Thomas, VI 00802
(809) 774-2991

VIRGINIA
Commissioner of Insurance
1200 Jefferson Building 1220 Bank
St.
Richmond, VA 23219
(804) 371-7694 or (800) 552-7945

WASHINGTON
Insurance Commissioner
Insurance Building AQ-21
Olympia, WA 98504
(206) 753-7301 or (800) 562-6900

WASHINGTON D. C.
Superintendent of Insurance
613 G St. NW 6th Floor
Washington, DC 20001
(202) 727-7424

WEST VIRGINIA
Insurance Commissioner
2019 Washington St. East
Charleston, WV 25305
(304) 348-3394 or (800) 642-9004

WISCONSIN
Commissioner of Insurance
121 E. Wilson Street
Madison, WI 53702
(608) 266-0102

WYOMING
Insurance Commissioner
Herschler Building 122 West 25th
Street
Cheyenne, WY 82002
(307) 777-7401

National Sources of Help and Information

The insurance profession involves both private industry and government programs. Below are some useful sources of information for citizens.

Insurance Information Institute (III) 110 William Street, New York, NY 10038, (800) 331-9146. This institute compiles extensive data on all aspects of the insurance industry. Their annual *I.I.I. Fact Book* provides a wealth of detailed information on natural disasters and their costs to the insurance industry.

National Insurance Consumer Helpline (800) 942-4242. The helpline is sponsored by three councils of insurance. Currently the helpline answers service requests on all kinds of insurance, particularly health and fire. The helpline has informational brochures for consumers that cover some natural disasters, but none currently on geologic hazards. Usefulness of this helpline on insuring against geologic hazards will increase as personnel serving on the helpline become more familiar with the topic.

National Committee on Property Insurance (NCPI), Ten Winthrop Square, Boston, MA 02110, (617) 423-4620 NCPI provides the property insurance industry with advice on a wide variety of issues that include losses from geologic hazards.

Property Insurance Plans Service Office (PIPSO), Ten Winthrop Square, Boston, MA 02110, (617) 423-4620 PIPSO is a special division of NCPI which provides advice on special risk coverage that may not be locally available.

National Underwriter Company, 505 Gest, Cincinnati, OH 45203, (513) 721-2140. This firm publishes books for insurance companies. Their annual compilation, *Who Writes What*, has information on insurers for unusual health hazards such as asbestos and for those in the geological, mining and drilling professions.

National Flood Insurance Program, (NFIP), P. O. Box 459, Lanham, MD 20706, (800) 638-6620. This agency also supports seminars for producers and lenders, and serves as a map distribution center with 78,000 maps compiled for 21,000 communities. Flood study reports are available for over 10,500 communities. There are currently 2.4 million policies in force in over 18,000 communities that cover both single-family dwellings and 2- to 4-family buildings. Average rates as of current time of this writing are approximately $275 for about $85,000 worth of insurance, but rates vary by location. Policies written by 85 companies are sold through 130,000 insurance agencies and brokers. From 1983 through 1990, the program paid over two and a quarter billion dollars in losses, with annual losses ranging from 45 million (1988) to 592 million dollars (1989).

Index of Key Terms

This index also serves the function of a glossary. Technical terms have been kept to a minimum, and all terms that are used are defined. The page on which the definition appears is highlighted below in standard **boldface type**. *Boldface italics* below indicate the page on which particular features are illustrated by photographs or drawings.